D0132088

# The Big Book of Benefit Auctions

Jay R. Fiske
and
Corinne A. Fiske

**WILEY**

John Wiley & Sons, Inc.

WITHDRAWN
UTSA LIBRARIES

Copyright © 2009 by John Wiley & Sons, Inc. All rights reserved.

Published by John Wiley & Sons, Inc., Hoboken, New Jersey.

Published simultaneously in Canada.

No part of this publication may be reproduced, stored in a retrieval system, or transmitted in any form or by any means, electronic, mechanical, photocopying, recording, scanning, or otherwise, except as permitted under Section 107 or 108 of the 1976 United States Copyright Act, without either the prior written permission of the Publisher, or authorization through payment of the appropriate per-copy fee to the Copyright Clearance Center, Inc., 222 Rosewood Drive, Danvers, MA 01923, 978-750-8400, fax 978-646-8600, or on the web at www.copyright.com. Requests to the Publisher for permission should be addressed to the Permissions Department, John Wiley & Sons, Inc., 111 River Street, Hoboken, NJ 07030, 201-748-6011, fax 201-748-6008, or online at www.wiley.com/go/permissions.

Limit of Liability/Disclaimer of Warranty: While the publisher and author have used their best efforts in preparing this book, they make no representations or warranties with respect to the accuracy or completeness of the contents of this book and specifically disclaim any implied warranties of merchantability or fitness for a particular purpose. No warranty may be created or extended by sales representatives or written sales materials. The advice and strategies contained herein may not be suitable for your situation. You should consult with a professional where appropriate. Neither the publisher nor author shall be liable for any loss of profit or any other commercial damages, including but not limited to special, incidental, consequential, or other damages.

For general information on our other products and services, or technical support, please contact our Customer Care Department within the United States at 800-762-2974, outside the United States at 317-572-3993 or via fax at 317-572-4002.

Wiley also publishes its books in a variety of electronic formats. Some content that appears in print may not be available in electronic books.

For more information about Wiley products, visit our Web site at www.wiley.com.

*Library of Congress Cataloging-in-Publication Data:*
Fiske, Jay R.
The big book of benefit auctions / Jay R. Fiske and Corinne A. Fiske.
    p. cm.
Includes index.
ISBN 978-0-470-41292-3 (pbk.)
1. Benefit auctions. I.   Fiske, Corinne A. II.   Title.
HF5476.F57 2009
658.8'7–dc22                                 2008042572

Printed in the United States of America

10 9 8 7 6 5 4 3 2 1

Library
University of Texas
at San Antonio

# Contents

# About the Authors

**Jay R. Fiske** is a nationally recognized charity auctioneer and regular speaker for many different types of organizations related to auction planning, consulting, and fundraising. He has been a regular contributor to many media publications such as *Auctioneer* magazine, *Rotarian* magazine, and more. Jay regularly serves as a consultant on fundraising to national and local nonprofits.

**Corinne A. Fiske** manages many of NWBA's events and also teaches at the auction workshops, but it is through her own business, The PoliteChild (www.politechild.com), that she does most of her public speaking and media appearances. Corinne's publications include articles in *USA Today*, the *Wall Street Journal*, the *Washington Post*, and many trade and parenting magazines. She was featured in *Time* magazine and has appeared on the *Today* show, CNN, and more.

# Why This Book Was Written

Welcome to *The Big Book of Benefit Auctions.* Your stress level (and we know you ARE stressed about having to manage an auction!) is about to be reduced. We wrote this book to help volunteers and employed staff of charities, foundations, schools, museums, service clubs, and the myriad of other organizations that have discovered that auctions are good business and can be very profitable for their respective organizations.

Make no mistake about it, auctions are big business. Literally billions are raised each year at more than 350,000 charity auction events, as reported in the *Wall Street Journal*. And, in spite of recent challenges in the economy, those numbers are only increasing. According to a recent issue of *Auctioneer* magazine, charity auction revenue steadily increased from $13.4 billion in 2004 to $15.6 billion in 2006 and $16.2 billion in 2007, a 4.1% increase from the previous year. Charity auctions represent the fourth fastest growth area of all auction segments during the period of 2004–2007.

But these statistics relate to overall trends, not individual results. For many organizers, the fact that any money is raised at their event at all borders on a miracle. For others, stopping the flow of money that just seems to "pour in" would be a difficult task. Why the difference? It all has to do with how organizers go about setting up their events. What we will do in the *Big Book* is break it down for you in simple step-by-step fashion, in easy-to-digest pieces and parts, with sample documents, checklists, and reminders, so your event will be the one where the money seems to pour in, instead of the one where it is questionable if any profit will be made.

What differentiates the profitable event from the one that struggles to make it all worthwhile? Much of the difference starts with an *attitude*: the attitude of the leaders, the volunteers, and staff charged with raising the money. There are no shortcuts in the fundraising business. It all comes down to just how businesslike you and your committee are willing to be. If your committee is all about the party, then you will struggle to make money. If they are all about business, then you will hit your goal and most likely exceed it. In other words, you and your committee need to have a businesslike attitude. If you "throw a party" and hope it makes money, you will underachieve (except maybe in throwing a great party). On the other hand, if you create a great business with proper business tools and a great businesslike attitude, you will exceed your financial goals (and probably also have a great party).

There is no conflict between being businesslike and having fun. Don't believe us? Ever heard of Disney? "The Happiest Place on Earth" started out and remains one of the best-run businesses in the world. It's not only possible, but it's true: The more businesslike you and your committee are, the more fun you and your committee will have in running your business. The stress that would take the fun out of your event comes from disorganization, reinventing, and not knowing what to do. We will solve all of that for you in this book.

You will find tried-and-true techniques, systems, concepts, ideas, and profitable processes that have all been honed over many years and thousands of successful events. You will not need to invent anything, reinvent anything, or leave anything to chance—it's all here in *The Big Book of Benefit Auctions*.

We aren't going to discourage you from being creative. In fact, we want you to be creative. But we want you to apply your creativity where it makes sense. Don't mess with the basics—thousands of pioneering committees have gone your way before you, and we have captured in this book the tried-and-true, surefire techniques that will work *every time*. Why mess with success? As long as you stay with the basics as outlined within this book, you can let the creativity flow, because that is part of the fun of serving on the event committee.

Look at it another way. Do you cook? Do you use a recipe for those dinners or desserts you only make once in awhile? Of course you do, because trying to remember every ingredient, every cooking time, every combination of element that goes into the meal would leave too much to chance. Think of the *Big Book* as your basic cake recipe—once the cake is mixed, you can create shapes and layers, add flavors, icings, decorations, and create an unlimited number of cakes. Just remember that if you replace the flour with sand or forget to add an egg, you may have a collection of ingredients, but not a cake!

Whether this is your first auction and you don't know where to start, or you are a seasoned veteran in planning and putting on auctions, you're sure to find plenty in this book that will help you maximize your effort and increase your results. We promise!

# Acknowledgments

## Jay's Acknowledgments

So many people have contributed to the expansion of my knowledge about auctions, which I have used as the underpinnings of this book, that it would be impossible to acknowledge them all for fear of leaving one, or several out. However, clearly there are a few who must be listed for special recognition if anyone is to be listed at all. First and foremost is my wife and coauthor of this work, Corinne, who not only encouraged this project but negotiated with the publisher, taught me how to write a work that can get published, and has been a supporter of what I do for a living since I met her. She has never grown tired of me talking about auctions and has become an active partner in what I do, offering creativity and solid advice to the business, and for that I am very grateful. I must also thank my son, Rian, who is to "blame" for getting me into this business nearly 20 years ago when he was in high school. It was his invitation to a parent meeting at school that resulted in my first encounter with benefit auctions, and the rest, as they say, is history. My other son, Dale, and my three daughters, Alana, Alexis, and Regan, have withstood many days, nights, and weekends of Dad being away from home, missing the football games, soccer games, and other activities, all due to the demands of working weekends as an auctioneer. Their collective tolerance for "Daddy bye-bye" must be acknowledged.

On the professional side, I must thank Dick and Sharon Friel, who have been huge supporters and good friends. They never saw me as a competitor, but as a partner in helping their clients do a great job of fundraising. They opened their considerable wealth of knowledge for me to learn along with their clients, and referred me to anyone they were unable to help. Having these two on your team is one of the best assets anyone could hope for. I am grateful to Ken Kleve of MaestroSoft, who has been a steadfast friend and manager and was able to keep the company running and in fact growing while I spent most of my time focused on auctions and consulting. Tim Chapin helped me with my original printed work, *The Benefit Auction Resource Book*, by editing and formatting my words so they would make sense. Thanks, Tim!

Finally, I will always have in my heart the memory of my good friend and confidant, Michael Bader, who helped me form the vision for MaestroSoft.

Although he is gone thanks to the brain tumor that he could not beat, he is never far away, and will always serve us as our Chief Inspirational Officer.

## Corinne's Acknowledgments

You've heard the saying, "It takes a village to raise a child." Well, much the same can be said for writing a book. And, for this book, quite a village so far has helped raise it.

First, to the wonderful folks at John Wiley & Sons; thank you to Susan McDermott, for seeing the potential for this book and welcoming us to the Wiley family! Judy Howarth and Natasha Wolfe both played important parts in helping move the manuscript along from words to the formatted, finished piece you now hold in your hands. There are many others involved behind the scenes—reviewers, production specialists, editors, and more. These are people whose names we may never even learn, but who have all added their talents to bring concept to reality.

Then there's the support network behind those who wrote the words. First, I owe a tremendous "thank you" to my husband, best friend, and co-author Jay. Without him, his expertise, and his experience, I wouldn't have learned all I have to contribute to this book. Learning this business at his feet has been a lot like drinking from the proverbial firehose; fortunately, I haven't drowned yet! I'm always humbled and awed at the benefits our clients derive from the process, procedures, and wisdom he brings to each and every event. And we discovered that we not only can write a book together, we've managed to stay friends throughout the process! Bonus!

Also a big "thank you" goes to our daughters, Alana, Alexis, and Regan. Thank you for being patient and understanding when Mommy and Daddy had to dedicate those many hours over a summer to meet a promised deadline. To my parents, Eva and Druse Neumann, thanks for believing in me, supporting me, and instilling in me a work ethic so stubborn that yes, I will get up at 2:00 A.M. to finish editing a section, because it has to get done on time!

\*\*\*

Finally, thanks to the many clients and staff of Northwest Benefit Auctions and MaestroSoft, without whom we couldn't say with confidence that the concepts in the book have been tested and proven thousands of times on tens of thousands of events.

# A Brief Introduction to Successful Auctions

Putting on a successful charity auction isn't a matter of chance. Regardless of the size and goal of your auction, there is a step-by-step process that will guide you from the very beginning of deciding to have an auction through the end result of getting money in the bank and sending out your final thank-you letters. While some of the steps in the process may be optional, or may depend on the type of auction or the kinds of activities you'll have during your event, the fundamental basics are generally the same. These basics form the essential components of your event, and when they are used properly and consistently, you'll find your event will not only achieve expected results the first time, but can be depended on and used to predict and direct results for subsequent years.

While the complete auction process is made up of many individual activities and discrete steps, in general the following five main phases are involved:

- Phase I—Pre-Event Planning (4–6 months out)
  - Setting financial and attendance goals
  - Defining the mission
  - Establishing committees
  - Identifying a date and preferred location
- Phase II—Event Planning and Organization (4 months out)
  - Finalizing the date/time/location
  - Deciding on a theme and colors
  - Designing invitations/"Save-the-Date" cards
  - Identifying a short list of vendors
  - Holding kickoff rallies/meetings to initiate procurement, audience development, and volunteer staffing
- Phase III—Procurement, Audience Development, and Event Preparation (3 months out to 1 month out)
  - Creating list of invitees
  - Mailing out invitations and/or "Save-the-Date" cards
  - Soliciting donations and other procurement activities
  - Planning auction activities and revenue enhancers
- Phase IV—Event Execution (2 weeks out to day of event)

- ◆ Planning for registration/check-in needs and processes
- ◆ Scheduling day-of volunteer staff
- ◆ Coordinating auction recording, filing, cashiering
- Phase V—Post-Event Activities and Planning for the Next Event (1 day after to 1 month after current event); includes:
  - ◆ Conducting post-auction audit
  - ◆ Hosting post-event recap meeting
  - ◆ Generating and mailing thank-you letters to attendees and donors
  - ◆ Hosting volunteer party
  - ◆ Launching pre-planning for next event

Notice that the phases we refer to here are sequential, flowing naturally from one to another, based on a recommended timeline. Also, they are circular—when you finish the current event, you are ideally set up to begin planning for the next one. The cycle then repeats itself as shown in Exhibit I.1.

You'll notice that the diagram is a circle in which every activity not only feeds but blends into the next. This depiction is intentional, because that's the way auction planning really is. While you may have hard-and-fast deadlines for certain activities, some—like procurement—may not really be completely "finished" until the day of the event, because you may continue to receive auction items until the last minute. Likewise, as soon as you have completed your current event, you essentially begin the analysis of that event, which feeds into the planning of the next one. Successful auctions continue to be that way, because they are treated as a continuing cycle.

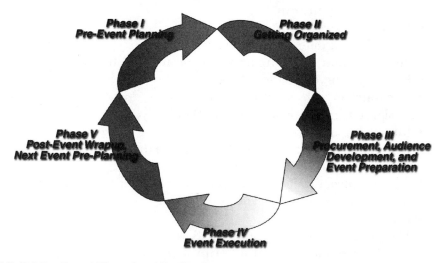

**Exhibit I.1   Event Planning Life Cycle**

## The Importance of Five-Year Planning

But wait just a minute. You are thinking to yourself, "I am not going to be working on the auction *next* year. I only signed up for one year!" That may be true, but *someone* is going to be working on the auction, and one of the best gifts you can give your organization is to break the cycle of one-year planning, which keeps the auction as a perpetual start-up business. Too many new auction chairs approach their "tour of duty" as something they must get through, instead of an opportunity to build something new, different, and lasting. They see their mission as needing to throw a great party, and then hope that it makes money. While this approach may result in some success, it will never yield maximum results. True success comes from realizing your auction is a business (when you end up with more money than you started with, you have a business). How successful a business is or can be depends directly on how well organized that business is from the start. Too many charity auctions are started as businesses that plan to go out of business the day after their first sale! Of course, any other "business" would never succeed long term with this kind of attitude. Imagine a business that sold Christmas decorations that planned to go out of business on December 26, only to wait until June to decide to become a start-up company once again selling Christmas decorations! How many charity auctions do you know that take this perpetual start-up approach? Unfortunately, nearly all charity auctions do this start-and-stop cycle, but here is your chance to break this pattern and leave a real legacy for your organization. In this book, we will show you how to build your auction business with a five-year outlook and truly leave your mark, which will have those that step up to fill your shoes praising your efforts long after your "tour of duty" is complete.

## The Planning Timeline

You'll notice we offer a suggested timeline for these events. The reality is that it takes six months or more to plan a successful auction. Now that doesn't mean it can't be done in a shorter period of time, but the amount of effort that it takes still remains; you can compress the schedule, but you'll find you are still accomplishing six months of effort even if you try to get it done in three or four months. Less than that and it becomes nearly impossible to pull everything together in time without totally annihilating your committees or volunteers in the process. Having said that, if you find that you don't have the ideal timeline, you can still pick up from where you are currently and implement the recommended processes. You'll have a bit of catch-up to do, and you can check off where *you* are in the process against the recommended timeline shown on the next page and continue from there.

## Auction Countdown Calendar

| Days to Event | Activities Performed |
|---|---|
| 180 | First Meeting: Pick date, set auction's financial goal, discuss location options, identify auctioneer, order procurement forms, pick theme, create a budget, choose major committee chairs |
| 150 | Designate all auction committee chairs, conduct walk-through of location, schedule meetings of all chairs |
| | Establish procurement and attendance goals based on financial goals for event |
| | Create Web site for auction |
| | List auction in planning calendars |
| | Choose theme and colors |
| 120 | Send out ``Save the Date'' notice to all members and target audience |
| | Have a procurement kick-off party, hand out procurement packets |
| | Start Audience Development process |
| | Secure major items for auction (focus on Live Auction items) |
| 100 | Identify a secure location to store items |
| | Enter items in database, begin creating item descriptions |
| | Live and Silent Auction Committees design displays |
| 90–45 | Create mailing list of potential invitees |
| | Finalize costs, layout pricing options |
| | Create and send invitations. List Web site in invitations |
| 40–30 | Begin ``phone tree'' calls or e-mail broadcasts to invitees as follow up |
| | Gather RSVPs and enter in database |
| 30 | Cut-off date for procurement |
| | Sort items into Live and Silent categories |
| | Sequence of Live Auction created *with* Auctioneer |
| | Order bid cards; create agenda for evening; gather pricing on catalog printing and finalize layout |
| 21 | Catalog goes to printer |
| | Final telephone or e-mail follow-up of attendees done |
| | Live and Silent Committees complete display preparation |
| 10 | Catalog (or ``Hot Sheet'') sent to RSVPs, if mailing |
| 7 | Agenda and addendum printed |
| | Registration committee prepares bid packets |
| | Print auction bid forms |
| | Volunteers, registration, cashiering training conducted |
| 1–0 | Final walk-through of auction location, set-up and AUCTION |
| –7 to –14 | Recap meeting; party and critique |
| –21 | Thank you notes sent |
| | ``Save the Date'' notice sent regarding next year's auction |
| | Location and date selected for next year |

As you review these activities, keep in mind this is not meant to be an exhaustive list; more detail will be provided in the following chapters, which discuss each phase of the auction planning and execution process.

## For Further Information

You can find more information about many aspects of conducting a successful auction—including auction timelines, supplemental resources, ebooklets on common auction pitfalls, handy tips for your auction, and more—at www.auctionhelp.com.

# PHASE I

# PRE-EVENT PLANNING

- Chapter 1: Pre-Planning Activities
- Chapter 2: Establishing Auction Committees
- Chapter 3: Getting to Work

## CHAPTER 1

# Pre-Planning Activities

Pre-event planning, as outlined in this section, will be among the most important steps you will take on your path to a successful event. You may have heard the phrase, "If you don't know where you are going, any path will take you there." It's true. Without knowing where you are going and why, you might as well set out on your journey and be content wherever you happen to arrive. You would not start a family vacation with this attitude, would you? At the very least, you would decide

- Where you wish to go
- How long you plan to stay
- What you will do when you get there
- Who you plan to take with you (like the kids, for instance!)

You would also make some financial plans, such as how much you need to budget for accommodations, food, travel, and entertainment. You would plan for some contingencies, such as what to do if your day at the beach is rained out. You would decide when you plan to leave and when you plan to return. Believe it or not, many auction committees do less planning for their event than they do for their family vacations! It must mean that whatever results they achieve are perfectly okay. Of course, you bought this book, so clearly you are already way ahead of *those* committees.

Pre-event planning should begin at least four—and ideally six—months or more before the event date. As we will discuss later in Phase V of this book, the first year of your Five-Year Plan is the only time where pre-event planning begins this close to the event date. Once you cycle through your first year, pre-event planning for the following year begins the day after your event. In other words, what is best and most successful is to *never go out of business*— to have one event's conclusion lead directly into the next event's pre-planning. This is the best way for organizations to continue to improve, reduce burnout of volunteers and staff, and break the cycle of reinventing the wheel. In fact, the more you follow planning as a continuum from one event to the next, the easier it gets to achieve success. In other words, as we discussed in the Introduction, does a business that makes Christmas decorations go out of business on December 26 only to go back into business in June? Of course it doesn't. Yet many auction committees go "out of business" the day after their first sale, only to start up again six months later, typically with a new, unfamiliar committee.

## The Auction Steering Committee

The best way to eliminate the constant starting and stopping of the business, along with the related need to begin planning after a six-month or more layoff, and to ensure the process continually improves from one event to the next, is to do away with the concept of the traditional *auction committee* and replace it with a *steering committee*. What's the difference? An auction committee has the event as its focus—getting through the auction and then being done. In contrast, a steering committee guides the business of fundraising, which includes the event. It never really goes out of business. Unlike the auction committee, a steering or standing committee, by definition, never has a termination date. Of course, this is not to suggest that once you are on the steering committee you can never leave, but rather that the steering committee operates on a continuum, with a line of succession, very much like a company's Board of Directors. Some members serve on the committee for three years; some for two, and some for one year. Leadership comes from within the committee, so the chair does not walk into the position untested and has at least a year of observing the committee's operations. This is a much more orderly approach that will reduce the stress and strain on those serving, and it eliminates the need to beg people to take on the awesome responsibility of being the auction chair with little or no prior experience.

The steering committee still consists of all the essential elements needed to manage the event, but they manage it as an ongoing business, not just a discrete event. Lines of succession within the committee are clear and established, and recruiting to replace those that are in their final year is simpler because the new recruits get at least a year to learn "on the job" before taking on direct responsibility. An example of an effective Auction Steering Committee appears in Exhibit 1.1.

Once you have recruited your steering committee and convinced its members that you collectively are not going to merely "put on an auction," but rather that you are creating a sustainable business that *includes* an auction, then you are truly ready to take on the activities in Phase I.

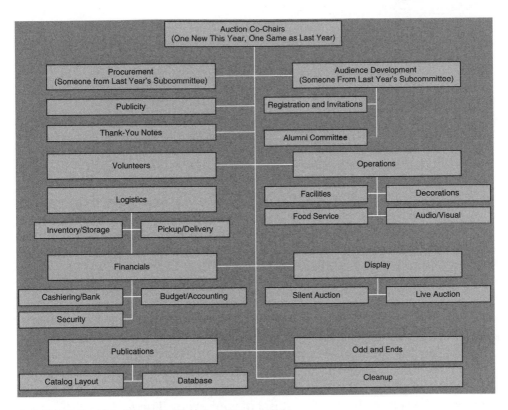

**Exhibit 1.1  The Auction Steering Committee**

## Defining the Purpose of Your Event

A successful event begins with defining why you are holding the event in the first place. As simplistic as this may sound on the surface, it really is central to your success. If you, your committee, and your volunteers are not in sync about why you are doing all this hard work, you are destined to come up short. One common mistake many committees make is to think that the purpose of the event is to make money. Huh? Of course the purpose is to make money! What message are you delivering when the entire focus is on the money? How will that message come across when talking to potential donors and attendees and when recruiting volunteers? Naturally, it's important that your event make money, but that should not be the *sole* purpose of the event. More to the point, focusing on just the money will cause poor decision making and may actually result in lower returns than if the focus and purpose were broader. Or, to state it another way, making money is not your purpose for holding your auction, it is your *outcome.*

In reality, you will be able to do a more complete job of planning and will achieve greater success if you shift the purpose of the event from being just about the money to being the mission of the organization for which you are raising money. The purpose is the answer to the question, "Why?" Look at the two examples below, and think which has a stronger impact on potential donors:

- "We are having a fundraiser and need to make $100,000 for our school. Would you consider donating to help us?"
- "Our school believes every child deserves a quality education, and our mission is to see that no student is denied that education because of an inability to pay for tuition. Our goal is to raise $100,000 for tuition scholarships for those that need help. Would you consider helping us get there?"

When you focus more on the *why* of your fundraiser than on the *what*, you will be communicating a positive message and will be able to rally support easier. Of course the money is important, and when we talk about goal setting, we will show why it is critical that the goal be specific, achievable, and measurable. The answer to "How much do you want to make?" should *not* be "As much as we can," because that is not a focused goal—or any kind of a goal, for that matter. Goals need to be specific—the more specific, the better. But be clear, the *goal* is a subset of your event. The *purpose* of the event is what drives it.

## Setting Financial and Attendance Goals

Now that you understand that "making as much money as possible" isn't a good goal, let's examine how you can go about defining a goal that is realistic and reachable.

There are some general guidelines that you can use in your process for determining a realistic goal. Of course, there are no absolutes, but if we were to create a bell curve of all historic results, from "barely getting it done" on one end to "far-and-away super success" at the other, what we are about to explain will fall near the middle of that curve. Within our guidelines there is also a bell curve, and using the processes and techniques as outlined will certainly push your results well above the "just getting it done" end of the curve and move you more toward the middle. Of course, you could also find your results more toward the end of "far-and-away super success," as well— that is up to you.

Having been involved in literally thousands of auctions, we know that a *buying unit* (a single bidder or a couple attending the event together is considered one buying unit) has the capacity to spend, on average, from $250 to about $1,000. Of course, there are exceptions, but the range of $250 to $1,000 per buying unit as a potential amount you can extract on the day of the event gives you a realistic goal. It would be unusual—but not impossible!—to realize more than $1,000 per buying unit, and many events *are* able to do this. However, these events tend to be mature, well-organized, and highly selective about their invitees, so they are able to skew their results off the bell curve on the high end. The key is to use the middle of the curve ($500 to $750 per buying unit) for your initial planning; you can adjust your expectations for the following year based on actual results from the first year. So, here are some examples of what you should expect to earn, per buying unit, at your event if you follow our planning processes:

200 people (100 buying units) = $50,000–$75,000
300 people (150 buying units) = $75,000–$112,500
400 people (200 buying units) = $100,000–$150,000

This chart assumes two things, which are critical to the success of the formula:

1. You have invited people to your event who are there for your cause (i.e., they understand the purpose of your event and have opted to help) and have the capacity to spend some discretionary funds.
2. You provide enough ways for them to spend their money at the event. In other words, you can only get out of the audience an amount relative to the value of the items on which they can spend their money.

It would make no sense to expect an audience of 300 people (150 buying units) to spend $100,000 collectively on items that are only worth $25,000, $50,000, or even $75,000. In fact, if the auction has $100,000 worth of items, the audience still isn't likely to spend $100,000. The event would need to have items worth $150,000 to expect $100,000 as a result of the bidding process, because not all items sell for their fair market value. Some items will sell for less than they are worth, and some for more. For planning purposes (but adjusted based on actual results) you should assume your items will sell for about 60% to 70% of their total value, on average.

But, on the other hand, it would be just as unrealistic to expect the same audience of 150 buying units to spend $150,000 just because you offered $300,000 worth of items for sale. This would exceed the per buying unit expectation of $500 to $750 per buying unit. You would need to reach $1,000 per buying unit in this situation, which is not impossible, but you should not

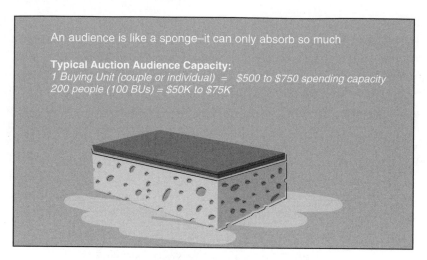

An audience is like a sponge—it can only absorb so much

Typical Auction Audience Capacity:
1 Buying Unit (couple or individual)  =  $500 to $750 spending capacity
200 people (100 BUs) = $50K to $75K

**Exhibit 1.2    What Is Your Audience's Capacity?**

use that as your expected parameter during the goal-setting process. The number of people expected or needed to attend your event must be in balance with the total dollar value of your procurement for you to both set a reasonable goal and then be able to achieve it. The charts and illustrations in this book will help you select some reasonable goal ranges, based on your ability to gather auction items and on your confidence in being able to fill your room with buying units (see Exhibit 1.2).

As previously mentioned, it is unreasonable to expect to earn 100% of the fair market value from each of your auction items. Part of the fun for your auction audience is their trying to get an item for less than its value. Of course, when they are in the frenzy of bidding, bidders often will spend more than the value of some of the items, and that is just fine! Bidders will often pay more than fair market value, justifying their decision to overpay by saying "Well, it *is* for a good cause," and this is to be encouraged. In fact, an ideal auction is one where about 25% or more of the Silent Auction items are sold for more than they are worth. When we discuss bidding techniques for the Silent Auction in Phase IV, we will use a term called *Guaranteed Purchase*, which allows a bidder to close out the bidding and be guaranteed to win the item *if* they are willing to pay a premium for the item, generally about 50% over value. This is analogous to eBay's *Buy It Now* option.

As you are planning your auction, figure that you can expect from 50% to 60% yield from the Silent Auctions and 75% to 85% or more yield from the Live Auction. You will receive about 65% of the auction revenue from the Live Auction and 35% from the Silent Auction. These figures are *very*

**Exhibit 1.3  Expected Goals Based on Procurement Value versus Bidding Activity**

| Revenue Desired | Live Procurement | Live Yield | Live Net Rev. | Silent Procurement | Silent Yield | Silent Net Rev. | Gross Yield | Total Procurement |
|---|---|---|---|---|---|---|---|---|
| **$40,000** | $34,667 | 75% | $26,000 | $28,000 | 50% | $14,000 | 64% | $62,667 |
| **$50,000** | $43,333 | 75% | $32,500 | $35,000 | 50% | $17,500 | 64% | $78,333 |
| **$60,000** | $52,000 | 75% | $39,000 | $42,000 | 50% | $21,000 | 64% | $94,000 |
| **$70,000** | $60,667 | 75% | $45,500 | $49,000 | 50% | $24,500 | 64% | $109,667 |
| **$80,000** | $69,333 | 75% | $52,000 | $56,000 | 50% | $28,000 | 64% | $125,333 |
| **$90,000** | $78,000 | 75% | $58,500 | $63,000 | 50% | $31,500 | 64% | $141,000 |
| **$100,000** | $86,667 | 75% | $65,000 | $70,000 | 50% | $35,000 | 64% | $156,667 |
| **$125,000** | $108,333 | 75% | $81,250 | $87,500 | 50% | $43,750 | 64% | $195,833 |
| **$150,000** | $130,000 | 75% | $97,500 | $105,000 | 50% | $52,500 | 64% | $235,000 |
| **$175,000** | $151,667 | 75% | $113,750 | $122,500 | 50% | $61,250 | 64% | $274,167 |
| **$200,000** | $173,333 | 75% | $130,000 | $140,000 | 50% | $70,000 | 64% | $313,333 |

conservative, and your results will likely exceed these figures, but with these ratios in mind, you can set, with some accuracy, your goals based on Exhibit 1.3.

Remember, auction item procurement is only the first part of the formula. *Audience development* is also a very important part of this mix. If people in attendance at the event are not also willing to spend money on these items, the results will not be as predictable. Generally speaking, an audience of 200 is the minimum size required for competitive bidding. It is possible to have very successful auctions with less than 200 people, but you will need to be very selective in who you invite so that active bidding can occur. A room full of "eaters not bidders" in a small audience is a disaster, so if you are planning a smaller event, make sure you hand-pick your audience for their enthusiasm in supporting your cause as much as possible. Larger events have the luxury of natural selection to build a room full of bidders; that is, larger audiences will include people there just for the party, but because the quantity of attendees is larger, you can expect that many would also be active bidders.

As you are about to learn, the night-of revenue is only one piece of how you account for your event revenue. Total event revenue will include other sources of income, such as entry RSVPs, sponsorships, raffles, matching gifts, underwriting, advertising, tiered pricing structures, table sales, merchandise sales, and Internet auction sales.

A final note on your procurement goal setting: More is not necessarily better. It is possible to overprocure, that is, to have too many items for the number of people who are attending your event. It is always desirable to maintain a seller's market rather than a buyer's market for your items. A seller's market comes from having fewer items to sell than buying units to buy them. A buyer's market happens when there are more items to buy than buying units to buy them. It stands to reason that, in a buyer's market, items sell for less value, and conversely, in a seller's market, they sell for more value. Therefore, it is of little value to continue to add more items once you have crossed over in quantity from a seller's to a buyer's market. More information about determining how many items to procure to maintain the right ratio of items to buying units will be covered in the section on Procurement in Phase III.

When establishing your auction goal, you ideally plan to achieve your procurement goal based on the attendance of the number of buying units that will allow you to reach your desired revenue range for your event, while maintaining a seller's market condition for your items. Having fewer high-value items, so there is more competition for them (a seller's market), will almost always create a better financial outcome than having a number of low-value items that exceeds the number of buying units (a buyer's market), resulting in less competition for each item.

## Planning Your Budget

As you get ready to plan the budget for your auction, we suggest you start with the sample budget worksheet we have prepared, which is included in the Resources section in the back of this book. However, for a moment, let's discuss the purpose of a budget and why it is so important not only to have one that works, but also to do all you can to stick to it. Of course, you have heard the saying "it takes money to make money," which is true. You will need to spend money, much of it in advance or at least committed in advance, to reap the rewards of a successful event. Many new committees try to do their entire event planning on a shoestring, so to speak, attempting to get every aspect of their event donated or at discounts. Getting auction items donated is good, and it's great if you can get decorations, centerpieces, printing services, wine, or similar items donated. When it comes to professional help, such as a caterer, sound system installation, and an auctioneer, you should plan on spending some money if you want to maximize your results. Our experience is that it is impossible to save your way to prosperity. At some point, you will have expenses, and that's expected and okay so long as those expenses are reasonable and help you achieve your goal when you could not get to your goal without the expense.

As an example, if you expect to get real support from high net-worth individuals, you must plan to serve a dinner, and a good one, at that. Asking the high-net-worth folks to come to a spaghetti feed or potluck dinner is just not going to work. A good dinner costs money, and you need to set a budget for that; however, the cost will be offset by the price of attending your event. You could save money by serving a low-cost dinner, but then you would not get the audience you really want to attend or have them come again the following year.

Similarly, you will want to budget for an auction-quality sound system, because built-in sound systems in nearly every hotel ballroom, community center, and country club are designed for after-dinner entertainment and luncheon speeches, not for the energy and "commotion" of a benefit auction. You should also budget for auction management software and professional help, including a professional benefit auctioneer, if you plan to have a Live (oral) Auction. Volunteer auctioneers will cost you much more in lost bids and irritated guests than a professional who knows how to make the audience understand the process and ties the bidding to the cause in a positive way. Because they can keep the auction on track, sense when opportunities present themselves, and know several ways to increase your bid activity, professional auctioneers often pay for themselves in just a few items sold. The guest experience and entertainment value becomes a bonus, long after the cost is justified, in the increased bid activity. Like an adequate sound system, this is another area where you cannot save your way to prosperity.

The Budget Planning Worksheet in Exhibit 1.4 will help get you in the ballpark, but your committee will have their own ideas of what expenditures they need to make along the way. The first page of this Worksheet follows this discussion to give you an idea of the format and content, but the complete Worksheet appears in the Resources section of this book. As a rule of thumb, targeting a budget that leaves about 75% of your gross revenue after the event for your cause is in the right area. If it looks like you will be retaining much below that, then you have two choices: 1) cut some expenses, or 2) plan to raise more money on the same expenses. It is not a good message when you say to your guests and supporters "We raised well over $100,000 [gross] tonight!" Later they find out that the actual amount raised that went to your cause was less than $65,000 [net] because you spent too much to get there. In this example, you spent $35,000 of your gross income on expenses, which means you should have raised closer to $150,000 before expenses. Without a budget, and the committee's willingness to stick to it, you may find yourself overspending and underachieving. That's not good stewardship of your funds, and it's not good business.

**Exhibit 1.4  Budget Planning Worksheet**

**Sample Auction Budget Template**
**Page 1**

**Net Event Goal      $100,000**
*Income*

| Income | Number of Guests | Cost/Person | Budget | Actual | Variance |
|---|---|---|---|---|---|
| **Pre-Auction Revenue** | | | | | |
| Underwriting–Corporate Cash Donations | | | $1,500 | $0 | ($1,500) |
| Underwriting–Non-cash Services or Materials (in kind) | | | $1,000 | $0 | ($1,000) |
| Underwriting–Individual Cash Donations | | | $1,000 | $0 | ($1,000) |
| Catalog Advertising | | | $5,000 | | ($5,000) |
| Sustaining Funds (carryover from prior year) | | | $7,500 | | ($7,500) |
| Misc. Contributions | | | $1,000 | | ($1,000) |
| **Subtotal** | | | **$17,000** | | ($17,000) |
| **Admissions** | | | | | |
| **(Target 300–350)** | **350** | | | | |
| General | 200 | $75 | $15,000 | | ($15,000) |
| Faculty or Special | 20 | $50 | $1,000 | | ($1,000) |
| Patron Level | 10 | $100 | $1,000 | | ($1,000) |
| Benefactor Level | 20 | $250 | $5,000 | | ($5,000) |
| Sponsorship Level | 5 | $500 | $2,500 | | ($2,500) |
| Table Sales (10 per) | 50 | $75 | $3,750 | | ($3,750) |
| Complimentary (honored guest) | 10 | $0 | $0 | | $0 |
| Other (media, staff) | 10 | $0 | $0 | | $0 |
| Total Guests | 325 | | | | |
| **Subtotal** | | | **$28,250** | | ($28,250) |
| **Total Income (Pre-Auction)** | | | **$45,250** | | ($45,250) |
| **Income, Auction** | | | | | |
| Auction Revenue | | | | | |
| Limited Ticket Raffle–Donated Prize | | | $5,000 | | ($5,000) |
| Silent Auction | | | $20,000 | | ($20,000) |
| Live Auction | | | $40,000 | | ($40,000) |
| Fund-an-Item (20% of live and silent income) | | | $13,800 | | ($13,800) |
| Grab Bags or Balloon Sales | | | $1,500 | | ($1,500) |
| Centerpiece Sales | | | $1,500 | | ($1,500) |
| Merchandise Sales | | | $1,000 | | ($1,000) |
| **Subtotal** | | | **$82,800** | | ($82,800) |

*Planning Income Level Based on Buying Units (2 guests = 1 BU)*

| | | | | |
|---|---|---|---|---|
| *$500/BU Average* | *Number of BUs* | 175 | **$87,500** | *(not in totals or recap)* |
| **Other Auction Revenue** | | | | |
| Guests' Employer Matching | | | $10,000 | ($10,000) |
| Funds (post-event), estimated | | | | |
| | **Subtotal** | | **$10,000** | ($10,000) |
| **Total Income (Auction-Related)** | | | ***$92,800*** | ($92,800) |
| ***Total Revenue, All Sources*** | | | **$138,050** | ($138,050) |

# CHAPTER 2

# Establishing Auction Committees

In the previous chapter, we discussed the differences between the Steering Committee—the group responsible for the overall vision of the "business" you are building—and the Auction Committee, which refers to the group responsible for all the functions needed to complete this year's event. In this chapter, we will look at the specific areas of responsibility the Auction Committee has, and how the Chairs of each committee are related to, and interface with the Steering Committee to get the job done.

While your committee chairs have the responsibility to take ownership of their area, they are expected to recruit helpers to assist them. The section chairs work with their subcommittees and then report back to the Steering Committee on the progress made in each area. Recruitment for these committee chairs, therefore, should be based on their ability to be organizers and motivators, not just on the assumption that they will do all the work in their specific area of responsibility. Building a team made up of both workers and leaders is the ideal situation: From the current workers come the leaders of the future, along with the continuity you desire, so your "business" never goes out of business.

## Auction Committee Co-Chairs

The first item on the agenda needs to be the assigning of committee chairs. Later in this section, you will find a form you can use for assigning and tracking those chairs. We will also discuss the responsibilities of the various committee chairs in greater detail, but for now here is a brief definition of each committee chair's responsibilities:

1. *Procurement*: The Acquisitions Chair is responsible for organizing those people who will go out into the community to gather items for sale at the auction.
2. *Audience Development*: The Audience Development Chair is responsible for designing and distributing invitations, coordinating the sales of

15

corporate tables, coordinating a phone tree for all committee chairs, and receiving reservations from guests planning to attend.

3. *Operations*:

   a. *Facilities*: The Facilities Chair is responsible for coordinating the venue in which you will hold your event. The many different factors involved will be discussed later in this chapter.

   b. *Decorations*: The Decorations Chair is responsible for turning the venue selected into a festive room coordinated with the theme the auction committee selected. This person is also responsible for organizing people to show the Live Auction items while they are up for bid.

   c. *Food Service*: The Food Service Chair is the person responsible for making sure that the guests attending the auction are treated to the best service regarding food and drink. This person selects the catering company and (if additional) the bar service.

   d. *Audio/Visual*: The Audio/Visual Chair has the responsibility of deciding whether the venue selected has enough light, and, if not, where lighting can be augmented. This person is responsible for rental of the sound system (microphones and speakers) for the event. Sound must be high quality and available in both the Silent and Live Auction rooms.

4. *Publications*:

   a. *Catalog Layout*: The Catalog Layout Chair is responsible for designing, compiling, and publishing the catalog. It is important that this committee keep track of new and last-minute items, and any packaging that may occur. Also, the Catalog Layout Committee needs to know the order in which the items should appear in the catalog.

   b. *Database*: The Database Chair (or Committee) is responsible for *all* data entry into the computer. We strongly recommend against trying to conduct your auction without some professional way of tracking donations, attendees, and finances. The best way to do this is with a computerized database system—preferably a respected commercial auction management software package. This person is responsible for keeping and organizing records of all items and reservations so the paperwork the night of your event goes smoothly. More often than not, the Database Committee consists of just one person. This prevents confusion and double entry. The Database Chair may decide to delegate guest reservations to someone else, as necessary. If you are using a web-based auction management system the workload for both item and guest list data entry can be spread over several committee members, which is the preferred approach rather than requiring a single person to do the work.

5. *Publicity*: The Publicity Chair is responsible for speaking with the local media and getting word out to the local community about your event via newspaper, radio, and even television. This includes registering the event on local community event calendars.

6. *Financials*:
   a. *Budget/Accounting*: The Budget/Accounting Chair is responsible for properly managing the budget money for committees that need funding and for tracking how much money is to go to each chair. In addition, this chair is responsible for accounting for how much money was made and making the final report to your organization. Professional auction management software can often make this process much easier.
   b. *Cashiering/Bank*: The Cashiering/Bank Chair is responsible for the money that comes in before, during, and after the auction. He or she is also responsible for taking the final deposit to the bank and working in conjunction with the budget committee in the final audit. If your organization has a treasurer or accountant, this is the perfect place for that person.
   c. *Security*: The Security Chair is primarily responsible for helping successful bidders find their items at the end of the Live Auction.

7. *Display*:
   a. *Live Auction Display*: This person or committee is responsible for delivering items to the auction venue, for setting up the live auction preview, and for other such displays. Decorations in the Live Auction area are also a part of this person's responsibility.
   b. *Silent Auction Display*: This person or committee is responsible for all aspects of setting up the Silent Auction tables and display elements.

8. *Volunteers*: The Volunteer Committee is responsible for coordinating, training, and keeping track of all people assisting as volunteers in the logistics of the event.

9. *Logistics*:
   a. *Inventory/Storage*: The Inventory/Storage Chair is responsible for tracking and storing all auction items until the night of the auction.
   b. *Pickup/Delivery*: These responsibilities start where the Inventory Chair's end. This person or group is responsible for organizing pickup and delivery of any larger items from the storage area to the auction. They also need to have a plan for delivering the larger items to the successful bidders' homes or destinations of choice, when within a reasonable distance of the event, or a contingency plan, for exceptions.

10. *Cleanup*: The Cleanup Chair's responsibility is to ensure that after you leave, the venue is in the same shape, or better, than it was when

your organization arrived. This committee is also responsible for making a final check for personal belongings or property of your organization that might have been left behind and is done at the end of the event.

11. *Thank-You Notes*: This person or group is responsible for thanking not only everyone who attended the auction, but also those who donated items. Often, this task can be automated with auction management software, but still requires an individual to perform quality control.

12. *Odds and Ends*: If there is a duty that needs to be performed, not only during the time of your event but in preparing your event, it is this person's or group's responsibility to step in and help to the best of their ability. This is also known as the "Miscellaneous" group because of its catch-all nature.

It's very important that you assign a specific person to each of these roles, even if the same person is assigned to multiple jobs. Some roles are more easily combined with others. For example, one person could volunteer to take on the chairs of all the item-related committees, such as Inventory/Storage and Pickup/Delivery. Be careful, however, that you don't overwhelm anyone by assigning them more than they can practically do, given their own abilities, availability, and interests. A sample worksheet for assigning committee chairs can be found in Exhibit 2.1.

### Budget/Accounting Committee

The Budget/Accounting Committee will have two primary responsibilities. One, they will work with the other committee chairs to establish the initial budget for each separate subcommittee and make sure all committee chairs understand that the money they have to spend is part of an overall event budget. Second, the Budget/Accounting Committee will monitor expenses along the way toward the event, to be sure all the chairs are staying within their budget or, should they need to go "off budget," that they come to the Steering Committee first and get approval for an exception.

There are legitimate cases where a budget item or category just cannot be met due to circumstances beyond the control of the chair, such as selecting a venue that requires a sound system that is more costly than the budget had allowed. Certainly, you would not expect to host the event without a proper sound system, and this is not an area where it makes sense to pinch pennies. It may be necessary to increase the budget for sound midstream, and as long as the new cost fits within the overall budget for the event, that's okay. The Budget/Accounting Committee will oversee

**Exhibit 2.1    Auction Committee Chair Assignments**

### Auction Committee Chair Assignments

| Committee | Person Assigned | Telephone # |
|---|---|---|
| Procurement | _____ | _____ |
| Audience Development | _____ | _____ |
|     Corporate Tables | | |
|     Invitations | | |
|     Telephone Tree | | |
|     Reservations (RSVPs) | | |
| Facilities | _____ | _____ |
| Decorations | _____ | _____ |
| Food Service (food/bar) | _____ | _____ |
| Audio/Visual | _____ | _____ |
| Database | _____ | _____ |
|     Catalog/Items | | |
|     Donors | | |
|     Attendees | | |
| Catalog Layout | _____ | _____ |
| Publicity/Web site | _____ | _____ |
| Budget/Accounting | _____ | _____ |
| Cashiering/Bank | _____ | _____ |
| Security | _____ | _____ |
| Live Auction Display | _____ | _____ |
| Silent Auction Display | _____ | _____ |
| Volunteers | _____ | _____ |
| Inventory/Storage | _____ | _____ |
| Pickup/Delivery | _____ | _____ |
| Cleanup | _____ | _____ |
| Thank-You Notes | _____ | _____ |
| Odds and Ends | _____ | _____ |

the expenditures and monitor the adherence to budget so the event is profitable and achieves the financial net goal that has been established. Payments to vendors; establishing or managing the bank account for the event; and finding and applying for the payment processing to be used during the event are also part of this committee's responsibilities.

### Cashiering Committee

The chair of the Cashiering Committee is specifically responsible for col-lecting the money or charge authorizations at the event, as well as assuring that all the bid activity is properly entered into the auction database. This committee chair will organize a subcommittee that works throughout the evening and, after the event, will also be responsible for the post-event audit and for processing credit card charges and bank deposits.

As you might imagine, this chair works closely with the Budget/Account-ing Chair, as there are some overlapping responsibilities. The easiest way of differentiating the duties is to assume that if it has to do with finance leading up to the event, the job falls to the Budget/Accounting Chair and Commit-tee. If it has to do with financial transactions during or immediately after the event, then it is most like the responsibility of the Cashiering Chair and that committee. Many organizations will combine these duties and use the same staff for continuity, and that is appropriate and acceptable.

Some of the duties of the Cashiering Committee include:

- Preparing the Live and Silent Auction bid forms, or at least ensuring that they have been created and available for the day of the event
- Preparing forms for tracking walk-up bidders or guests who need to pay at the door
- Ensuring that the payment system for credit cards is in place and that all the registration volunteers are trained in the qCheck or similar process, if one is used (the qCheck process, which is sometimes referred to by similar names such as Express Checkout or QuickCheck — is discussed in detail in Chapter 12, in Phase IV)
- Prepare or have prepared the Registration packets in advance so registration does not create check-in lines
- Registering guests and capturing guests' addresses, or verifying current addresses for guests
- Staffing the registration tables and ensuring all guests receive a bid packet
- Monitoring the Silent Auctions and closing the tables at the proper times
- Entering data into the auction database throughout the evening
- Capturing the Live Auction bids and providing runners to return the bid forms to the data entry area
- Filing the bid forms by bid number after the information is entered into the computer
- Preparing the final auction-night statement for the guests and collect-ing any payments from guests who did not qCheck
- Ensuring that guests collect their proper items and receive help removing them from the premises

- Conducting a post-event audit to account for all sales and then making all payments through the credit card system or bank deposits
- Preparing a post-event report and turning over all files and materials, along with a backup of the auction database, to the Steering Committee Chair

More detailed explanations of the way to set up registration and cashiering are provided in Phase IV.

### Venue-Related Auction Committees

There are four distinct committees that are generally involved in the specific selection of a venue for your event. Although other committees and members may also have input and issues that come into play, it is imperative that all four of these chairpeople coordinate and work closely with one another and with the Audience Development Chair to choose and set up a venue that will work best for all involved.

Before we get into the details of the four committees, here are several things that these chairs will need to consider when evaluating and choosing a venue:

- *Convenience*: Is the location easy to find and well-known? Does it have easy access for your guests? Does it have ample and accessible parking, or will you need to consider off-site parking, valet service, and shuttles? What about access for guest with special needs or challenges? Sometimes, "creative" locations aren't suitable for someone who is physically challenged or uses a wheelchair, so add this to your list of considerations before you settle on a location.
- *Food Service*: Will the caterer be able to comfortably handle service for the size of your audience? Does the facility provide an onsite caterer, or will you have to bring in somebody from the outside? Must you use the location's alcoholic beverages and services, or can you provide your own wine for dinner at a discount from another source? If the answer is yes, will the facility charge a corkage fee for this option? What about other potential "service" costs, such as a dessert plating fee, a minimum bar tab, or minimum number of guests?
- *Room Space*: Having too little or too constricted space can be a huge challenge for auctions. Make sure that the facilities you are considering allow your guests to move freely within the space and from one area to the next. Is there enough room to set up your Silent Auction and still have room to enable guests to walk around and check their bids? Is the Silent Auction area enclosed or configured so secure redemption of items will be easy and secure in case unclaimed items remain after all

guests have left? It's also important to look for areas that can conveniently be used for the other support functions like cashiering, registration, a volunteer room, storage, and so forth.

- *Decorations*: Look for a location with some flexibility. While hotel ballrooms and their related facilities are popular choices, don't limit yourself to consider this as your only option. Art museums, trade or convention centers, golf or country clubs, cruise ships, or converted historical landmarks in your area are also creative venues that allow unique ambiance for your event, making it more memorable.
- *Lighting*: Pay close attention to the available lighting at your venue. Your Silent Auction and Live Auction display tables need to be placed in well-lit areas; if that isn't possible, consider bringing in auxiliary lighting. Make sure your venue's policy doesn't preclude that as an option.
- *Sound*: Rarely do the facilities that are used for auctions come equipped with the right amplification systems for this kind of event. "House sound" is rarely adequate, and "band sound" is *not* designed for auctions. Be sure to budget for rental of speakers, microphones, speaker cable, etc. Also be sure to hire somebody to operate the sound system once it is in place, if you haven't engaged the services of a professional sound company that provides this service. Poor sound can cost your event *thousands* in lost revenue if people can't hear or understand the auctioneer.
- *Availability*: Often, popular facilities (e.g., cruise ships or convention centers) are booked well in advance—sometimes months or even years. Before you get too attached to a certain location, and certainly before you begin promoting it as your venue, make sure that it is available on the night your event is being held.

These are just a few very important considerations you will face when selecting a site for your auction. In describing the different subcommittees under the blanket of Venue Selection, we will educate you further so you will be sure to choose the right location. Be creative, but get all the information first. Don't take a place simply because it's free, and be sure read *all* the fine print before signing any binding agreements and committing to your location and your date.

**Facilities Chair** The Facilities Chair has the overall responsibility for the location of the event. This includes finding the location, negotiating the contracts, and arranging for the logistical support required for the event. Included in the Chair's scope of responsibility are such issues as:

- Moving into (and out of) the facility
- Facilities setup and timing

- Arranging for temporary storage onsite
- Availability of lighting, tables for display, registration, and cashiering and cashiering areas, and so on

A floor plan of your location is an important tool that is used to lay out the event; the facility can usually provide you with one if you ask. Your layout of the floor plan for your event should include: Live and Silent Auction locations, stage area, auxiliary lighting locations, audio locations, seating and kitchen locations, and cashiering and registration locations. Getting to know and building a relationship with the facility supervisor in advance of your event will help in getting last-minute changes taken care of with minimal difficulty.

Before signing any agreement to rent a location you should be aware of the following types of fees, services, or considerations (and if you don't see them, be sure to ask):

- Cleaning fees
- Deposits (refundable or nonrefundable)
- Room rental costs, especially if you are renting more than one room
- Catering minimums or overages
- Possible discounts for using venue catering and/or bar services
- Check-out with facility supervisor at end of night
- Fire codes that will affect room set-up plans
- Pipe and draping needs
- Fees for carpeting, tables, chairs, linens, and so on
- Any special restrictions on use
- Additional or specific insurance requirements

Sometimes hidden fees can add up and make your "perfect" location a very expensive mistake. Make sure you carefully read *all* the fine print before you sign any contract for location rental.

**Decorations Chair**   The responsibility of the Decorations Committee is to dress up the evening and showcase it in the most festive way possible. The chair of this committee has the overall responsibility for overseeing the many elements involved in planning for the feel and decorations of the event and, in principle, should have the final decision-making capability. The Decorations Committee brings the event to life by choosing color schemes and decorative pieces that incorporate and support the chosen theme. Bright elements and festive colors surrounding your guests will make for a fun and lively evening and will enhance the auction's energy level. This is a job for a creative person with an eye for transforming what might otherwise be a blank and boring room into a location that brings out the party mood in your guests.

It's the Decorations Chair's job to be creative, and he or she is encouraged to experiment, as long as it remains within budget. The best decorations are creative items that serve as decorations during the event, but which can be purchased by guests during the event to take home. This allows your organization to recoup some of the cost of the decorations, and cuts down on cleanup afterwards. Therefore, this chair should be someone imaginative enough to develop decorations that have appeal after the auction. Some ideas for items like this are:

- Table centerpieces and favors
- Stage decorations
- Silent or Live Auction display materials
- Balloon sales
- Medals or other recognition "rewards" for successful bidders in Live Auction

You don't have to always play safe in this area and go with what's worked in the past; don't be afraid to be creative in your decorations. Many ideas can come from walking through a craft store, looking around other people's homes, or attending banquets and other auctions. All of those decorations were put together on a budget as well. Get ideas wherever you can, and don't be afraid to incorporate elements that you like from others' ideas. You can find a host of successful themes and decorating ideas on our Web site too, at www.auctionhelp.com.

### One Word about Centerpieces

You should pay attention to one caution about your table centerpieces. Sometimes, an overeager Decorations Chair or committee member decides to unleash their creativity on the centerpieces, to the detriment of the event. Centerpieces that are so elaborate or tall that they interfere with line-of-sight across the table (guest-to-guest) also impede the auctioneer's ability to see your bidders. If the auctioneer cannot easily see a bid card, that can cost you money. Even more important is the auctioneer's ability to see the *guest* who may be considering a bid, but hasn't made the bid yet. Being able to see the guest, read body language, and interpret it quickly and easily can make the difference in getting that incremental or final bid. Word to the wise: Keep centerpieces low and fairly simple—ideally, they should be no taller than 18 inches from the top of the table.

Below are some examples of successful and fun themes you might want to consider for your next event:

- Mo' Rockin' Knights (the school's mascot was the Knights and they had a Moroccan-themed event)
- The Wonderful Wizard of Oz
- Chocolate Holiday
- Starry, Starry Night
- Hollywood themes (e.g., Hooray for Hollywood, Oscar® Night tie-ins, or connections with hot movies)
- Tropical/Hawaiian themes (e.g., "Jamaica Me Crazy!"—tropical with steel drums)
- Flower Power (1960s theme)
- Flashback to the 1970s, 1980s, and so on
- Western
- "Jungle Book"
- Safari
- Nautical
- Literary characters from books (especially good for schools)
- Carnival and Mardi Gras
- Broadway (especially tied to specific Broadway shows)

**A Western-Themed Silent Auction Display**

**Live Auction Stage for a Nautical-Themed Event**

It can be tempting and fun to select themes that allow your guests to come dressed up to match the theme or in costume. Costumes can be a great energy builder, but avoid themes that encourage people to wear masks. Psychologically, masks can serve as a shield or allow people to be more anonymous, resulting in a tendency for people to be something other than themselves at the event, often with negative results. Also, keep in mind that a good auctioneer is reading guests' body language and assessing their interest and willingness to bid. Having guests wearing masks at the event makes this impossible.

**Food Service Chair**   The foods and beverages you'll be serving your guests are an important factor in the success of your event. As you are evaluating and selecting your location, keep in mind that some locations are not designed—or are not ideally suited—for catering services. The Food Service Chair needs to work closely with the Facilities Chair to help choose a location that either offers onsite catering or has adequate kitchen and service facilities so you are not restricted in your food service choices. The Food Service Chair has the responsibility of coordinating all food and beverage service for the event, including:

**The "Yellow Brick Road" Leads the Way Through the Silent Auction for a *Wizard of Oz*-Themed Event**

- Planning the menu and food selections
- Determining and negotiating the cost of meals
- Coordinating the scheduled times that courses should be served (timing can have a significant effect on the success of your auction, so don't minimize the importance of establishing an effective service schedule with your banquet or food services staff at your location)
- Determining who will provide bar services and source/cost for beverages
- Special requests (e.g., kosher/vegan/vegetarian meals and other dietary requirements, allergies, etc.)

Here are some preliminary questions to ask when evaluating a food service provider for your event:

- Do they allow for a choice of meal selections for guests? How many?
- Do the caterers bring the food in already prepared, or do they require an onsite kitchen facility? If they need access to a kitchen, how does that fit with the facility's policy?

- Do they provide waiters and waitresses or do they have a "buffet" setup?
- What wine lists do they offer?
- Are there corkage fees associated with their service?
- Do they offer discounted prices for charity events?
- Have they provided services in your chosen location before? How familiar are they with the layout of the venue and its facilities?
- How much overage do they allow for in estimating costs? Will they be able to provide emergency or backup meals for a certain percentage of guests who may show up unannounced?

These are all very important questions to consider as you select and negotiate your food service. Also, because the food costs are directly related to the number of guests, it's important that the Food Services Chair keep an open line of communication with the Audience Development Chair, to make sure that there will be enough meals to account for:

- Guests that have sent in their RSVPs
- Honored guests (if applicable)
- Nonregistered (walk-up) guests
- Volunteers and event staff, if you will be providing meals for them

As you plan for your meal, one temptation might be to cut food costs by serving a buffet dinner. Buffets are generally a bad idea for auctions, because they are counterproductive to the spending process. The last thing your organization or your auctioneer needs is people getting up out of their seats to get in the food line or to go back for seconds. This distracts from the momentum of the evening and can make visibility difficult for the auction-eer. Worse, people who are out of their seats are typically *not* paying attention to the auction and, therefore, are not spending money. Your Food Services Chair will also probably find that a buffet dinner will cost just as much per person as a sit-down dinner at most upscale venues. So, instead of saving yourself money, you'll find it actually *costs* you to feed your guests this way, both in upfront food costs as well as in lost revenue the night of the event.

Good hors d'oeuvres during the Silent Auction, a good meal during the Live Auction and great wine and other beverages throughout the evening will help keep your event running smoothly and your guests happy and in the mood to bid for your cause. If you aren't sure who to go to for catering, ask friends and relatives for recommendations. Get references for the company and make sure they are reputable and can handle your type and size of event. Nothing can spoil a great auction like bad food service, and nothing can make a great event even greater than a great meal!

**Audio/Visual Chair**   Proper sound and lighting are essential to the success of any auction. This Chair will be responsible for working with the Facilities Chair to arrange for proper lighting and sound for the event, including rental of auxiliary lighting, as necessary. If the guests cannot see the items (or the bid sheets) properly, read the catalog, or hear the auctioneer's bid increments, bidding activity will be reduced. Good lighting can enhance the appearance and perceived value of physical items, particularly artwork, which can be specially lighted to enhance its appearance.

The sound system used during your auction is as important as lighting, if not more. Many facilities will tell you that they offer an adequate in-house sound system when, in reality, it isn't. A built-in system will rarely work for auctions. The built in sound at nearly all hotels, country clubs, and banquet venues (99.9%) is designed for an after-dinner or lunch guest speaker, a wedding, or another quiet social gathering where the entire audience is expected to listen to the one person in the room with the microphone, the guest speaker. Not so at an auction. Built-in sound is *never* designed for an auction, where hundreds of people are all talking, *plus* the auctioneer and emcee must be understood. In a noisy room, the built-in sound systems are just mush, and there is a good reason for this.

Consider that speakers in a built-in system are installed in the ceilings. These speakers are small and useless for anything more than a moderate level of sound. The louder the volume is set in these small speakers, the worse the sound gets. Sound travels in a straight line and does not bend; it must be *reflected* to change its direction. Since no one has ears on the top of his head (they are on the sides, remember?) the only sound you can hear from built-in systems will have been reflected several times before it enters the ear. Because it's reflected by numerous things in the room—chairs, tables, walls, the floor, even people—several iterations of the same words enter the ears at slightly different times. This reflected sound loses its clarity, and when it is combined with the buzz of potentially hundreds of conversations in the audience, the result is essentially a sound soup. A potential bidder who is unable to hear the auctioneer's bids is reluctant to hold up a bid number. Cumulatively, across your entire audience this could result in several missed bid steps on each item. For a ten-item Live Auction, with an average value of $2,500 per item, the loss of a few bid steps on each item could mean losing several thousands of dollars. Bad sound is a thief, literally stealing your money by keeping the audience from enjoying the evening, as it inflicts loud, unclear and increasingly annoying noise on them. Your bidders will tune out early, and no amount of pleading with them to pay attention to the auctioneer will bring them back.

While many committees will scale down their sound requirements because of reluctance to pay for an adequate setup, understand that a proper sound system will add significant revenue to your event—much more than the cost of the system—by allowing bidders to follow the bidding process more easily. The Audio/Visual Chair should engage a professional sound company to arrange the setup, operation, and removal of the system. It's important that the sound system provide balanced, clear sound at relatively equal levels to all parts of the auction room. Sound that is too loud in one area and not loud enough in another will cause people to lose focus on the auction and tune out. A typical mistake is to place the speakers at the front of the room or on the stage area. This causes the sound to be clear and strong at the front of the room, while the people in the back of the room will strain to hear the auctioneer. Increasing the volume so that the back guests can hear causes a different problem: The sound will be too loud for the guests seated at the front, to the point where it can be painful. This is a typical scenario faced by auctions that have bands for dancing or entertainment, when the committees decide to rely on the band sound for the auction. Band sound is a front-loaded speaker system; the band puts its speakers on the floor in front of the stage where the dance floor is. For the people at the back of the room to hear, the sound must travel *through* all the people between them and the stage. By the time the sound travels to the back of the room it is mush, and so loud in the front as to be uncomfortable for the guests sitting there. The people in the front are blasted and leave early, while the people in the back can't hear and leave early.

Most of the high-budget events today include a slide presentation of Live Auction items or video presentations for the Fund-an-Item or emotional appeal of the event. The best sound and light services can also provide projectors, large screens, and all the sound equipment you need to add a professional touch to the Live Auction.

There is much more information available about sound and lighting for your auction. The Resources section of this book is one place for you to start. Also, don't hesitate to ask people at other charitable organizations to recommend a reputable company in your area and remember to ask for references.

We can't say this too often: it's *very important* that you not cut corners with lighting and sound when budgeting for your event. If the guests cannot hear and see the action, or if they are sitting in a place where sound is blasted at them, momentum will be lost as guests try to figure out what is going on or where their attention should be focused. Bad sound will cost you many times over the price you'd pay for good sound.

### Catalog-Oriented Committees

The two committees that are involved in catalog construction are the Database and Catalog Layout Committees. It's critical that both these committees work cohesively with one another to create a catalog that is functional and informative as well as eye-catching and fun. With the help of the Procurement Chair and the auctioneer, auction items need to be numbered, sequenced, and adequately described. This section is dedicated primarily to the function and duties of each committee, but further information about catalog layout and design appears in Phase III.

**Database Committee** The Database Committee is the group responsible for working with the auction software to ensure that all data related to the event is properly tracked and accounted for. As a result, the Database Committee has three primary responsibilities:

1. Entering all information on items procured for the auction
2. Entering all critical information on auction donors so that thank-you letters (and potentially invitations) can be sent out
3. Entering all guest information for reservations

The Database Committee may also have the overall control of any online sites that you may choose to use, such as an event Web site or online auction. While the look and feel of these components may include help from other committees, such as the Decorations Committee, to make sure design elements of the sites are consistent with the theme of the event, the Database Committee has the ultimate responsibility for knowing and using the technology portions and the working with the data.

In this section, we will discuss primarily the specifics related to the duties of the Database Committee, not the underlying aspects of the technology or tools used to get the job done. Because a discussion of the benefits and purpose of auction management software would be fairly extensive, this topic is covered in detail later in Phase II. In this section, we will focus on what needs to be done, and not muddle the issue by bringing up tools and technology, which really relates to more to *how* the tasks are done.

*Item Entry* As mentioned in the previous paragraph, in Phase II we will talk further about the details of automating your event and event site, but for now, let's merely point out that most auctions today are managed using a specialized computer database system. Consequently, the person responsible for data entry should be computer literate and familiar with the program being used. Initially, they will be responsible for entering *all* items from the original Procurement Forms into the database. As auction day approaches, they will have a significant and growing workload that includes item tracking, packaging, and sequencing, so this person should not be assigned to any other auction preparation tasks or committees.

The Item Entry person will also be working with the Catalog Layout Committee to enter good item descriptions of the items that will later appear in the catalog. The individual selected to do this job will be one who has a creative mind, reasonably fast typing skills, and good writing abilities. Ideally, while more than one person can do preliminary item entry (assuming you have an auction management tool that provides for multi-user capability), one person should be responsible for final checking and cleanup of that data in the computer, as that will keep all information and entries consistent.

*Donor Entry*    The Database Committee is responsible for entering the names and critical information of the item donors into the computer database, as well. This information is helpful, as it provides a list of those companies and individuals who may have further interest in helping your cause. These people will be sent thank-you notes, as well as invitations to your next event. They can also be kept on file for next year's Procurement Committee. Having a list of companies who donated items the previous year can make procurement easier the following years.

If your organization uses a constituent management software system, you may be able to handle this task another way. Some auction management software products will export and import data to your constituent management software system, saving a tremendous amount of time and ensuring accuracy while simultaneously coordinating with the effort to build and maintain relationships with donors and potential donors. Blackbaud's The Raiser's Edge and Maestrosoft's AuctionMaestro Pro are two available products that provide a seamless integration between the two databases. As a minimum, your auction management software should have an easy way to export data and import data, so you can develop and track long-term relationships with donors.

*Guest RSVPs*    Your guests should have an easy way to register for your event, and it's the job of the Audience Development Committee to set up a system to handle the RSVP process. Note that we are not talking about ticket sales. We do not *sell* tickets to a gala; we invite guests, and expect them to respond, which is what RSVP (répondez s'il vous plaît) means. When you sell a ticket to an event, the guest may feel that he or she has made a contribution by purchasing a ticket, and, therefore, need not attend the actual event. This is not the case when you use an RSVP system, where it is expected that the person who is invited either decides to attend or not to attend and then sends in a registration card to let you know. Those who do RSVP to attend are actually expected to show up at the event, and while some are ultimately "no-shows," that number is much smaller than it would be if a ticket sale approach was used.

An RSVP system will also make it much easier to prepare registration packets and assign tables. Knowing how many guests are coming also helps you calculate the proper number of meals and tables that need to be set. Trying to capture guest information—name, addresses, telephone numbers—and then assigning tables and bid numbers at the event is a sure way to create long check-in lines and irritated guests. Once you irritate the guests, you may never get them back in a happy and generous mood, plus you have given them a great reason not to attend the following year. As much as possible, get all of the data and do all of the work that can be done ahead of time, and leave the day of the event only for things that must be done at the last minute.

One of the new trends is to use the Internet and an event Web site as a place to advertise and promote your event, display your auction items as they become available, and register guests online. This has several advantages. First, by sending these potential guests to your Web site to register (list the address on your RSVP card); you are also letting them preview your auction items. Also, in this day of credit card fraud, identity theft, and security concerns, asking a high net-worth individual to send an RSVP card back in an envelope with his or her full name, credit card number, expiration date and signature is just asking for trouble. You provide a much safer method when you can send them to your auction Web site and take a secure payment at that time, assuming your Web site has a secure payment process available. Companies like cMarket and MaestroSoft, with its MaestroWeb product, provide online registration and catalog viewing features so your guests can register for your event, take a tour of the items that will be up for bid, make on-line donations, and even bid on items on-line, if that is something your committee would like to include as part of your pre-event revenue.

**Catalog Layout Committee**   The responsibility of the Catalog Layout Committee is to decide on the designs and presentation of all the printed material used to support your auction, particularly including the auction catalog. This is one of the most visible responsibilities, as every invitee and guest will be the recipient of one or more of these items. More details on how to design and produce effective materials for your auction will be discussed in Phases III and IV.

## Security Committee

The Security Chair plans for, organizes, and supervises a simple security team for the auction. Often the team is a group of volunteers who assist guests with finding and retrieving their items after the auction, verify their paid receipts against tracking forms, and then sometimes help guests to their car or to the entrance of the auction if you don't have a separate Carry Out group.

While some auctions contain items that are expensive and valuable enough to warrant traditional security activities, such as keeping the area guarded and closed off when not in use, most of the time the security team's function is to prevent items from being mistaken for others and avoiding the confusion that results when someone takes the wrong item, thinking they were the successful bidder. At some auctions, police cadets, fraternity and sorority volunteers, or other service groups perform this function. These volunteers also work before the actual auction during setup to make sure the public doesn't stray into the setup area and to monitor the Live and Silent Auction tables before the auction begins.

Since the security team is primarily present to help with redemption, they should be familiar with the items in the auction and particularly aware of the items that could potentially be mistaken for something else, or of duplicate items that could be confused.

### Inventory/Storage Committee

The Inventory/Storage Chair is responsible for arranging a proper and secure location for all auction items once they have been received as a result of Item Procurement activities. When an item is received, an inventory system is used to assign a tracking number, which is attached to the physical item or certificate. The tracking number is then copied to the original procurement form, a copy of which is given to the Database Chair for entry into the database system. The tracking number is coordinated with the catalog number when catalog order is determined. Auction management software can help greatly in automating and coordinating these activities.

This committee has the overall responsibility of ensuring all items are properly tracked and stored in a clean, dry location that is easily accessible before procurement, during procurement, and on auction day for delivery to the auction site. This storage facility should have the following attributes:

- Be large enough to fit all auction items, no matter how small or large
- Be in a secure location with locks and (ideally) a theft deterrent system
- Be a clean area (if a garage is used, it needs to be a clean garage)
- Be dry and free of drafts and excessive amounts of moisture
- Be sufficiently spacious that, even with all items in the storage facility, people are able to walk through and check tracking numbers
- Have adequate access, so that it requires only a reasonable effort to move all items to the auction venue before the auction

Your auction guests expect that their items are in the same quality condition as if they had gone into the store and purchased them brand new.

The only difference is that your committee has been storing them for a couple of months between the time they were received and the auction date. The better the condition of the items, the more people will bid on them, and the more money your organization will make.

### Pickup/Delivery Committee

The Pickup/Delivery Chair works with the Inventory Chair to ensure auction items are delivered to the storage area before the auction, that the items are delivered to the location on the day of the event, and that arrangements are made picking up the items by the successful bidder after the auction has concluded.

The Pickup Chair coordinates with the Procurement Chair to make sure that items are delivered to the storage facility by the auction representatives, or, if necessary, that a date and time is arranged to pick up the item from the donor.

Remember that the auction guests expect items to be in perfect condition when they bid on them. If the items look like they have been moved around a lot, or are damaged in any way, this will decrease their value, resulting in lower bids. Items in transit from the storage facility to the auction, or from the donor location to the storage facility, must be treated with care so they arrive to the event in pristine condition. Here are a few helpful hints regarding item transport:

- Wrap any breakable objects with popcorn or bubble wrap if the donor didn't provide such protection.
- Place clothing or material items in plastic bags or clothes boxes to stop them from getting dirty and wrinkled.
- Keep framed items in a safe place where they won't be broken or cracked.
- All certificates should be put in separate envelopes and filed in a file box until they are assigned catalog numbers.
- Any electronic items should be kept in their original packaging and free of moisture or dust.
- Food items should not be delivered to the storage location. Instead, they should be delivered directly from the donor to the event on the day of the auction.

By following these simple rules, you increase the odds of keeping your items in perfect condition so they will fetch a high price at your auction.

### Cleanup Committee

After the auction, the event space will likely require cleaning up. While the degree of cleanup may vary depending on the facility, the service provided by the venue or caterer, and the degree to which decorations and staging have been used at your event, in general these activities include:

- Removing decorations
- Performing inventory and storage of items not sold or unclaimed
- Removing all items owned by or brought by the organization to the venue

If tables or any other furniture were moved around during the auction setup, these items must be returned to their original locations. All tape used to hold down speaker or microphone cables must be removed and cleaned up, as well as all balloons and other party decorations. All leftover food not provided by the venue or caterers needs be thrown away or taken home, and in some locations, vacuuming and cleaning is necessary to bring the facility back up to its state of pre-event cleanliness.

If a commercial location is used, such as the banquet room of a hotel, your catering crew will likely handle all cleanup beyond those activities described in the bulleted list. This is generally part of the service you pay for as part of your contract. Check with the Venue Committee Chair to find out the terms and conditions are regarding the facility's post-event cleaning.

Some organizations find it difficult to get volunteers willing to help with this task late at night, when everyone is tired and wants to go home. Some organizations have turned to paying for a separate cleanup crew so the committee chairs, executive staff, or board members don't get left with the job in their formal clothing after everyone else has gone home. High school and college students are great resources for this purpose, because they are frequently willing to do a little extra work for money or need hours for their school's community service requirements. Perhaps you can even make their "pay" a charitable contribution to their particular need or cause, which then serves a dual purpose. If you can find a board member or event sponsor to underwrite the clean-up crew, this can help alleviate the cost.

### The Odds and Ends Committee

By definition, this committee's responsibilities cannot be strictly defined, since the primary role of the Odds and Ends Chair is to have a team of volunteers ready to go to fill *any* duty not specifically planned. The Odds and Ends Committee picks up all the loose ends and fills in the gaps that sometimes develop when people become ill, or are needed in other areas, or when a larger number of guests than expected turns out. Some of the miscellaneous tasks these team members perform include:

- Providing greeters at the door
- Adding an extra cashier as needed
- Jumping in with more spotters, runners, or Silent Auction table closers
- Adding extra volunteers to help with item redemption or carry-out
- Handling any other responsibility as the need arises

Because of the catch-all nature of the potential tasks this committee performs, it's important for the committee members to be familiar with *all* Auction Committee responsibilities and have a working logistical knowledge of the entire auction process. This way, the committee members are able to jump in wherever it is necessary without a lot of training or explanation.

CHAPTER

**3**

# Getting to Work

## The First Committee Meeting

Your first committee meeting sets the tone for future meetings and gives you an opportunity to create a positive impression of both your leadership skills and the way future meetings will be conducted. There is, of course, the old expression, "You don't get a second chance to make a first impression," so you will want that first impression to be a positive one. Here are some ways you can get everyone focused quickly, set a positive tone, and send your committee down the path toward success:

- Start on time (even if all your committee members are not yet present)
- Have a printed agenda to give to all attendees
- After your welcome, explain that future meetings will follow an agenda, and stay "on the clock"
- Set the next several committee meeting dates—monthly for six months; weekly as you get closer to the event date
- Ask those present if they wish to add any agenda items; accept those that are appropriate
- Include copies of financial results of your last event (if there was one)
- Confine discussions to the agenda item—don't allow the meeting to drift off subject
- Discuss expectations and job descriptions for each committee member
- Allow the committee members to volunteer for the roles on the committee they feel best match their talents—ask for suggestions of other people who could join the committee
- Ask each committee member to fill his or her own subcommittees and to bring a list of their team members to the next meeting
- Monitor the clock—stay focused to respect everyone's time

Your first meeting is designed to let everyone get to know each other, get comfortable with the process you are establishing, and be on board with the concept of this being a business that will be fun, not a party that makes money. Right from the start, it is very important that your committee buy into the fact that they are setting the standard for the future, that they are being asked to be businesslike, and that they are expected to manage this joint effort with an eye toward what happens after their tour of duty is concluded. In other words, you are asking them to help you build the business and be part of your start-up company even though they may intend to serve on the committee for only one year. They need to see, right away, that the focus is on making decisions for the good of the cause on a long-term basis, not just to be expedient for the moment. If you sense reluctance from any or several of the committee on this subject, it's best to get it on the table and discuss it at the first meeting. If you don't, you will be fighting negativity for months, and it will ultimately limit your success. The process of getting all the committee members to buy in to this long-term, businesslike approach is critical to your success.

Each of your committee members will come with his or her own ideas of what should and should not be done, based on personal experience. You don't have all the answers, nor should you suggest that you do (even though you are reading this book!), because it is important for your committee members to take ownership of the process. Ownership comes from having one's ideas accepted—or at least given a fair consideration—as part of the total process. However, remember the old adage that "A camel is a horse that was designed by a committee." You don't want to be trapped into building something you did not set out to build by being inclusive for its own sake. Test new ideas and ask how they fit with the overall objectives. Sometimes, great ideas can be misplaced and become counterproductive, so always ask "How does this idea fit with our goal, our theme, our objectives, our process?" and so on. As an example, say a committee member suggests that you have dancing for the audience before dinner "to get everyone loosened up and enjoying themselves." Ask, "Okay, so with our schedule—which must include a Silent Auction and Live Auction—what do we cut back or eliminate to make time for the dancing?" In other words, you want to add ideas that enhance the objectives and planning, not pull in an opposite direction.

One point that the entire committee must understand from the very beginning is that you do not have an endless amount of time on the day of your event. If you follow a typical schedule, you might open the doors at 5:00 P.M. and you *must* be done by 10:00 P.M., so you have only five hours to make your fundraising work. Every minute is a "revenue minute," which means that every minute is an opportunity to earn money. You may choose to use that time for other things (such as welcome speeches, awards, thanking the committee, dancing, video presentations, games, entertainment, singing, etc.), but when you do, be mindful that there is a cost associated with it.

To make the point, consider the following example:

Assume you wish to make $100,000 from your guests on the night of the event. Your "hours of operation" are from 5:00 P.M. to 10:00 P.M., which gives you five hours total for selling auction items and raffle tickets, soliciting cash contributions, and selling merchandise. That works out to $20,000 per hour, or $333.34 per minute. If you take away 15 minutes for moving your guests from the Silent Auction to the dinner tables, and another 15 minutes for socialization at their tables, you now have four and a half "revenue hours," which means you now need to make $22,222 per revenue-hour, or $370.37 per revenue-minute. When you take away more time for welcome and thank you speeches, add in a video presentation and some other distractions, you could easily lose another 30 minutes, so now you are down to four "revenue hours" and must earn $25,000 per hour, or $417 per minute.

Do you see what happens? Time really is money! So, when a committee member suggests that a choir give a performance, or you hire a magician, or have an hour for dancing, these activities actually *cost* your event $X per minute, which needs to be factored into your plans. Twenty minutes of dancing costs your event more than $8,000—and that doesn't include the actual cost of the band! We aren't saying you shouldn't have a band, or have dancing or entertainment. Just be mindful of the real costs associated with those decisions. If you compress the number of revenue minutes by using them for something not directly related to generating revenue, you will need to raise more money in the time remaining, and at some point you'll find that "you just can't get there from here."

By the way, you should use the above example when someone wants to give a speech to get everyone ready to bid, or to explain the cause they are supporting. Remind the speaker that every minute is a revenue minute, and you are "willing to give them $1,000 of your revenue time" for a three-minute talk. After that, however, you expect them to write a check, at $333 per minute, to make up the difference. You will be amazed how short the welcome remarks become!

Your first committee meeting should include these elements, which are explained in more detail on the following pages:

- Agree on the event's mission
- Establish committee responsibilities
- Select a date for the event
- Discuss potential themes
- Discuss possible venues
- Set a preliminary financial goal
- Work on preliminary budget
- Establish a meeting schedule

## The Mission Statement

Earlier in this book, we mentioned how important it is to be clear on the purpose of the fundraising event in support of your efforts. We discussed how it's most effective to sell the purpose to potential donors and supporters, rather than merely the need for the money. The mission statement you develop supports that purpose. While it may seem redundant when you are also defining the purpose, the mission statement is not the same thing. The mission statement should be a single line or two that briefly defines why you are asking for a donation or support. All that you do, whether it is asking for donations, sponsorships, or volunteer involvement, should be in support of that mission. If you cannot condense it down to one or two lines as a mission statement, then it will be difficult to convey your intentions to potential supporters; they will not have the attention span to listen to a lengthy discussion about your purpose and goals. Here are some examples of effective mission statements.

- "We believe every child deserves a quality education regardless of financial ability, and we are dedicated to providing that at our school."
- "Quality health care for our senior citizens is a must. We are committed to seeing that all the seniors in our community are cared for."
- "We exist to fund the necessary research that will someday find the cure for cancer."

Armed with a solid mission statement, you will be able to cut through the clutter of lengthy justifications and get right down to business with potential supporters. Open with the mission statement, then do the "ask." As an example, you might say the following:

> Our organization exists to fund the necessary research that will someday find the cure for cancer. As such, we are seeking like-minded members of the community who also care about finding a cure, and asking that they assist us by becoming a sponsor of our event.

The mission statement removes the uncertainty of potential mixed messages by keeping it simple and getting immediately to the point of why you are asking. All committee members should be armed with written copies of the mission statement and should be encouraged to use it when explaining why they are asking for support.

## Establishing Committee Responsibilities

Earlier in Phase I, we discussed the various committee responsibilities and expectations. Your committee members should be given responsibility for areas where they can use their abilities and experiences, as well as their potential connections within the community. As we discussed, allowing members to volunteer at the initial meeting gives them a chance to take on the responsibilities with which they are most comfortable. This option will greatly increase the chances that they will successfully meet their obligations. We always have a better attitude and increased likelihood for success when we are doing a task we enjoy than when we're doing one we do not enjoy. Therefore, as much as possible, try to match the person and his or her individual talent to the task at hand.

There will be some tasks, however, that you may not be able to fill through a self-selection method. As an example, the role of Procurement Chair is often one area of responsibility for which people rarely volunteer, because they are worried about how much work it will be or that they won't be successful. Often it is necessary to "draft" the chair for this position. One way to make this task appear more achievable and acceptable to the potential chair is to remind that person that they are not in this alone, but that "everyone is on the procurement team." That is, the chair is not personally responsible for getting all the auction items, as, in reality, everyone on the Auction Committee—and many others not on the committee—will all be helping to get auction items. The Procurement Chair's responsibility is to coordinate and report on that effort, and subsequently, the job of the chair is a management position with lots of help.

Certainly the most creative people on the committee will likely volunteer for the decorating tasks, and those with financial experience may become your Budget/Accounting Committee members or handle the event cashiering. By allowing your committees to select their areas of responsibility and recruiting specific people as needed to fill in additional roles, you will have a solid committee that will share their depth of knowledge and real world experience to help you establish your business. They will, of course, recruit their own subcommittee members, but you can assist in that process when you make your general call for volunteers and accept sign-ups for various subcommittees.

## Selecting the Date for the Event

There is no ideal day of the week, month of the year, or season in which to hold a successful fundraising event. Successful events are held every day of the week, and at all times of the day, including breakfast events, lunch events, and dinner events. In general, it makes little difference in terms of auction yield whether you conduct an auction in the morning, at mid-day or in the evening, and it also makes no difference what day of the week you hold your event. Sunday events can be as successful as Saturday night events, and a Wednesday luncheon can produce as much revenue as a Friday night gala. How can that be? It really comes down to when you can fill your room with supporters. For some organizations, it is easier to draw their supporters at a mid-week luncheon than it is to get the same supporters to attend a Saturday night gala. Your committee should begin the search for a date by answering the following questions:

- What time of year are we most likely to be able to get people to attend?
- What conflicting events or holidays must we avoid?
- Will our preferred venue be available on that date or potential dates?
- Will we have enough planning time to be successful if we select that date?
- Will that date or those dates support our theme?

It's not necessary or accurate to assume your event will be more successful on a Saturday night than on any other day of the week. Remember, on Saturday other conflicting events may draw from your potential guest list. A Sunday afternoon event may be just as successful, as long as you feel you can draw your supporters on that date. Once there, they will spend just as much as they would have on Saturday night.

There is also a case to be made for trying to keep your event on the same weekend of each year, so it can be predictable for your constituents. If you select the first weekend in February, for example, then always have your event on the first weekend in February. You do need to keep in mind that this same weekend may have built-in conflicts with other events that also select that weekend each year, so if you happen to share a constituency with other events on that weekend, you will always be vying for the same people. Moving it around on different weekends solves that issue, but creates the potential for new conflicts each year, so there really isn't one "best" method. Also, keep in mind that some holidays don't fall on fixed dates, but "float" around during the calendar. One such example is Easter; if you plan to have your event on the same weekend each April, realize that in some years this may fall on Easter weekend, which could possibly affect your turnout, depending on your audience base.

You should be aware that, on average, audiences "turn over" about 20% each year through natural attrition. This is due to people moving, children graduating from schools, loss of interest in a cause, schedule conflicts, and other reasons. As a result, you will have a totally new audience every five years. Changing a predictable weekend date or a location every few years will really not harm your planning, because you are dealing with a new audience makeup every few years anyway.

## Identifying Potential Themes

When selecting a theme, bear in mind that the theme you select must carry through on all printed material, advertising, publicity, decorations, and at the location for the event. For example, if you select a sports-related theme such as "Show Your Colors," where you encourage guests to come dressed in their favorite sports team or college team colors, it would make sense to find a sports stadium as a possible venue. An "Orient Express" theme would be great for an event held at a train station, and a western theme, such as "Denim, Dudes, and Diamonds," would fit wonderfully at a horse stable or riding arena. However, many themes will work at generic locations, such as schools gymnasiums, community centers, hotel ballrooms, and convention halls.

Themes are good because they help create a party atmosphere, and they suggest decoration ideas that will frame the venue properly as a backdrop for your event. More information about how themes and decorations go together, including ideas for possible themes, was provided in Chapter 2, in the section about the Decorations Chair.

## Selecting a Preferred Venue

One of the most important decisions for your auction is where to hold your event. Accessibility, facilities, and usable space are all very important factors that you need to keep in mind while looking for the ideal venue. In addition, your location should enhance your theme, if possible, as discussed in Identifying Potential Themes.

Early in the planning process, your agenda should include time for brainstorming locations for your event. Don't necessarily think that you must limit your options to hotel ballrooms or convention center meeting rooms. You know your home town and its meeting venues better than anyone else, so *be creative*. Your location will need to be a place that is easy to find and centrally located, someplace that will be an attractive venue for people to want to spend their time (not to mention their money).

The word brainstorm means exactly that. Don't immediately discount any idea, no matter how farfetched it may seem. Some of the best, and most unique, auctions have taken place in the wildest locations. If the organization has a western theme, for example, you might consider finding a barn that has been converted into a meeting hall. If a cruise ship is the theme of the evening, you might think about finding a large yacht that can host a dinner cruise.

Take some time and really think about where you want to have the event. You might come up with an idea that no one has thought of before. If a lot of guests are coming in from out of town, trying a location that is unique to your particular town or area might be fun. For example, an auction in California might take place in a winery, or an auction in Washington D.C. might be held in a famous historical landmark or building. Keep in mind that your location takes a backstage to the event itself, but scenery is an important contributing factor.

It may be that the theme you select requires that you hold your event in a location that is going to be more costly. There is nothing wrong with that, but consider all costs of the event in total.

Schools will be tempted to try to hold their event on campus as a way to reduce costs, and often that will work. At some point, however, depending on your goal and who you want to attend, you may need to move offsite to attract guests from outside the immediate school family. In addition, many schools have policies restricting the ability to serve alcohol on campus, so if you are planning to serve wine, beer, or mixed drinks as part of your event you may have no choice but to go to a non-campus site.

Remember, don't over commit your organization's funds when searching for a venue, but don't choose a location simply based on the idea that it is inexpensive or free. If your sponsors and benefactors see that you have spent some money so that they can have an enjoyable evening, they will be more generous in their giving. Sometimes venues will discount their rates for nonprofit organizations so they can write off part of the rental fee. A great way to save on fees would be to consider having your event on an "off night," like a Sunday or Monday evening. Selecting an event because it was the only free location available is really backward logic. A location with a cost may actually be more cost effective and valuable in the long run. Here is an example:

> Your committee is committed to only finding free locations, so they decide to accept the offer to use a large aircraft hangar owned by a friend of the organization. While the committee is getting the location for free, they must now find a caterer to handle the food service away from their normal place of business, typically at an increased cost. The serving staff must be recruited to work at an offsite location as well. The Decorations Committee discovers that they now need to rent all the dinner tables, as well as the Silent and Live Auction display tables. Then, of course they need to rent the linens to cover the tables—and they also need to rent the serving dishes, plates, silverware, and more.
>
> The hangar does not have adjustable lighting (it's either all on or off), and the Decorations Committee will not accept a "brightly lit" room so they need to rent auxiliary lighting to set the mood. An aircraft hangar does not have great acoustics, so the Audio/Visual Committee

learns that the cost to rent a sound system is higher than what they had budgeted due to the need for additional equipment to make the sound correct for an auction, and there are no built-in screens for a PowerPoint presentation of auction items or video during the event, so those rental costs go up as well.

Are there adequate bathroom facilities, or will the committee need to rent portable toilets? Will there be any additional costs for post-event cleaning crews to restore the location back to its original state? There may also be a cost for portable heaters or cooling systems, depending on the time of year.

In addition, the owner of the hangar may require an insurance policy or bond to cover injuries to guests, or liability for damage to the hangar or its contents, which could also add to the total cost of use.

Finally, costs to arrange for parking or valet at the hangar may be higher than if the event was held elsewhere.

By the time all of the amenities, rentals, and other costs are added in, your "free" location may not be such a bargain after all. Having the event at a hotel might be a more cost-effective decision, because there are no added costs for tables, linens, serving utensils, lighting, insurance, or other items that are typically part of the package. Many hotel caterers will not charge for the ballroom, as long as you meet certain minimums of food and beverages to be served. It is best to do a comparison of *total* costs, not just location rental costs, when evaluating potential venues.

When selecting a venue for your event, you also need to consider what kind of items need to be transported. If there is a lot of really heavy furniture that needs to be delivered to, and carried into, the event, it might be best to choose a location where the least amount of lifting is required.

Above all, don't be afraid to ask questions about the building that you are renting. Some locations (meeting halls, convention centers, etc.) have an exclusive contract with only one catering service. Inquire about conditions like end-of-the-event clean-up, fees for staying after midnight, janitor fees, table or linen fees, and how much each would add to the cost of the rental. Be sure that decorating restrictions will not get in the way of your plans, and be prepared to provide all materials from tape to extension cords. Also, follow safety rules like taping electrical wire down over door thresholds so the guests and wait staff are not in jeopardy. And make sure, before you sign on the dotted line, that you are certain of your choices.

Finally, set some goals and a budget for your venue and stick to them. If you have a vision of what the space should look like, don't compromise simply because you found a space that was free or was the first one available; that's the wrong reason to choose a site for your classy event.

**Some unique locations that offer interesting possibilities for your event include:**

- Hotel ballrooms and convention halls
- Sports stadiums and athletic fields
- Wineries
- Shopping malls after hours
- Private country clubs
- Tennis courts (indoor and outdoor)
- Train stations
- Corporate building lobbies
- University or college clubs, community centers, and church halls
- Restaurants
- Zoos, botanical gardens, and public aquariums
- Amusement parks (e.g., Sea World, Universal Studios, Magic Mountain, Six Flags, etc.)
- State fairgrounds
- Theaters and music halls
- Cruise ships or other large boats
- Horse arena/stables/barns
- Private mansions or exclusive homes
- Museum display halls
- Aircraft hangar or aircraft carrier deck
- Circus tents

**A Venue Selection Worksheet**  Exhibit 3.1 is a sample venue-selection worksheet you can use when evaluating locations and facilities for your auction.

## Establishing a Goal

One of the most important tasks you will have is establishing a goal that will make sense. One of the reasons we start with a goal is so everyone will know where we need to be after the event. Many will say that their goal is "to make as much money as possible." This is no more valid and effective than deciding on a vacation location "as far away as possible." As we discussed earlier, the success of your event has everything to do with how thoughtfully you have created your plan and how well you execute that plan. If you have no goal, as Yogi Berra used to say, "Any path will take you there."

**Exhibit 3.1   Sample Venue Selection Worksheet**

1. Occupancy
   a. Number of people attending: _____
   b. Maximum occupancy of building: _____

2. Display Space
   a. Estimated number of Silent Auction items to display: _____
      Calculation: (2a multiplied by 2 ft/item): _____
   b. Estimated amount (in linear ft.) of table space: _____
      (*answer from calculation above*)

3. Parking
   _____ Covered parking?
   _____ Inclement weather plan?
   _____ Cost of parking: $_____
   _____ Availability of valet service?
   _____ Proximity of parking to venue?
   _____ Safety and security of parking?

4. Lighting
   _____ Current venue lighting optimal?
   _____ Auxiliary lighting needed for _____ tables?

5. Sound and Amplification Systems
   _____ Building is open and large (larger sound system needed)?
   _____ Halls, corridors, different rooms (more speakers and speaker cable
            needed)?
   _____ One banquet hall and satellite rooms for Silent Auctions. (standard
            4-speaker system)?

6. Move-in and move-out considerations
   _____ Elevator access or loading dock?
   _____ Other events sharing facility earlier in the day? (How soon will we have
            access?)

7. Additional room for volunteers and ``war room'' for computers?

Establishing a clear goal also helps you parse the variety of options available to you for earning income. If, for example, you set a goal of $100,000 (net), then you can start to break out the subset pieces you'll need. Perhaps you plan to make $50,000 from your Live Auction, $25,000 from your Silent Auction, have a $10,000 raffle, make $5,000 from RSVP entries, and make another $5,000 from advertising. This would leave an additional $5,000 that will need to be come from other sources. Of course, your organization can only spend what is left after all the bills are paid, so your goal should be a net goal, not a gross goal. However, you will have to pay for the expenses that get you to that goal, so having a gross income number needed is very important. Ultimately, you will also want to be sure you meet normal guidelines for net-to-gross income, which tests whether you did a good job of earning your net with a reasonable cost.

Many nonprofit organizations use a range of 17–23% as an acceptable amount that can be spent to create the income from an event. This means that it is acceptable to have a gross income of $120,000 to end up with a net income of $100,000. It would not be acceptable to gross $150,000 and end up with a net of $100,000, because that would mean too much money was spent in proportion to the amount returned to the bottom line for the cause. Some organizations take this "spending amount" so seriously that their development executives are strictly graded on their net-to-gross percentages, even to the point of being replaced if they consistently exceed their limits.

## Creating a Budget

As you manage the business of your event, periodically you will want to evaluate how you are tracking toward your goal. As you monitor the progress of procurement and assure yourself that you will be able to meet the income goal based on the procurement activity as well as the other sources of income from sponsorships, advertising, and so on, you will want to be equally concerned with tracking expenses. It will do you little good if your committee does a great job of procurement but a lousy job of staying on budget. Therefore, you will want to create a budget that is reasonable and, more importantly, one that everyone on the committee will buy into.

As mentioned previously, a good working number for an expense budget is in the range of 17–23% of the gross revenue for the event. To get everyone on the same page, it's a good idea early on to have a budget meeting with your entire committee. At this meeting, all branches of the committee will have the opportunity to request budget money for their areas of responsibility. The Decorations Chair will present ideas and potential costs, the Audio/Visual Chair will do the same, and so on around the table until all have expressed their "wish lists" for the budget. At that point, it may be necessary to trim or repurpose some budget money. The key point here is that you need each discipline on the committee to understand that they are not operating in a vacuum, but that their efforts and good stewardship of the budget affect everyone and can help keep the Net Goal as an achievable result. As an example, we have experienced many events where the Decorating Committee went way overboard on making the room spectacular but in the process pushed the net-to-gross ratio way out of whack. By having a budget meeting at the very beginning, you will allow all committee members to have input and express their needs while refining the budget; at the end of the meeting, everyone should be comfortable with their budget line parameters.

## Setting Future Committee Meetings

Your Steering Committee will be composed of nearly all volunteers, and it's important that you respect their time and reward their participation. Ad hoc meetings should be kept to a minimum and replaced with a schedule published right from the initial meeting through the post-event recap meeting. Early in the planning cycle, you may hold your meetings monthly on the second Wednesday at 6:00 P.M. Then as you get closer to the event, move to an every-other-Wednesday format. In the month before your event, you may move to weekly meetings, again on Wednesday at 6:00 P.M. since your committee has already gotten accustomed to this day and time. The point is, if you all agree on a schedule and stick to it, you allow your committee members the opportunity to plan well in advance to schedule their other obligations around this standing meeting, and you assure your team of having a quorum each time they meet.

Additionally, if you have a published schedule, your committee members can get a stand-in from their subcommittee to fill in for them should they have a schedule conflict on any given meeting day. Having continuity of representation from each committee is important. Progress from each area of responsibility, reported at each meeting, will help keep the planning on track.

Begin each meeting with a published agenda and then stick to it. It's best if you can e-mail that agenda to your committee ahead of time, so any reporting or materials can be ready and you don't have to waste time discussing what is on the agenda. Remember, the purpose of the meeting is for each committee member to report on progress in his or her area of responsibility. Each member should be allocated a block of time, and the chair should keep track of the allocated times, out of respect for all the members' time. A crisp, well-orchestrated meeting that starts on time and ends on time is the best way to ensure maximum participation from your committee.

# P H**A**S E **I**

# CONCLUSION

Now that your first meeting is over and you are underway toward your event, you can move from Phase I to Phase II, where you will dig deeper into the details and begin implementing the plans you have been working on and preparing for in Phase I. Phase I is an important step, because it lays out all you and your committee will need to ensure you are headed down the correct path. As we mentioned before, if you don't know where you are going, any path will take you there. Having properly and diligently orchestrated your planning by establishing your committee; setting your goals and preliminary budget; and considering dates, locations, and themes; it is time to move forward with specific decisions in these areas.

In Phase II you will solidify your location, theme, date, goal, and budget; have your kickoff rally; select table captains; and hire vendors. The pre-planning and setting the stage are over. It's now time to get to work, because in Phase II, everything starts to come together and your committee begins to look like a real business that is getting prepared for its big annual sale!

# PHASE II

# EVENT PLANNING AND ORGANIZATION

Phase II
Getting Organized

Up to this point, you have been focusing on the basic activities for getting started. At this stage in your process, you should be comfortable with your Steering Committee and your preliminary goal, which will be finalized in this Phase. In fact, Phase II is where your business really starts to take shape: You will assemble the volunteers; lock in your goal and the elements of achieving it; and nail down the event date, location, and logistics. This is the "meat and potatoes" part of the planning, because you will be making commitments to vendors, hiring an auctioneer, placing deposits, and giving shape to your business as manifested in your event.

You will also hold your kickoff rally, which will be your first opportunity to go public with your plans. At the rally, you will add volunteers to your list of helpers, and you also will launch your procurement process and the first part of the audience development process. You will discuss space considerations for your event location so that you will be comfortable that the selected venue will meet your needs, and layout considerations for the Live and Silent

Auctions will come into play. We will share with you many "revenue enhancers" that you can consider making a part of your event, should you see fit.

Before getting too detailed in the planning for this event, however, we hope that you will take a short pause and read and digest the first part of Phase II, which discusses the Five-Year Plan. As tempting as it might be to bypass that discussion, we believe it is well worth the time to read it thoroughly and see whether you should integrate this philosophy into your planning strategy. It would be easy to assume that a long-term plan will make little difference, because you may not have plans to continue on after this year. However, when you realize how managing your event this year according to the Five-Year Plan can not only help your replacement in the future, but will help *you* achieve greater success immediately, you may see it in a different light. And now, on to Phase II.

# CHAPTER 4

# The Five-Year Plan

Before diving into Phase II, where we are going to get very busy implementing the strategies and plans we made in Phase I, let's detour for a brief moment and discuss Five-Year Planning. Your immediate reaction might be "Who cares? I just want to get through this year!" Fair enough. However, consider what you do in your normal life. When you buy a car, do you think about transportation for only this month or year, or do you look at cars that won't have to be replaced right away? Don't you look at the cost of maintenance, warrantees, and, most importantly, resale value for when you finally decide to sell? These are all normal thoughts when buying a car—even though your need may be immediate, you give ample consideration for the future. When buying a home, you do similar long-range planning, and when you search for a job, while you might need work today, you typically look for employment as a long-term expectation.

By looking "down the road," so to speak, we make better decisions that not only will benefit us in the short-term, but also will keep us from having to undo decisions long-term. Let's look at a few examples where a Five-Year view of our auction planning might benefit us in the short term.

Assume at some point you and your committee are going to ask corporate donors to be sponsors, underwriters, or matching-gift or item donors. What message will resonate with those making a decision to assist you and your cause?

- "Our school is having a fundraiser this year to raise money for quality education in our community. We would really like to have your company on our team helping us. Would you consider assisting us as a [sponsor, donor, underwriter, matching gift donor]?"
- "Our school is on the path to raise $XXX over a Five-Year Plan to support quality education in our community. We would really like to have your company on board as a partner in achieving this five-year goal. Would you consider joining our team to support education in our community as a sustaining [sponsor, donor, underwriter, matching-gift donor]?"

Let's look at one more example:

- "Our school is having a fundraiser this year, and we need a sound system for our event. Can you provide a quote for us based on the provided specification?"
- "Our school is on track to raise $XXX over a Five-Year Plan, and we are selecting vendors that want to have a steady client for years to come. Can you provide a quote for us based on the provided specification, and can you show what discount will be applied if we commit to your services for more than one year at a time?"

Dealing with committee members is also easier if you ask them to manage a process that is well underway and has been for years, so they don't have to reinvent the wheel. There is nothing that will cause people to shy away from volunteering faster than thinking that they must create their job descriptions from scratch and be responsible for results that may be very subjective. If, on the other hand, you ask volunteers to take over a responsibility that has been managed successfully the previous year, with duties that are clearly defined and objectives that are well within their capability, recruiting becomes much easier. No one likes to fail or think he/she may fail, so an existing plan that carries forward each year lowers that risk and makes success easier to achieve.

Setting a proper goal based on experience from the prior year is also an advantage of using a Five-Year Plan approach. Goals can be set based on previous experience, and the chances of achieving the new goal increase when it is reasonably set and has been achieved in the prior year. Think of how easy it would be to set your goal this year if you had a three- to five-year track record of goals and results to draw upon for guidance. In fact, goal setting the first year is the most difficult, because it is primarily based on assumptions. In the second year, the goal is still partly based on many assumptions, but those assumptions can be tested against the prior year's experience. In the third, fourth, and fifth years, goal setting becomes much easier because you now have a trend, and that trend can be extrapolated to the following year, and years to come. Look at the chart in Exhibit 4.1.

Notice right away that the chart contains seven, not five, years' worth of information. It would make little sense to start a business using a Five-Year Plan, operate it for five years, then go out of business. Therefore, the chart assumes that while we look forward five years at a time, we renew the five-year planning cycle each year. In other words, we are always looking forward and using history to guide us. The longer we manage our business, the more data we have at our disposal to help look forward with our need for adjustments and setting of goals and objectives.

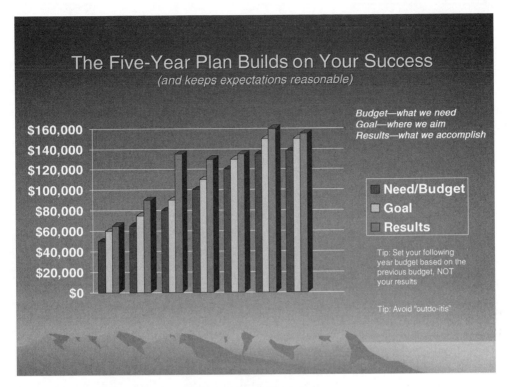

**Exhibit 4.1    The Five-Year Plan Builds on Your Success**

Also note that the goal for each year is slightly higher than the goal set year before. This new goal is *not* based on the results from the prior year. This is important, because it's not reasonable to assume that each year the new committee will automatically be able to "outdo" the results of the prior year, nor should they try. A goal should be based on the needs of the organization, tempered by the goal (not the results) from the prior year. Just because the results in any given year are well above the goal, that should not be a reason to dramatically increase the goal for the following year beyond the results from the previous year. To do so would create an exponential curve that gets increasingly steeper, which will most certainly lead to burnout of your volunteers, committee, and donors.

In reality, many committees suffer from "outdo-itis" where they feel obligated to outdo the prior year's results. This is not a competition where Mary must do better than Sally, and Bill must have a better event than Mary. When properly set up and managed, your organization will have a business, and future leaders of that business should be focused on *managing* the business and achieving agreed-upon goals rather than creating a competition. When you look at your business with an eye to a five-year projection, and renew that five-year outlook each year, you will find it much easier to stay calm and focused and not be so worried about making each year "bigger and better" than the year before. Just focus on the task of supplying your organization with needed funds in an orderly, businesslike fashion, without burning out your committee and volunteers. To do so will create a legacy that will pay dividends, make it easier to recruit, and will certainly reduce your stress.

## Managing Change

People typically hate change, because it takes us out of our "comfort zone." When you decide to start doing things differently from how they have been done before, you may encounter some negativity, typically manifested in the comments, "We never do it that way," "We've never done it that way before," and our all-time favorite, "If it ain't broke, don't fix it." To break the cycle of one-year starting and stopping, you may need to make changes slowly, over time. Consider that even positive change can be stressful. Start by gaining some support from your committee so you are not going it alone. *Maverick* may have been a hit TV show and movie, but typically, mavericks don't make many friends! So think of the changes you have to make as gradual, taken in small doses over a long period of time. If you are looking at a five-year window for real change, you don't need to do it all this year. And you don't have to be in charge for five years if you take this approach! Just set your committee up with a five-year viewpoint, make some changes this year, and build into your plan the changes you want the following year's committee to make. You can do this when you have a Steering Committee instead of an "Auction Committee," because the Steering Committee will maintain continuity from year to year; you will not taking away anything from those who replace you when you leave.

Here are some tips for managing change:

- Make changes slowly—sometimes over several years.
- Change must be *evolutionary*, not *revolutionary* . . . *because people get shot in revolutions.*
- Don't attempt to do it all at once—slowly "boil the frog" in cold water.
- Gain buy in from management and volunteers so they embrace change.
- *"If it ain't broke, don't fix it"* must be replaced with *"If isn't perfect, improve it!"*
- Treat the first year of the Five-Year Plan as creating a legacy for the future.
- List the changes that need to be done, and attempt only a few in the current year.

With a Five-Year Plan approach, it's easy to see why it is so important to have auction management software to manage your business. You will want to be able to run reports that measure your income, yield, and profit in the current year and provide a history of these data points from prior years. Data is important for managing any business, and it is especially important when planning for more than one year at a time. At the very least, you will want to know "who bought what?" each year to plan for what to get for the following year. You will need to know who on the committee procured which items, and who made the donations. You will want a descending-dollar report, so you can see who the big contributors are, and of course you will want a list of categories that were the biggest sellers so you can procure similar items in following years. A complete budget from the prior year would help you set your budget this year, and having a database of donors and attendees to solicit will reduce the risk of reaching out to strangers with no relationship to your organization.

If you were only concerned with this year, having proper software tools might not seem very important. When you start to look at the tools you will need for not only this year, but the following years, decision making becomes easier, even if the payoff of that decision spans more than the current year. The cost of proper software can be amortized over several years, and should not have to be credited against the current budget year if a multiyear approach is being used. It becomes an investment then, rather than an expense.

You may be stepping into an existing job that many before you have done successfully. If that's the case, ask yourself: "What information have I been given to do this job well, and what tools has my predecessor given me to get me started the right way?" Were you handed a big box of records and perhaps a binder? Who is going to help you wade through all that data, and how do you know what is important and what isn't? How do you know what data is relevant to what you want to accomplish this year? Can you assume that the last committee "got it right?"

If you are lucky, your predecessor was an advocate of the Five-Year Plan as well, and you are being asked to take over and manage that process. He or she may have been highly organized, made great decisions, and laid out all that needs to be done for you so you can continue from where he or she left off. How relieved you would be right now! However, if you are not so lucky, you have a great opportunity to break the cycle of "one-year events" and begin doing it the right way, starting now. Ask your committee if they are ready to build a going business, and if so, whether they will assist you in making good decisions for the long term, not just to be expedient. Everyone will enjoy the challenge, appreciate the results more, and leave a lasting impression on your organization.

### Advantages of the Five-Year Plan Approach

- You create a businesslike attitude and are taken seriously.
- Each year leverages the previous year's success and knowledge. *You don't have to start over each year.*
- You develop long-term relationships with donors, vendors, attendees, and volunteers.
- Goals are realistically set based on need, not on the prior years' results. *Effective goals are reasonable, achievable, and measurable.*
- The Committee has a line of succession, and no person is "thrown to the wolves."
- Net income is a reliable resource for your cause.
- Committee/volunteer burnout is reduced or eliminated. Recruit for three years: observe and learn the first year, work the second year, teach and mentor the third year. *See one, do one, teach one.*

And now on to Phase II, where it is hoped you will make your decisions and organize your business from a five-year perspective.

# CHAPTER 5

# Planning the Details of Your Event

By now, you have committed to following the Five-Year Plan as discussed in Phase I. You have set up your committees, assigned roles to your committee chairs, picked a likely date and preferred location for your event, and established a proposed budget that is tied to your goals. It's now time to move forward with the detailed planning phase, where the planning becomes more specific and the activities surrounding your event will begin to take shape. In this phase, your committee will be working on the specific details of the event, including making the theme come to life, establishing the contracts with your vendors, and making plans for the Live and Silent Auctions, plus adding other revenue-enhancing activities you may need or want to meet your goals.

Now, in Phase II, we will work on finalizing the location by matching it to your needs, based on what venue will be required to host the audience you will need to achieve your goal. Since you know your goal and have a good idea of what it will take to achieve it (based on the goal-setting parameters outlined in Phase I), your committee can also take the first steps toward building the audience (Audience Development) and finding items to sell (Procurement). It is never too early to begin thinking about *how* you will fill the room (preferably with bidders, not "eaters") and *what* you plan to offer your guests. Once the date is fixed, and you have a contract with your venue ready to sign, it is time to send out "Save-the-Date" cards or letters to your most desired supporters.

Once the location and date are locked, the theme is set, and you are certain that the venue will be able to accommodate all the logistics surrounding your event, you will be ready to move to Phase III, where we get serious about building your audience and procuring your auction items. However, some key supporters may need plenty of time to lock in the date if their attendance is critical to your event, so be sure to informally get on their calendar as soon as possible, even during Phase I or Phase II, so you can mitigate any potential schedule conflicts. This is especially true if you plan to have an Honorary Chair or present an award to a deserving supporter of your cause. It just makes sense that the honoree be able to attend the event.

Another important part of Phase II is to begin planning the Live and Silent Auction display areas. Begin factoring in how many linear feet of table space will be required for each section, lighting considerations, and where bars are to be set up, both for your guests' convenience and to maximize your bidding. For example, it makes no sense to place bars in a hallway and arrange the auction displays in a different space, such as a room off the hallway, because the bars would become a congregation point that would prevent your auction items from ever being seen! Place the bars in the same general area as the item displays, but not where they would interfere with movement through the room or make it difficult for bidders to get to the items to place bids. Both the bars and the auction items can coexist happily in the same area and actually leverage each other in a positive way, as we will discuss in this Phase.

At this point, we need to highlight just how important it is to hire experts to assist you with your planning. Of course you will hire vendors for food service and for the venue, but there are a number of other services that you should just not try to get free, or have volunteers provide, regardless of how much of a deal their services appear to be. Volunteers are incredibly important to your success, but they cannot replace the specific expertise professionals bring. You certainly want to get professional help with your sound and lighting, because both will help you earn more money if set up correctly and will cost you money if done improperly. Likewise, hiring a professional *benefit* auctioneer can be the smartest decision you will ever make. It's nearly impossible for a part-time volunteer auctioneer to be able to sense the crowd and make the subtle adjustments needed on the fly to keep your event moving in a positive direction, on time, entertaining, and profitable. The hiring of professionals is a key to your success, and in Phase II we will discuss this subject in more detail, plus we will give you some guidelines on how to find, interview, and hire the professional help you will need. We will also discuss some typical costs, and what you should demand for your money.

Finally, the last part of this Phase concerns the official launch of your procurement and audience development process. The Kickoff Rally is designed to get all supporters on the same page, so to speak, and is a terrific recruiting tool to find volunteers, potential committee members, donors and table captains. A table captain is a person who agrees to attend your event and bring a table full of like-minded supporters with him or her. The table captain process will be discussed in more detail, and having the Kickoff Rally really sets up the process of finding and motivating potential captains.

By the time we finish Phase II, you will be well down the path with your planning steps and headed toward a successful event, and all you will need to move forward is the implementation of your excellent planning. Planning is what makes any business effort successful, and taking the time to move deliberately through Phase II—as you did in Phase I—will pay excellent dividends down the road. It will also greatly reduce your stress and that of your committee, because everyone will know that what you are doing is not left to chance but based on proven techniques that many before you have employed to great success. You won't need to reinvent things to be successful with your event. This doesn't mean that creativity is not necessary, because it *is* and it can be rewarding, but leave the creativity as the icing on the cake, and don't mess with the basics—as outlined here in Phase II.

## Determining the Elements of Your Goal

Before we head out looking for auction items and start locking in the logistics of the event, it is a good idea to take stock of just where the money we're planning to make is going to come from. Not all of the revenue has to come from auction item sales the day of our event. This is a good thing, because the more revenue we can get into the bank before the actual event, the easier it's going to be to achieve our goal. With that premise, let's look at a variety of elements that can add to the overall goal.

As shown in Exhibit 5.1, numerous elements contribute to the overall goal. Relieving the bidders at the event of the need to fulfill 100% of the event goal will make it much easier to achieve success. With some excellent planning and support from your community prior to the event, it is quite

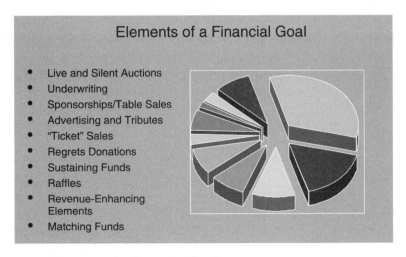

**Exhibit 5.1    Elements of a Financial Goal**

possible that only half of the goal will actually need to be raised in the Live and Silent Auctions, as represented on the right-hand side of the pie chart shown in Exhibit 5.1.

When planning your auction item procurement, assume you will receive about 70% of the value of the items when sold at auction. Therefore, if the pieces of the pie representing the Live and Silent Auction portions of your overall goal represent 50% of your needed revenue, you will need to get donations of items totaling more than 50% of the goal, but not 100% of the goal, because of the contributions from other elements.

As your volunteers and committee members go into the community to solicit support for your event, they should recognize that there are many ways donors can help. It does not have to be all about getting auction items. In fact, armed with some good data about your organization and mission, the same people asking for auction items can also ask for sponsorships, advertising, sustaining funds, raffle sales, and matching funds. They also can ask people they encounter if they would like an invitation to the event. By having a variety of potential ways a contact can help, as we have split them out on the chart, chances of hearing a ''Yes'' increase dramatically. For example, a professional office, such as a law firm, doctor's office, accountant's office, dentist's office, or real estate office may not have an auction item to donate, but all could underwrite a trip or other auction item, buy a table at your event, be a sponsor, or provide matching funds. Having a choice of ways to help enhances the asking process, and will yield more positive responses.

## Finalizing Your Date and Location

In Phase I, we talked about the various types of venues you can consider and suggested a number of reasons why you might select one over another. It's time to finalize that decision if you have not already done so. Of course, the desired date for your event may also play an important role in that decision process, as location availability can be quite competitive, especially on prime event dates. Before making the final decision, however, let's review the purpose of the event location and some of the minimum parameters you should consider before locking it in with a contract.

Remember, the purpose of the location is to be able to host your event in such a manner that you will be able to achieve your goal. If your committee says ''Gee, it is a great location, even if only 200 people will be able to fit in the room'' and you need 300 people to accomplish your goal (remember the revenue rule of $250 to $750 per Buying Unit), then the location is unacceptable. In Phase I, we provided a Venue Selection Worksheet, and now you should review it for each of the venues you have on your short list.

If the location is perfect, but you can't get it on your desired date, it is also not acceptable. Ask yourself the following questions:

- Will the location be able to accommodate the number of guests required to meet your goal?
- Is there adequate space to display the Live and Silent Auction items?
- Will the location be able to provide the meal service, or alternately, will a caterer be able to provide that service at this location?
- Are there any conflicting events at the location that would make it difficult for your guests to find parking or attend the event?
- Is your auctioneer available on the selected date?
- Does the location meet all or most of the desired objectives on our Venue Selection Worksheet?

If the location you have selected meets all or most of these requirements, you should get a contract signed and lock in the venue and date. Once that is completed, you can get ready to send out a Save-the-Date card or e-mail so your potential guests can reserve the date on their calendars. The Save-the-Date reminder should list just the basics, such as theme, date, and location. Items such as costs, RSVP levels, and a detailed schedule of events are not required on the Save-the-Date mailing. You are simply trying to get your potential guests to save the date. Period. Of course, on the actual invitation you will offer more information such as attendee levels, table purchase opportunities, and more. More on Save-the-Date cards and invitations will be discussed later in Phase III.

## Hiring the Experts

While it is not necessary to hire outside help for your event, you may find it well worthwhile to consider at least some professional assistance to help make it run smoothly. With a full staff of volunteers running the show, you have some risk. Experience is a great insurance policy, and hiring benefit auction experts to help train volunteers and to ''run the show'' the night of the event will allow the auction committee to sit back and enjoy themselves. It is much more pleasant to enjoy the evening than to worry about every detail. The Chair of the event should be the king or queen of the ball, having no responsibility except greeting and mingling with guests, and should be highly visible having a great time! If the Chair of the event is running around all evening putting out fires and is rarely seen, recruiting a replacement for the next event becomes very difficult. If you want to be able to pass the baton of leadership to new recruits, then be visible, smile a lot, and enjoy yourself the night of the event. Outsource or delegate all responsibilities during those times where guests are present.

Following are some key positions you should consider outsourcing.

### *Auctioneer*

The auctioneer is the face of your event once the Live Auction begins. Regardless of how careful you have been in your planning, how good the food is, how wonderful the decorations, or how efficiently you were able to handle the check-in, the Live Auction is the high-visibility part of your event. It is often also the last part of your event your guests will experience, before cashiering. An inexperienced auctioneer or volunteer can leave the guests in a sour mood, and that feeling can carry forward after they leave, making it difficult to recruit them for your event the following year.

It's quite probable that the cost of a professional benefit auctioneer will be covered in increased bids in just a few items. The professional will know what to say and just when to say it, and will be able to assist you in increasing your revenue by offering suggestions that you may not have thought of. The ability to sell items twice, sell a choice of items, handle an auction sweep (discussed under revenue enhancers), and professionally handle the Fund-an-Item portion of your event are all well worth a reasonable fee for a professional.

The best charity auctioneers are often booked six months to a year in advance on the prime nights, so you will want to begin the search as soon as you set your event date. You will want an agreement with your selected auctioneer that allows you to renew your agreement on the same day the following year, should you and your guests like the way he or she works. Often the best auctioneers will allow for a renewal period (typically 30 days) after the event to lock them in for the following year. Under no circumstances, however, should you accept a perpetual or multiyear agreement that automatically renews, as some auctioneers request. You and your committee will want to evaluate the performance and gain feedback from guests before being locked in to that auctioneer for the following year. The National Auctioneers Association (listed in the Resources section of this book) maintains a list of auctioneers that specialize in charity auctions, and they actually have a special rating (the Benefit Auction Specialist designation), which some auctioneers obtain. The BAS designation is not a guarantee that you are getting a quality auctioneer, however, as the requirement for this getting this designation merely involves attending a class.

A good benefit auctioneer is as much an entertainer as auctioneer, and you can't teach someone how to be entertaining. Most of the top benefit auctioneers are in fact not BAS-designated, because that designation is only a few years old; most auctioneers have not completed the course of instruction, and, frankly, may choose never to do so. That said, the NAA Web site is still a good place to start to find an auctioneer in your area. Be sure to select one that specializes in charity and benefit auctions, not art sales, estate auctions, or liquidations. Your goal is to raise as much money as you can from your items, not to have them liquidated!

You can also ask around for a referral from other charities in your area. If you call the chairs of the largest events that host auctions in your city, you will certainly discover that most use a professional. Get referrals for a few, then call and ask if you can visit an event to see if his or her style will work for your organization.

One final caution when selecting an auctioneer: a free auctioneer, even a free professional auctioneer, may *not* be what you need. Many commercial auctioneers are taught at their auctioneer schools that, since they earn their living in the community it might be a good idea to donate their time by serving as an auctioneer to some local charities. While this sounds like a dream come true, think before you leap at the chance to use one of these free auctioneers. Let's start with the fact that, if they donate their time, they can't do it very often, perhaps just a few times each year. Consequently, their experience in a charity auction will be limited. Second, if they are a commercial auctioneer, they are trained to liquidate items as quickly as they can, because that is what they normally do in their day job. Third, if they volunteer their time, they have no obligation to actually show up at your event, and if a commercial paying event comes along the same day, you can plan on getting a last-minute call that the auctioneer can't make it to your event because he has to work elsewhere. When you pay a fee, and sign a contract, you can insist the auctioneer show up.

Benefit auctioneers are specialists in fundraising, and this specialty is quite different than selling art, used restaurant equipment, or cattle. You would not take a child to a podiatrist when they are sick, you would go to a pediatrician. Just because they are both doctors does not make their specialty irrelevant. When you fly, you want your airliner to be flown by a professional pilot, not a student pilot, so don't put your auction in the hands of a student auctioneer volunteer unless you are willing to live with the consequences.

### Spotters

Having competent professional spotters can significantly increase the income from the Live Auction. The auctioneer can only be looking one direction at any given point in time; therefore, he or she might miss bids on opposite sides of the room. Also, the auctioneer doesn't have the ability to socialize with all the bidders during the evening. It is the job of the spotters to help bidders get comfortable with the auction process and to mingle with the guests and encourage friendly competition. This will result in increased Live Auction yield percentages. While it is possible for volunteers to perform a similar function, their attention span and performance can be limited, and part way though the Live Auction they may lose focus or interest. One or two bid-step increases on a single item in the Live Auction can often pay the cost of hiring professional spotters. More than likely, your professional auctioneer will be able to supply the spotters as part of the base fee for auctioneer services, or at a reasonable increase in the fee.

### Consulting Services

Some auctioneers offer full consulting, some offer minimum consulting. It may be beneficial to hire an expert to help guide you toward the right decisions while you are planning your event. Remember that the auction consultant has experience with many prior events and can guide you through some of the areas in which your committee might not have that experience. Consultants can be as hands-on or hands-off as you want them to be. As with any other consultant, however, they can only make suggestions based on previous experience. It is up to the Auction Committee to evaluate those suggestions and then implement them.

### Event Coordinator

The event coordinator's job is to be your day-of-the-event choreographer, making sure all the necessary pieces of the auction puzzle are in place and all the people associated with the day-of-event functions are trained and ready to go. The event coordinator will train your volunteers so they help guests in the most efficient manner possible, from when they first register to when they check out at the end of the evening. While a professional event coordinator is not required for your event, having one allows the volunteers who did much of the preparation for the auction the opportunity to take the night off and enjoy the fruits of their labor. This is also an excellent insurance policy against "crisis" issues that can only be solved by someone with experience.

### Event Staff

If you have a larger event with many guests to check in and check out, you may find it worthwhile to hire a few event staff helpers to work alongside your volunteers. This will help your volunteers feel confident about the event logistics and will also provide a competent experienced person to step in should any difficult situation arise. Event staff can perform any of the positions a volunteer would do, including help with registration, cashiering, data entry, and more.

Hiring professional consulting, coordinating, and staff to assist you is entirely optional, but can increase revenue significantly for most organizations while making your guests' experience more pleasant. Outside help will also allow the event organizers—that would be you and your committee—to actually be able to enjoy the event that you so painstakingly prepared. After all, volunteering to serve on the committee should not be considered cruel and unusual punishment! The most important person to hire, however, is your auctioneer. Most good auctioneers aren't available at the last minute, so make your decision early to ensure a good return on your investment. Remember also, that even the best auctioneer cannot replace proper planning. The auctioneer is the pilot of your airplane . . . it's up to you and your committee to build an airworthy vehicle.

## Tools for Getting Organized—Auction Software

Almost all businesses, whether they are doctors' or dentists' offices, retail stores, manufacturing plants, or restaurants, have one tool in common: specialized software to manage their business. The doctors and dentists use specially designed software to schedule their patient's visits, track their billing, and keep a history of patient's procedures. Retail stores track their inventory, pay their vendors, and collect money from their customers, using specialty software custom-designed for their type and size of business. And we have all experienced how restaurants use software to track table seating reservations. When we place our orders at a restaurant, the server enters them into software that eventually will produce the customer's bill while also tracking the restaurant's inventory of meals produced, which helps organize the reordering of ingredients and provisions so the restaurant never runs out or has to maintain a large inventory just in case. Tracking the popularity of certain meals helps the restaurant plan ahead, analyze pricing, and make adjustments to the menu. Manufacturing companies track inventory of raw materials, schedules of employees, stages of products in production, shipping schedules, and billing. It is clear that no matter the business, specially designed software makes that business more efficient and successful.

If you think about what needs to be tracked for a successful auction, many elements found in other businesses are also present. You have inventory tracking issues, scheduling issues, budgeting issues, RSVP tracking, employee (volunteer) tracking, materials production, financial reporting, sales and payment processing, and much more. Imagine trying to manage your local doctor's office or favorite restaurant using a home-grown database or an Excel spreadsheet! Yet so many auction committees try to manage their business without software specifically designed for managing auctions. This is a symptom of only caring about the current year, and not looking forward to the years to follow. If you are committed to making this year the first step of a five-year plan, with the intent of building the business so you can hand off a viable successful enterprise to your successor, then please invest in your business by starting with auction management software. Your job and the jobs of your committee will be made easier not only this year, but in subsequent years, as well. Success will be much easier to attain, because there will be a history to which you can refer, and reports specific to your business to help analyze results and plan for the future. The commitment to finding and implementing an auction management software suite will pay dividends for many years to come, and will also pay off immediately by taking one more task off your agenda—figuring out how you are going to track all your donations, donors, attendees, and financial information. Unless you are committed to keeping your event small-time, you simply cannot replicate all the hundreds of tasks automated by specialty software by creating a home-grown system.

There are many choices when selecting auction-specific software for your event, and a Web search will reveal a number of vendors. One immediate decision you will have to make is whether your software should be PC- or Mac-based, if it should reside on one computer or several, or whether it should be Internet-based, accessible via any computer through the Web. It is also possible that you may prefer a combination software approach, one that uses the Internet for data entry but transitions to a run-time or local computer-based system for the day of your event. One strong recommendation we make is that if you select an Internet-based program, make sure there is a corresponding offline component that will allow you to manage your processes the day of your event, because having to rely on Internet access at your event is not a good idea. Many venues simply cannot provide reliable access to the Internet, and even if they can, there is no guarantee that access will be operational 100% of the time during your event. You cannot let the success of your event hang on whether a third party is able to provide Internet access at the exact time you need it, and you can't afford to have your guests inconvenienced because "the net is down." You don't get any do-overs, so don't build in any traps you can easily avoid.

Exhibit 5.2 includes some specifics to look for when selecting your software. The Resources section in the back of this book can also help get you started.

Other features are not required, but are very handy if available. Notice, in the "very handy" list in Exhibit 5.3, we mention integration with donor management software. Many companies make software to track and manage donor information, also known as constituent management software. It's quite likely that your organization already has some form of constituent software for managing contacts and their multiple relationships to your organization.

As an example, one person might be new to your committee, but that same person could be a well-known alumnus of the school or a big supporter during capital campaigns for your charity. In another example, a particular

**Exhibit 5.2   Auction Software Checklist**

Software must be able to do the following:

- ☐ Track donated items and donors
- ☐ Produce reports showing donation status (tracking reports)
- ☐ Track RSVPs for attendees, including payments
- ☐ Provide a budget tracking system for expenses versus income
- ☐ Track committee milestones
- ☐ Filter and sort names in database for periodic mailings
- ☐ Track sponsorship sales and produce sponsorship statements
- ☐ Prepare the catalog of items, bid sheets, and table easels
- ☐ Produce certificates for any items arriving without one
- ☐ Able to easily package or bundle multiple items together to create a new item
- ☐ Assign bid numbers to registered guests
- ☐ Arrange seating of guests and provide a seating chart
- ☐ Produce the check in guest list
- ☐ Track successful bids and the winning bidder
- ☐ Easily track cash contributions during auction from Fund-an-Item
- ☐ Track other income sources, such as raffle and merchandise sales
- ☐ Tie the winning bidder to the payment method and produce a consolidated statement of account and final receipt for purchases
- ☐ Prepare the payments for uploading to credit card processors and bank deposits
- ☐ Produce post-event analytical reports
- ☐ Handle the pre- and post-event thank-you letters for donors and guests

person may have not only attended the auction, but also played in the golf tournament for several years, and made regular cash contributions for years, even though they might not have purchased anything at the auction; this is important information. Being able to look at a person's total connections to your organization is very beneficial because it paints a more complete picture of that individual's involvement.

**Exhibit 5.3   Optional Features for the Auction Software Checklist**

Optional Features

- ☐ Seamless synchronization with donor management software for constituent tracking
- ☐ Seamless integration with Microsoft Office products for exports to Word, Excel, and e-mailing through Outlook
- ☐ A Web-based component for sharing workload across your committee and for publicizing your event and your auction items with an online catalog
- ☐ Direct importation of ``foreign'' databases through a common bridge, such as Excel or CSV (comma-separated values)
- ☐ Ability to handle credit card payments directly for auction items, cash contributions, and RSVP payments

The data you provide to your organization before and after the event will help your organization develop a more complete picture of their constituents. If you can import constituent information from the donor management software into your auction software, and then are able to send the post-event data back to that donor software, your organization will be better able to manage the relationships of your guests, donors, and volunteers over time, resulting in better event outcomes and easier fundraising for the organization as a whole. Ask questions of your auction management software vendor to be sure that they can easily, if not seamlessly, take data in from constituent software and send it back out to the same place after the event. This is a key feature that will pay long-term dividends.

You will find a number of auction management software vendors to choose from, each with its own advantages and disadvantages. Be sure to find out about the *total cost of ownership,* such as whether there are annual renewal fees, charges per event, or penalties for discontinuing use. As an example, some auction software suppliers will "give" the software away for free or charge only a nominal cost, but require that you use their payment processing, pay a per-event setup charge, and/or rent the credit card terminals from them. Some also require you sign a long-term contract that you will be unable to cancel without harsh penalties. In the long run, when you factor in the cost of payment processing fees, event setup charges, and terminal rentals, you would be well ahead to just pay for the software up front, so be sure to look at total cost of ownership over several years, not just the first year. Be sure to read the fine print on any agreements!

## Holding the Kickoff Rally

The Kickoff Rally or party is designed to be informative and fun, and is an opportunity to introduce everyone in your auction circle to the theme, location, goal, mission, and process that you have planned with the help of your committee. This is a great time to introduce your committee as the Steering Committee, setting the expectation that you will be doing business in a new way by making the auction part of the normal fundraising of your organization. You can present this new Steering Committee as the inaugural group and ask that those interested in future membership let you know.

You will also use this opportunity to sell the value of the event, tie it to your mission, and demonstrate to everyone that they can share in the success in some capacity. You will want to have clipboards for people to sign up as volunteers, ask for table captains (discussed in detail in Phase III), and, of course, kick off the item procurement process. This is your first opportunity to share with your supporters the goal and how you plan to get there.

The Kickoff Rally is meant for anyone who can assist, in any capacity, in making the event a success. The list of people to invite (besides the Steering Committee, of course) includes board members, past donors, past vendors, prior contributors, current staff and volunteers, friends of the organization, and anyone else associated with the organization in any way. For schools, you would also include faculty, parents, and alumni. Of course, not everyone invited will attend, but they all should receive an invitation, because this is the first step toward solicitation items, attendees, sponsorships, and vendors.

The format of the rally is quite simple. Pick a date and location where many, if not most, of your potential guests could attend. For some organizations, such as a school, this might be in the morning after the students are dropped off for class, or perhaps in an evening at a private home. Location is important to the extent that you can accommodate the expected attendance and for the convenience of people who will attend. Parking may also be a factor. It is not necessary to hold the kickoff at the event location, especially if there is an extra cost involved, it would be inconvenient for people to get there, or parking would be an issue. Convenience for optimal attendance is the key for choosing a location for the rally.

Keep the agenda short and to the point. The entire amount of time to have your guests there is one hour—no more. You want to respect their time, and you will find that you are more likely to get attendance if you promise to take no more than an hour total.

Here is a sample agenda for the Kickoff Rally:

## Sample Agenda for Kickoff Rally

| Time | Activity |
| --- | --- |
| 6:00–6:15 P.M. | Hosted drinks and snacks (could be wine in the evening or coffee in the morning). |
| 6:15–6:30 P.M. | Welcome and introduction of Steering Committee and guests. Discuss the event mission and goal, as well as the date, location, and theme. |
| 6:30–6:45 P.M. | Item procurement discussion, using the ABCs of Procurement (see the Resources section for a sample; the full document is available online at www.auctionhelp.com). Ask everyone to help solicit items. |
| 6:45–7:00 P.M. | Discuss volunteer needs and ask for help serving on committees. |
| 7:00 P.M. | Thank everyone for attending, ask them to take a procurement packet as they leave, and adjourn. |

You will want to include the following in the procurement packet:

- An envelope or folder to hold all materials
- Two letters to potential donors outlining your request for donations and highlighting the mission of your organization; let your solicitors make copies of letters
- Two procurement (donation) forms
- A one-page prompt sheet for solicitors to help with sample "Ask" questions
  - Include information about the event such as date and theme
  - Provide the tax ID number of the organization
  - Be sure to ask if the donor would like an invitation to the event
  - List the procurement due date
  - Ask for backup marketing materials to use for displays
- A list of sample auction items. You can use a copy of the ABCs of Procurement, which can be downloaded at www.auctionhelp.com.
- Optionally, a list of sponsorship and underwriting opportunities for donors who would prefer to make a cash contribution
- Instructions as to returning the completed forms

Of course, your committee may wish to add other information in the packet as well. This list will get you going, but be sure to discuss this with your committee and be creative. Bear in mind that the more information you stuff into the procurement packets, the less chance it will all be read, so keep it to the essentials.

The Kickoff Rally is a great way to reach out and identify members of your community who share your passion for your cause. It is a recruiting bonanza—most people who attend will end up accepting some role in the success of your event. It might be that you will add a member or two to your committee or to one of the subcommittees. You may find some hidden connections to the local business committee, or a person willing to find some underwriting for services you'll need for your event. At the very least, you will be sending all the attendees off to get auction items, and you would be amazed at the hidden wealth of items that await you when you get your supporters excited about networking to get items rather than cold calling. The discussion on Procurement (Chapter 8, in Phase III) will show you how to get items without ever cold calling on strangers, which nearly everyone hates doing. It is really unnecessary to cold call, and at the Kickoff you will excite people when you share with them how to get those items easily without ever having to make a cold call!

# Planning Your Silent and Live Auctions

In this chapter, we will discuss some long-range planning for the Live and Silent Auctions. Each auction serves a different purpose. By looking at the ways you will be using these two pieces of your fundraising puzzle at your event, you can more clearly focus on considerations such as space requirements, lighting, sound, and table displays. You will find that when it comes time to actually set up your displays at your venue, the move-in process will be much easier if you have planned ahead. It is all about merchandising. Your bidders (customers) in the Silent Auction can't bid on items that they are physically restricted from reviewing and for which they can't access the bid forms. There is no faster way to constrain your bid activity (which costs you money) than to have your Silent Auction room too tightly packed with items and guests. As you begin your procurement process, you will want to visualize how those items will be displayed and therefore how much total room you will need, based on your goal.

You will also want to instruct your volunteers who are finding those auction items to ask for supporting material when they receive an item. For example, when receiving a donation from a restaurant, ask for a menu or copy of a menu for the display. If you get a donation of a weekend cabin, or vacation condo, ask the donor if they have any pictures they could provide showing the view, the rooms, and the amenities. If you receive a donation of an airplane ride, get a picture of the airplane; likewise, for boat cruises, you would want pictures of the boat. This is logical, of course, but often missed in the excitement of hearing "Yes" to a request for a donation.

## Effective Silent Auction Displays

Most benefit auctions consist of several Silent Auctions and one Live Auction. Silent Auction setup is vital to the success of any auction, because this is the part of the evening that people experience first. Silent Auctions close at various intervals, often 15 minutes apart. They are the precursor to the Live Auction, and get your guests in the bidding mood. For planning purposes, here are some guidelines to follow when doing advance planning for your Silent Auction:

- Plan to close your Silent Auction in sections, not all items at once. This is to allow for compression of the bid activity due to supply and demand. As you take items away (close a section) you make the remaining items more valuable, because there are more bidders for fewer items.
- When setting your schedule for the evening, plan to close all Silent Auction sections prior to moving on to the Live Auction. *Never* keep a Silent Auction open until after the Live Auction. To do so will make it impossible to have a smooth checkout process.
- Assume you will need, at a minimum, two linear feet of table frontage for each Silent Auction item. Do *not* ask the facility how many tables they will give you. Plan for how many linear feet you require for the anticipated number of items you will sell, and then tell them how many tables you will need. If necessary, rent more tables and be sure the facility can handle the space required for the additional tables.
- Place bars at the most remote area of the Silent Auction so guests will need to walk past your item displays to get their drinks. If you place the bars in a hallway or outside the Silent Auction area, your guests have little incentive to walk through your Silent Auction. Be careful that any lines forming at the bars do not block your bidding tables!
- If you plan to serve food during your Silent Auction, avoid a buffet island filled with food. This will draw bidders to the food, and away from the bidding tables. Instead, get passed appetizers if possible, or at least spread the food around the Silent Auction area, with cheese and crackers at one station (between silent display tables) and vegetables on the other end of the area. By placing the various food items around your Silent Auction room, you create a flow through the bidding area and eliminate congregation at the food tables.
- Make sure your Silent Auction area has plenty of lighting during the time the sections are open for bidding. Try to visit the event location at the same time of day as you are planning your event, so you can see the existing ambient lighting. Doing a site visit at noon will not tell you what the lighting will be like at 7:00 P.M.! Plan for auxiliary lighting if needed. Candlelight dinners good; candlelight Silent Auctions, bad!
- Try to keep your ratio of Silent Auction items to buying units on a one-to-one basis. That is, if you plan on having 200 Buying Units (approx. 400 people), then the ideal number of Silent Auction items would be 200. If you have fewer auction items than that, you have lost opportunity, but the yield on each item should go up. If you go much over that ratio (more than one item per buying unit), you start to spread the

same bid dollars over more items. The one-to-one relationship is optimal. To get there, plan to assemble packages of synergistic items if you have many more items than buying units.

- Carefully check how much room is available for item display and guest access at your venue. Your silent tables *must* have at least eight feet of available walking space between them, if you set up islands or columns of tables. If you allow less than eight feet, your guests will not walk between the tables, and this will cost you bids.

- Plan to use a catalog numbering system to make it easy for guests to find items, assuming you provide a catalog to follow. If, for example, you have three Silent Auction sections (closings), then you would want a system that places items in Section A, B, and C to correspond to closings 1, 2, and 3. Therefore, the numbering of the items for the first closing should be Section A, numbers 101, 102, 103, and so on. The second closing would be Section B with a numbering system of 201, 202, 203, and so on. This logic is easy for people to follow and will help guide your bidders quickly to the items they wish to view. Do not start your numbering system at number 1 because you will end up with single-, two-, and possibly three-digit numbers, which makes cross-checking correctly entered bids in the auction software more difficult. Being consistent with your numbering pays dividends during the heat of the battle on auction night.

- Plan to use props to tastefully display items. If possible, build "sky-lines" with your item displays. To do this, cover cardboard boxes or crates with cloth at varying degrees of height. Bring smaller items up closer to the eyes of your bidders by placing them on taller boxes. When displaying jewelry, try to use a jewelry display case, which often can be borrowed from the jeweler who donated the item.

- Display gift certificate items with pictures, murals, drawings, magazine clippings, props, anything you can find to make the item more appealing. Be creative.

- Plan to use a bid system that will preset bid steps on three-part bid forms. Using a three-part form (white, yellow, and pink copies of each form on carbonless paper) will greatly assist the checkout and item retrieval processes. This is discussed in more detail in Phase IV.

The Silent Auction sets the stage for the Live Auction, so having an area in the Silent Auction where your guests can preview the Live Auction items that will be up for bid is also a good idea. When planning your space allocation, therefore, include enough space in a prominent area for the Live items to be displayed, with excellent lighting and easy access. This will contribute to your Live Auction by giving your bidders an hour or two to think about the items and for couples to discuss their interest.

**Silent Auction Sections Using Effective Skylining and Display Techniques**

## Effective Live Auction Promotion

Planning for the Live Auction display and promotion is fairly straightforward. The items you sell in your Live Auction may represent a full two-thirds of the value you receive from auction items. As a result, it is well worth your investment to make sure these items are displayed beautifully and are the centerpiece of your auction area. As previously mentioned, displaying the Live Auction items in the Silent Auction area will provide a preview for your guests. If the Silent Auction is in a separate room from where you will conduct your Live Auction, it may be necessary to move the Live Auction items to another display area in the room where the Live Auction will be conducted. For planning purposes, you should allow three feet to display each Live Auction item, because it is important for each of these high-end items to have its own visual space. You will also want larger signs describing the items, especially when the item is an intangible such as a dinner or trip.

In addition to the display of the Live Auction items in your Silent Auction, you should consider using presentation software (such as Microsoft's PowerPoint) during the Live Auction to display a picture and a brief description of each item while it is being offered for sale. You will likely want

**Live Auction Preview Examples**

to have a video presentation highlighting your mission anyway, and since you have paid for the video display equipment, it makes sense to use it during the Live Auction to enhance the value of the items, as well. Remember, your guests will have many distractions, so the purpose of the video display of each item is to refocus the guests' attention on the auction. It is also possible to creatively include musical bumps along with the presentation—not only does the display change with each item, but the introduction for each item includes a 10-second tune to reorient the audience. Something as simple as 10 seconds of "Take Me Out to the Ballgame" to introduce an autographed baseball or jersey, or "New York, New York" for a trip to that city, or perhaps the theme from the "Love Boat" for a cruise will all add some fun to the auction and keep your bidders tuned in.

CHAPTER 7

# Other Auction Activities

## Revenue Enhancers: Adding More to Your Bottom Line

In this section, we will offer you a shopping list of revenue enhancers that can be added to your event. Perhaps you will be tempted to do all of them, figuring they will all help you get to your goal. As we discussed earlier, however, change must be evolutionary, not revolutionary, because people get shot in revolutions, so proceed cautiously and think in terms of implementing these changes over three to five years. It is possible to overwhelm your committee and guests with too many changes, so pick a few for this year, then know you have many more tricks up your sleeve for next year (even if you pass the baton of leadership, you can still offer your ideas for your successor.)

### Additional Auction Revenue Ideas

Here is a list of suggested revenue enhancers you may want to consider for your event. This is by no means intended to be an exhaustive list, but it contains several of the most popular ideas.

- Use pre-auction *Corporate Underwriting* to offset hard costs. If you are able to get local businesses to agree to fund part or all the cost of your event, then more of your revenue goes to the bottom line. Often a local bank, real estate office, printing company, or similar business can write off support for your organization as an advertising expense.
- Get rid of small gift certificates profitably by using *Balloon Sales* or *Grab Bags*. It makes no sense to put a $20 or $25 gift certificate on a Silent Auction table and have it take up valuable space. They will sell for about half of what they are worth on the tables. If you put each one in a helium balloon and sell the balloons for $20 each, you make more money and save valuable table space. You can have $20 to $50 items in balloons selling for $20, $30 to $75 items in $30 balloons, and $50 to $100 items in $50 balloons. A variation: At golf tournaments, insert

certificates into sleeves of golf balls instead of using balloons. Golfers love it! And get a sponsor to supply the golf balls. They will do it gladly, because it puts their logo into the hands of the buyers.

- Add 10% to 20% to the total Live Auction bids by adding a *Fund-an-Item Goal.* If you have a specific goal for a special item or project that represents about 10% of your total auction goal, you can get it from a Fund-an-Item drive during the Live Auction. It's like a mini-telethon where the audience pledges by holding up their bid cards at different dollar amounts.

- Gain another 5% to 10% of your auction bid activity in the weeks *after* your auction by establishing a *Corporate Matching Funds* program. It's likely that many of your bidders work for companies with a charitable corporate matching fund program. Be sure to ask the successful bidders whether they work for such a company. If so, have them submit their receipts for matching funding. Here is a tip: Place a check box on your invitation that asks if the guest's employer has a matching gift program. If they check the box, then capture their employer's name during registration and provide a duplicate cash contribution receipt specific to the guest to submit to their employer after the event. Track employers with matching fund programs in your auction software, tied to the guest record.

- Variation: the *Over Value Match.* Find a company willing to match any of the money bid *above* the fair market value of each item in the Live Auction. Prompt the auctioneer to mention the company's name every time the bid goes above fair market value. For example, a high bid of $1,500 on a item valued at $1,200 gains an additional $300 match ($1,800 total earned on the item) and a nice mention of the matching gift donor from the auctioneer.

- Offer some Live Auction items as *Choice to the High Bidder.* Place similar items in the catalog at the same catalog number, but as an A, B, or C choice. High bidders are given their choice of the A, B, or C item, or any two or three of them at multiples of their bid. This creates additional bid activity on each individual item.

- Let your auctioneer use the process of *Selling Twice,* or multiple times, to maximize the bid activity on a popular item. Make sure you get clearance from the donor ahead of time to sell their donation more than once if it reaches above a predetermined bid level.

- Have at least one item you can sell in a *Sweep.* A sweep allows you to sell one item to multiple people, one person at a time, or to one couple at a time. This works very well if you have a party that has room for 20 couples. Sell entry to the party by the couple to maximize your money. If the value of the party is $10,000, it will be much easier to find 20 couples who will pay $500 each to go to the party than to find only one or two bidders willing to pay $10,000 to entertain their friends.

- Use *"QuickCheck" cashiering* to stimulate increased bid activity—people queued up in the cashiering line do not spend any more money. Keep them at their tables during the Live Auction by encouraging the use of the Quick Check system. More on QuickCheck—also called qCheck or Express Checkout—is covered in Phase IV.
- Provide *Auction Scrip* to create bidding above item values. Auction scrip will add value to your Live Auction, because the bidders who have it will spend more just to get rid of it. Offer scrip to anyone who buys into your event at a premium. For example, if a regular admission is $50 and a patron admission is $100, offer the patron $25 in auction scrip, which is only good toward auction purchases.
- Insert a *Bidding Frenzy* to market items of similar categories. This is a great way to get rid of 10 to 20 restaurant certificates or sports ticket packages. It takes just a few minutes in the auction, and all frenzy items sell for full price. Rounds of golf at a variety of popular courses make a great golf frenzy. More information on bidding frenzy techniques appears later in this chapter.
- Try a *Bid-O-Gram* to save display space for the higher-ticket items (the Bid-O-Gram closes during the Live Auction, but bidders can do it from their tables). There are always items that just missed the cut for the Live Auction. These are good candidates for a Bid-O-Gram. They get focus throughout the night, and are sold as a blind bid. More on Bid-O-Gram techniques appears later in this chapter.
- Include *Raffle Ticket* sales to increase revenue. Your bidders are always looking for some new way to try their luck. Everyone likes to buy raffle tickets, so go ahead and add them to your evening. The best raffle items are those that generate more value as a raffle item than as an auction item. For example, a 21-inch television (value: $300) would sell for about $200 to $300 in the auction. Instead, you could sell 100 raffle tickets at $5.00 each, earning $500 on the same item. Note: Raffles should be drawn *after* the Live Auction. Once the auction is underway, the auctioneer is building momentum and getting the energy of the room worked up. When you stop to announce a raffle winner, the momentum needs to be started once again. This is costly to the value of the auction items. Variation: Sell a Best-of-Live Auction raffle ticket. If your state raffle laws allow, sell tickets at $50 to $100 each. The winner is drawn *before* the Live Auction begins. Winner gets their choice of any item in the Live Auction catalog! Make sure that the total you can make on the raffle tickets is greater than the expected value of the best item in the Live Auction, even though it is rare that the winner takes the most expensive item.

## About Raffles

Before you initiate any kind of raffle or gambling game, we strongly recommend that you check with your local or state gaming commission to verify the rules and regulations in your area. Rules and regulations can vary from area to area, so don't assume that what worked for an event in another town will be legal and fine in your town.

- Sell *Portable Billboards* to increase your sponsorship revenue. Billboards come in various sizes and shapes. The most common is on the back of the bid card. The front of the card has the bid number; the back of the card has a sponsor logo and message. This is an easy sale, because sponsors see the value in having their logo in the hands of every guest the entire evening. The back of the bid card is typically worth $1,000 to $3,000 to a sponsor. You could also award the back of the bid card to a "presenting sponsor" or major underwriter of your event.

### Pre-Event Revenue Opportunities

**Sponsorships**  Companies, corporations, and individuals with an interest in helping you fulfill your mission may not have items to donate to your event, but they can help by donating money to help underwrite your expenses. Any money you can receive before the event will help offset costs that would take profit away from the money raised at the event. You can offer different levels of sponsorship, as well as advertising for each level. Here are examples of some sponsorship opportunities:

- *Event Sponsor*—A company, corporation, or individual that underwrites all or the majority of the event expenses, including catering, venue rental, decorations, alcohol, valet parking, and administration costs. In return for their generous donation, they should be offered substantial advertising in conjunction with your event, they may receive premium seating or special service at the event, and their logo or name should appear on printed materials, such as banners, invitations, letters, table tents, and the catalog.
- *Partial Event Sponsor*—Also known as underwriting sponsors, these sponsors generally absorb (underwrite) certain specific costs of the event, such as food, music, beverages, consigned items, and so forth. Underwriting sponsors may receive an honorary table, banners, and special catalog advertising.

- *Bid Card Sponsor*—One of the most active and visible advertisements that you can sell at your event are sponsorships of the back of the bid card. Companies that sponsor the backs of the bid cards have their logo—or even a coupon—printed on the back of every bid card used that evening. Every time a bidder raises his card during the Live Auction, everyone in the room will get a view of the Bid Card Sponsor's logo.

  Note: Custom-printing a logo on the backs of bid cards is generally more expensive than using standard bid cards. Make certain, when you set the price for bid card sponsorship, that your printing costs are covered.

- *Item Sponsor*—Some companies or individuals, such as banks, attorneys, real estate agents, or accounting firms, will want to donate an item to your event, but the items that they donate will not necessarily have the cachet of some of the more popular items. In other cases, an item you would like to obtain for your event may not be available for a strict donation. For example, travel agents will rarely donate a cruise outright, but they may sell it at a significantly discounted rate. They will expect that you pay transportation fees and portage fees. Item sponsors can be used to cover item costs so you can still offer the item, but your organization doesn't have to lose incremental revenue. The item sponsor gets credit for all or a portion of the value of the item, just as if they donated the item itself. This is a popular way to minimize the financial impact to your organization for consigned items, too. More information on consigned items and how to use them judiciously is provided in Chapter 8, in Phase III.

- *Advertising Sponsor*—Unlike the other tax-deductible sponsorships listed above, these sponsors essentially pay a premium to your organization for the privilege of advertising at your event. They can pay money for an advertisement in the catalog or offer an in-kind service performed for the organization as trade for an advertisement. For example, a local printer might donate the printing of the catalog. There are many places advertising sponsors can be used at your event, including the catalog, your invitations, Save-the-Date cards, other printed materials, centerpieces—even the pens used during your Silent Auction can be donated by an advertising sponsor for a premium donation to your event. Think of it this way: If you have to pay for it for your event, chances are that there might be an advertising sponsor willing to show off their logo or message in exchange for helping you with the cost!

## Individual Donations

- *Tiered Pricing*—The difference between the regular price of entry and the actual price paid can be a tax-deductible contribution. Tiered pricing simply allows a guest to register for your event at a premium cost. For example, your normal entry fee might be $100, with a fair market value of $75. The deductible portion is, of course, $25. However, if you offer a patron-level admission at $150, and the fair market value remains the same, the deductible portion is now $75. You could offer a benefactor level as well for, say, $250, which would provide a deductible amount of $175. In addition to the extra deduction, the patrons and benefactors would receive special recognition, perhaps in the catalog or program, and could also be offered auction scrip, which is a discount on purchases during the auction.

- *Donations in Lieu of Entry*—Often called "regrets donations," these is generally handled by adding a line on the invitation that says, "I am unable to attend, but please accept my gift of $___."
- *In-Kind Donations*—Donations of products and services that will be needed in the course of the event or event planning are called in-kind donations. These might include printing services; postage for mailings of invitations; software or computers to manage the event; wine or other drinks for the event; or reduced or free rental of tables, tents, and chairs.
- *Auction Scrip*—Used in conjunction with the Tiered Pricing, this is paper money that patrons and benefactors can use at the event as discounts on their auction purchases. It is nontransferable and non-refundable. By introducing scrip into the bidding, you will get greater participation in your bid activity as the scrip holders attempt to get rid of their scrip, since it expires and is worthless once the auction is over.

## Important IRS Revenue Ruling Language

For your organization to remain protected from potential IRS penalties, it's important to advise your guests of the fair market value of your event. To do so, one of the following statements, or some similar form, *must* be on the invitation, or the IRS could hold your organization liable for any taxes or penalties incurred by guests who claim the entire ticket price as a deduction. This language should be in a very small font near the bottom of the invitation. It needs to be visible, but it doesn't need to be prominent or highlighted; plain text is fine.

Per IRS regulation #67-246, the Fair Market Value of this event is: $< . . . >

Or, as an alternative:

Pursuant to IRS Rev. Rule #67-246, the Fair Market Value of this event is: $< . . . >

With this language on your invitation, your guest is notified that they can potentially claim only the difference between the fair market value of the ticket and the actual amount they paid. Therefore, it is in the guest's best interest to have a fair market value below the actual ticket price, but one that is realistic and justifiable.

As an example, a fair market value of the typical dinner auction, for the dinner only, might be $50. If your ticket cost for the event is $75 per person, then the difference between the fair market value of the dinner and the $75 entry cost may be a charitable deduction for your guest.

*Remember!* Get help from a tax advisor familiar with your specific organization. This information is for general guidelines only, and is not intended to be professional advice.

### Online Auctions

Online auctions are a way to reduce the number of items that will need to be displayed at the event, which helps you keep your auction as a seller's market. By removing many items from your item list and offering them online, you will not need to display as many items, which will allow for better display of the remaining items. Several companies, such as cMarket and MaestroSoft, Inc., can assist you in setting up an online auction.

Unlike eBay, you will not be offering your items to the general public. Instead, your online catalog will be directed to the mailing list and e-mailing lists your organization maintains. In the case of a school, this might be the parents, extended family, and alumni of the school. One of the bonuses of using an online service like cMarket and MaestroSoft's MaestroWeb is that the entire catalog of items in your inventory, including all the items that will be sold at the event, are displayed online. This isn't possible with eBay. As a result, when you direct potential bidders to your auction Web site to bid, they will also be exposed to a catalog of items only available at the event. This could create additional interest in attending the event, or at least could provide a preview of the items available at the event so event guests will not be experiencing the items for the first time. Conversely, if you make your registered guests aware of your online catalog, they may visit to preview items they wish to bid for at the event and then decide to bid online too.

Also, understand that the mentality of an eBay shopper is different from that of the people coming to your event. Typically, people come to eBay to find a great deal or to locate a very unique item. They are trying to pay as little as possible for that item. Your supporters, on the other hand, are not so much looking for a deal as they are looking to help your organization. If they can get a great item at the same time, well, then that's a bonus.

These days it is so simple to set up an online auction that most organizations are making the Web-based catalog a standard feature of their event, and many are adding online bidding capability as well.

### Chance Items

**Raffles**   For those guests who want to take a chance, you might want to include some kind of raffle. The best raffle items bring in more money than the raffle prize would have made in the auction alone. For example, if you are able to procure a 36-inch flat-screen television, it might bring in a selling price of around $500 on a Silent Auction table, but if you sell 100 tickets at $10 each for the same television, you would make double what you might have otherwise made.

Any raffle items should be sold by bid number (unless it directly violates any gambling laws for your state) so your guests won't be limited by the cash in their pocket. This way, the charges will automatically show up on their invoice at the end of the evening, or, if they have signed up for qCheck, it will just show up as a charge on their credit card statement. It also keeps volunteers from having to walk around with cash and make change. Some auction chairs might not want to hamper volunteers with the liability of carrying cash.

Before you begin selling the raffle tickets, here are some specifics to consider:

- How many will you be able to sell? Will you have a finite number of tickets, or will it be unlimited?
- How will you sell the tickets? Will you have volunteers roaming during the Silent Auction?
- When will you draw for the prize?
- Does the winner need to be present to win?

These questions will be answered by the type of raffle you are using. Here are several types of creative raffles to consider:

- *Best-of-Live Raffle*—Tickets for the Best-of-Live Raffle should be limited, and the winner definitely needs to be present to win this one. You sell a limited number of tickets during the Silent Auction for either $50 or $100. You have an honored guest or emcee draw the winner right before the beginning of the Live Auction. The winner gets to pick any item they wish out of the Live Auction. You will need to make sure that the total amount raised by the sale of raffle tickets will more than offset the fair market price of the most expensive item in the Live Auction. If the most expensive item would have sold for $5,000, you might sell 100 tickets at $100 each for a total income of $10,000. You might talk to as many donors of Live Auction items as possible to see if they would be willing to donate the item a second time if their donated item is picked as the Best-of-Live prize.

Note: It is possible to set limits on the Best-of-Live Raffle. For example, if you are a school and have class projects, you can restrict the winner to anything except class projects. You can also limit the choice to only items equal to or less value than the amount raised in raffle sales.

- *50/50 Raffle*—Tickets for this raffle can be sold for any price that is legal in your state, and the goal is to sell as many tickets as possible. The winner does not necessarily need to be present to win, and you could even sell tickets well in advance of the event. After the ticket sales are closed, the income is tallied so it is known exactly how much was brought in by sales. The winner then splits that financial pool with the organization, 50/50.

   Note: In some states a gambling license may be required for this kind of raffle, and cash prizes may even be illegal. Be sure to check your state gaming commission rules before offering a raffle that might require a license.

- *Bucket Raffle*—Also known as pot raffles or opportunity raffles. In this raffle, bidders are sold a long strip of raffle tickets, and they place tickets in buckets, boxes, or pots that represent each available prize. In this manner, the bidder is able to select the prize(s) they wish to win by placing the tickets in specific containers.

- *Diamond Bar*—If you have a local jewelry store that is willing to be part of the show, you might try setting up a diamond bar. You etch 100 champagne glasses with your event logo or your organization's logo. Set all 100 glasses, full of champagne or sparkling cider, out on a table, and sell the glasses for $25, $50, or $100 each. Each glass has a felt bag wrapped around its stem. All but one of the bags contain a cubic zirconium, but one of the bags has a real diamond in it. The jewelry store sends a jeweler onsite to verify who won the diamond and to sell settings for the cubic zirconiums as well as for the real diamond. Whether the bidder wins the real diamond or not, he or she at least gets something worth their initial investment in the form of a souvenir glass, champagne, and a cubic zirconium, with a chance to win a real diamond.

**A Diamond Bar Raffle**

## Item-Related Chances

- *Opportunity Boards*—You will likely receive many gift certificates during your procurement process. By their nature, certificates do not display well. Rather than trying to create displays to "sell" the certificates, which will merely tie up valuable Silent Auction table space, you can clear all the low-value certificates off the tables and sell them on an Opportunity Board, also known as a Buy It Now Board (see the picture on the next page). Each certificate is described on a small card with the certificate's value. Certificates with values from $50 to $100 can be combined on the same board; the patron pays a flat rate of $50 to select any of the certificates offered. The $100 certificates are the less desirable ones, such as car washes, pizza coupons, and chiropractic examination services. The lesser value certificates, such as restaurant certificates, will be the more popular items. Bidders willing to pay closer to full price get the more desirable certificates, and those wanting a bargain get the less desirable certificates. All of the certificates will sell, because everyone likes to win something at an auction! Of course, you can also have a $100 board with certificates from $100 to $200.

You can have fun creating a version of the Opportunity Board that ties in with your theme. Some themes we have seen that work well are "Angel Boards" (tied to a holiday theme), where the guests selected their certificate by placing an angel sticker with their bid number on it, and "Star Boards" tied to a Hollywood theme.

**An Opportunity Board**

- *Balloon Sales*—Get rid of small gift certificates by putting a slip of paper representing each in a helium balloon and selling the balloons for $25, $50, and $100. Put certificates worth $25 to $50 in the $25 balloons, certificates worth $50 to $100 in the $50 balloons, and those worth $100 and up in the $100 balloons. Each denomination is color-coded, and guests buy a balloon for the face value and pop the balloon to see what they won. This gets rid of many of the certificate items that do not sell or display well, and it frees up considerable table space for items that must be displayed.
- *Treasure Chest*—Fill a safe, treasure chest, or other locked box that matches your theme with valuable items. Sell keys that all look the same to your guests for a price, such as $25 per key. Over the course of the Live Auction, people will go up and try their luck at unlocking the Treasure Chest. If you have 100 keys to sell, you will sell out, and make $2,500. You should not allow anyone to test one of the keys in the lock until all keys are sold.

### Cash and Other Tax-Deductible Donations

Throughout the event, guests bid on items or purchase items. In either case, they are receiving something for their money. Unless they bid far above the fair market value of the item, there is little or no tax deduction for their bidding activity. Many guests will respond enthusiastically if given a chance to donate directly to your cause. Here are some ways you can make it easy for them to do this.

**Fund-an-Item**   The Fund-an-Item, which may also be called Raise the Paddle, Fund-a-Need, Fund-a-Cause, Fund-the-Mission, Emotional Appeal, Cash Call, or many other names, is essentially a mini-telethon during the Live Auction. Bidders are given an opportunity to raise their bid card at various dollar amounts and make a straight cash contribution to a specific cause. The more specific and emotional the cause, the better. Avoid calls to support general operating funds, or for items that would be seen as normal business expenses (such as a new copy machine for the office), as these are assumed to be what the general event funds are for already. Try to stick with something that would be an extra, one that would not get funded without the direct generosity of the audience.

Some examples of excellent causes that really work for Fund-An-Item are as follows:

- School computer lab (school auction)
- Special tutors for students (school auction)

- Safety equipment
- Scholarships for disadvantaged students (school auction)
- Send a child to camp (YMCA, Boys and Girls Club, Campfire Kids, Boy and Girl Scouts auction)
- Research to find cures for diseases (any of the research organizations)
- Incubators for premature babies (children's hospital auction)
- Uncompensated hospital care (any public hospital)
- A special display at the museum (museum auction)
- A new community park (Rotary Club auction)

The timing of *The Ask* for a Fund-an-Item is fairly important. It is not a good idea to do this at the end of the Live Auction, because by that time some guests will have left (so they can't give you money!), and it will also slow down the checkout process. If you ask at the beginning, or early in the Live Auction, many bidders will be holding back on their money in hopes of winning an item. The best time to ask is about halfway through the Live Auction. At that point, most bidders have figured out whether they are going to be able to win in the Live Auction, and they will have their budget available for the cash contribution. Also, halfway through is generally before any guests have departed, so you have a full audience from which to accept donations. When we sequence the order of item sales in the Live Auction (discussed in detail in Phase III), we sell the most expensive item about midway through the list (following a bell curve of values), so the Fund-an-Item is best placed directly after the peak of the curve.

To set up the ask, have a very short (no more than three-minutes) video or presentation describing the item or need you wish to fund, and perhaps have a guest speaker who can describe how important this is to your cause. This *must be kept short*, otherwise the audience will tune out (keep in mind your revenue minutes, as we discussed in Phase I). Once the need is demonstrated, the auctioneer asks for generous pledges at various levels, starting with the highest amount reasonably expected to be received from the audience, and then working down to the lowest amount. It is always a good idea to have a Board member or supporter start the process at the highest level, so when the auctioneer asks at that level, there is at least one card in the air to "prime the pump." Resist the suggestion often made by an auctioneer to start at the lowest level and then increase bid amounts. If you present lower amounts first, guests willing to donate at the higher levels are let off the hook at the lower amounts and don't feel motivated to donate at higher or multiple levels when those amounts are called. There is collective energy in building momentum; you are more likely to gather energy by going from high to low bid levels rather than from low to high, because as the levels get lower, you'll get more people responding. This builds excitement (positive pressure) and energy as you get to lower levels, and you'll get more people willing to "Raise the Paddle" because they, too, want to be part of that energy.

As the auctioneer calls the bid numbers at each level, the recorders write them down on the recording sheet in the corresponding columns. The recording sheet is then brought to cashiering to be entered into the database so the guests' accounts can be charged for their cash contribution. A sample of a Fund-an-Item recording sheet appears in the Resources section of this book.

One point of note here: When you are interviewing your potential auctioneer, be sure to specifically discuss Fund-an-Item prior to hiring him or her. Not all auctioneers are experienced with this part of the auction, and they may not be comfortable doing it. This is another good reason to make sure your auctioneer specializes in benefit auctions, because commercial and memorabilia auctioneers never have to ask for cash contributions. Doing this well is an art and can add substantially to your event's bottom line.

**Silent Fund-an-Item**   As variation on the Fund-an-Item theme, if you have smaller projects that need funding, you might setup pledge forms on a Silent Auction table (usually the last one) and have a box where guests can place completed pledge forms. If a guest was outbid in the Silent Auction, they can just donate that money right there and then, and that money will show up on their statement at the end of the night.

**Dessert Auction, Also Called Dessert Dash**   To save the costs of paying for catered desserts, you can have the desserts donated by committee members, local bakeries, and restaurants. You need one dessert for each table and a form for guests at each table to make donations for the right to choose dessert first. The table that has the largest total donation gets the right to choose first, the table with the second largest donation chooses second, and so on. The donations are tallied by the auction staff. During the Live Auction, the auctioneer is handed the rankings by table. The auctioneer then announces the top table, then the second, then the third and so on down the list. As each table is called, one member of that table "dashes" to the dessert display area and places a flag with their table number on the available dessert their table wants.

### Other Bidding Opportunities

**Bid-O-Gram**   To save display space for higher ticket items, have a separate auction that closes during the Live Auction; guests can bid from their tables in a *blind bid*. These items are the ones that just missed the cut to be in the

Live Auction. Guests fill out their bid number, item number, and bid amount on a form and hand it to a Bid-O-Gram runner, who delivers the bid to a computer operator. The computer operator continuously enters the new high bid amounts, which are displayed on a large screen in the Live Auction area. At the closing of the Bid-O-Gram, the highest "offer" is the successful bidder. Class projects are frequently sold in this manner.

**Centerpieces** If you have centerpieces on your tables, the auctioneer can deputize one "auctioneer" at each table to auction off the centerpieces. This is a fun way to get the guests involved in the evening right at the beginning of the Live Auction (and dinner). Other ways to sell the centerpieces include selling them for a set price or having a Silent Auction form on each table, which is picked up at a certain time during dinner. We refer to selling the center pieces as "decorating with revenue items."

**Decorations** People are always looking for ways to decorate their homes and make them more festive and tasteful. One way of spurring more revenue is to offer to sell (or auction off) some of the decorations at the end of the evening. Centerpieces, lighting (auxiliary if donated), leftover cases of wine or champagne, memorabilia from the evening (banners, signs, etc.), can all be sold to the highest bidder to raise additional funds. Any equipment that is donated to your organization can be auctioned at the end of the evening. It is not uncommon for the auctioneer to see how many cases of wine are left over as the last item comes up for bid. After that item has been sold, the auctioneer will announce that there are [X] of cases of wine left that will be auctioned. People are always willing to purchase bottles of wine for entertaining guests at their homes.

**Bidding Frenzy** If you have 10–20 items in similar categories (such as dinners, parties, services, etc.), you can sell them quickly for full value or more by having a *bidding frenzy* during your Live Auction. The auctioneer describes the gift certificate and states the full retail value. The first guest to hold up a bid card after the auctioneer announces the value wins that item at the item's full value. This is a great way to raise 100% of the fair market value of an item when it probably would have reached only 50% of its value if placed in the Silent Auction. Another benefit is that the bidding frenzy helps generate excitement and energy during the Live Auction and can be strategically placed to reengage an audience who may have grown a little complacent or bored after their meal.

Exhibit 7.1 is a sample of a catalog page that shows one way to display your bidding frenzy. While we use restaurants in this sample, you can sell any number of types of related objects this way, such as gift baskets, gift certificates

**Exhibit 7.1   Restaurant Bidding Frenzy**

---

## RESTAURANT BIDDING FRENZY

**Here is your chance to try a new restaurant or return to some of your favorites, as well as support** [your organization here]. **These gift certificates for breakfast, lunch, or dinner will go to the first person offering the face value by raising their bid card.**

Angelo's Ristorante, dinner for 2. . . . . . . . . . . . . . . . . . . . . . . . . . . . . . . . . . . . . . . . . . . $25

Tucci Benucch, dinner for 2. . . . . . . . . . . . . . . . . . . . . . . . . . . . . . . . . . . . . . . . . . . . . . $30

Red Robin in Redmond. . . . . . . . . . . . . . . . . . . . . . . . . . . . . . . . . . . . . . . . . . . . . . . . . $35

Duke's Bar & Grill in Bellevue, dinner for 2. . . . . . . . . . . . . . . . . . . . . . . . . . . . . . $40

Mikado Restaurant. . . . . . . . . . . . . . . . . . . . . . . . . . . . . . . . . . . . . . . . . . . . . . . . . . . . . $50

McHigh Restaurants–FX McRory's . . . . . . . . . . . . . . . . . . . . . . . . . . . . . . . . . . . . $75

Ristorante Paradiso, dinner for 4. . . . . . . . . . . . . . . . . . . . . . . . . . . . . . . . . . . . . . . . $80

Eques Restaurant in the Hyatt Regency . . . . . . . . . . . . . . . . . . . . . . . . . . . . . . . $100

Trattoria Sostanza, dinner for 4 . . . . . . . . . . . . . . . . . . . . . . . . . . . . . . . . . . . . . . . $100

Spazzo Mediterranean Grill, dinner for 8. . . . . . . . . . . . . . . . . . . . . . . . . . . . . . $200

Spirit of Washington Dinner Train. . . . . . . . . . . . . . . . . . . . . . . . . . . . . . . . . . . . . $228

---

for services, parties, and more. To make it easier for you, most of the better auction software programs can print this page directly from the database.

There will, no doubt, be some gift certificates that will be more popular than others. If there are more than 20 bid cards in the air the auctioneer might use a technique sometimes called "Auction Chicken" to sell them off. The auctioneer will start by asking all the people with their card in the air to keep them in the air. He or she then increases the bid amount by $5 or $10 increments. As the bids rise, the number of cards drops. The last card in the air gets the item at that last bid. It's a great way to get 150% to 200% of the value of small items that might go for 50% of their value on a Silent Auction table.

**Pot of Gold**   The purpose of the Pot of Gold is to allow the guests at the event to be able to donate part of an auction item that will be sold at the end of the Live Auction. This is easily accomplished as follows: Get a clear container, like a fish bowl, and have volunteers go around the room having guests put something of value in the container (probably during cocktail hour and Silent Auction). Items might include cash, jewelry, and watches; a business card with a promise of a donation or service by that person's company; or anything else the guest may wish to contribute. What makes this fun is that no one in the room truly knows to what value the Pot of Gold has risen, because the only person who gets to count it is the winning bidder, after they purchase it. People who donate items to the Pot of Gold will want to stay to the end to see how high the bids go, and because of the intrigue of bidding on something that is unknown, some guests might stay around who would normally have left halfway through the Live Auction. The goal here is to keep people in their seats until the end of the evening, so that the momentum and energy in the room remain at a high level.

**Sweeps**   During the procurement process, a donor might give you an item that may be too big for a single bidder, such as a dinner cruise for 60 people. In this case, instead of auctioning the item to a single bidder, the auctioneer might recommend selling the cruise "by the couple." In this manner, it is quite possible that the total bids (30 couples all paying the same amount) will be larger than a single bidder buying the entire cruise for a private party. You will need to have a form ready for the recorders so they can write down each bid number and the quantity. The auctioneer will then treat this item just like a Fund-an-Item, except there are a finite number of couples' spots on this cruise. You will assign a price per couple, and the auctioneer will count the cards in the air at that specific price. If there are more cards in the air than available spots for the item, the auctioneer will increase the price per couple to get to the proper quantity available. As the price goes up, of course, the number of couples who want to buy goes down.

A similar situation might occur when you have 10 cases of fine wine, or 20 seats at a ballgame. Use the sweep process to establish a value for each, and sell one of each to the bidders willing to pay the most for each one. A sweep is a great way to sell that large item in smaller portions, so you can get a higher percentage of the fair market value.

You may notice that many of these game-like revenue enhancers are based upon guests taking a chance. When people know that putting their money on the line is a win-win situation, they will more freely part with it. If they win, they will receive the prize (e.g., a television, a $100 gift certificate, a gift basket, the Pot of Gold, etc.). If they don't win, they have the satisfaction of knowing that their money went to support your cause, and they had fun playing at the same time.

## Handling Class Projects

School auctions represent a great opportunity for a variety of people to get involved at any level they are able. For the teachers at the school, their contribution can be to coordinate a class project that can be sold at the auction as an instant heirloom. What parent wouldn't want a lasting memory of their child's third-grade experience?

If properly designed and constructed, the class project represents the best elements of the most desirable auction items: It is unique, has strong emotional appeal, has a "priceless" quality (no perceived upper limit of bid expectation), will be desired by a broad base of bidders, and (if possible) can be sold more than once. Class projects fit within these parameters.

There are some basic guidelines to consider when creating a class project. Here are some of the most important ones:

- The item must be handcrafted by the students (with some adult supervision)
- Each child must be clearly represented (include a "map" if necessary to show which part of the project each child constructed, painted, or designed)
- Use a variety of colors to appeal to the widest décor—a single color item may not fit a specific home and is too constraining
- Use quality construction materials—the item must literally last a lifetime
- Avoid items that will not get displayed once purchased—for example, a long mural would be impractical

The best class projects have both an emotional value and a practical value as well. Here are some examples of good class projects:

- Coffee tables
- Place settings, chargers, serving dishes or trays
- Toy boxes, craft boxes, or keepsake trunks
- Chess sets
- Decorative display art or custom frames for art or mirrors
- Quilts
- Planting workbench
- Tiles for a patio

Note that each of the above has a practical use that will allow the children's art to be displayed, plus has the emotional impact of being a one-of-a-kind keepsake. This combination helps the bidding process reach ridiculous heights—a very good thing for your auction!

Here are some additional ways to increase your income using class projects:

- Have two of the projects built instead of one—the auctioneer can sell the second one for the same price as the first.

- Create a "choice" situation, such as pictures representing seasons. The high bidder gets to choose any of the seasons, or can have a number of seasons at that number times the bid, or all four for four times the bid. This really helps the bidding process! Make sure each child is represented on *every* piece, so the buyer will be happy with ANY of the choices.
- Match the items to the anticipated audience. If only one or two people representing a class are expected to come to the auction, there will be little competition for the item. Focus on getting class projects for the classes that will have the largest attendance, if known.
- Use a class project coordinator to work with the teachers. This person surveys the parent community to see what will sell, gets the raw materials, and collects the seed money to pay for them, and then "leaks" a few choice comments about how the project is coming together. This creates anticipation and word of mouth marketing in advance of the auction!
- Get pictures taken before, during, and after the project is completed. Post the pictures on the school Web site, or circulate pictures of the projects under construction to build anticipation and desirability. Have a preview display of the items a few days before the auction or on your Web site, so potential bidders can start to bond with the item.
- Include only the best of the projects in the Live Auction. If all of them make the Live Auction, the audience will soon lose interest, because they will have too many choices. Keep in mind that, as a rule, only the parents of Mrs. Anderson's second-grade class will be bidding on that particular class project, so don't bore the rest of your audience with too many items that have, by their very nature, restricted interest. The items not designated for the Live Auction will still sell well in a spirited Silent Auction or a "Mini Live" at the end of the Silent Auction.
- Be sure to intersperse the projects throughout your Live Auction so that you retain a good mix of items and keep all your guests' interest and attention, not just the parents bidding on class projects.

## Summary for Revenue Enhancers

It's not necessary to confine your fundraising effort to just the traditional Live and Silent Auctions. As we have tried to establish in this discussion of revenue enhancers, there are many ways to get your audience to be generous. They all come to support your cause, and when you make it fun for them by providing some games or opportunities to win, they will respond in kind with generous support. Think of *fun-raising* as well as *fundraising*.

Don't be afraid to experiment. All of the good ideas haven't been thought of yet. If something has a chance to add value to your event, give it a try. As a final thought, be sure to use bid numbers for *all* purchases. Let it all go on one master bill and let the guest pay at the end of the evening. When people have to spend their cash, they feel like they are spending more than they had planned, but if they can pay by check or credit card at the end of the event, they are more generous. If their card is on file through the qCheck process, then you have all the more reason to "go cashless."

# PHASE II

# CONCLUSION

At this point, you are well underway with your planning, and you have decided what elements you wish to incorporate into your event. Consideration has been given to hiring expert help, you have surveyed and selected a location that can accommodate your event with plenty of space and lighting and has all the other essential elements for a successful event. You may have also decided to host an online auction in conjunction with your gala. Additional revenue-enhancing elements have been considered and may be used too, although some of these decisions can be made closer to your event.

We will now move on to the specific tasks of getting the auction items and marketing your event. It is now important to obtain the items that will be sold and fill the room with bidders. In Phase III, we will take on the task of creating forms and processes for getting auction items (we discussed this early in Phase II when we talked about the Kickoff Rally) and for filling the room with guests willing to bid. You will be sending out your Save-the-Date cards, creating your invitations, structuring your catalog, and finalizing all your operations for the event. Phase III leads you right up to event day, so get ready, because this is where the "rubber meets the road!" Phase III will be essential reading for everyone on your committee, because each of them will be affected by the action items that are accomplished in that Phase.

# PHASE III

# PROCUREMENT, AUDIENCE DEVELOPMENT, AND EVENT PREPARATION

Phase III
Procurement, Audience Development,
and Event Preparation

In this Phase, we move on to the nuts and bolts of preparing for the event. We will cover many items, all essential to your successful event. Moving well beyond theory, we start to assemble the pieces of the puzzle, preparing the materials needed to solicit auction items and sponsorships, determining how we will track those items as they are received, and identifying where and how we will store them. We will also discuss how to get unique and highly desirable items and trips that would not normally be donated, and we will cover audience development as well, so we have a room full of bidders to buy all these great items we are gathering!

Once the guests get to the party, we will want them to have a catalog to view, so we will cover the preparation of catalogs that work, what should be included, and what does not need to be included.

We will also review how to organize your silent auctions for maximum efficiency and optimum marketing of the items. This will include why we have several closing times for auction sections, instead of closing all Silent Auctions at the same time, and why we distribute the values across these closings in ever-increasing amounts, not equally. By the end of Phase III, you will be completely prepared and ready with auction items, a catalog, and people who are registering for your event. At that point, it is on to Phase IV, where we prepare for the event day.

# Procurement

To have a successful auction, you will need items to sell and people to buy them. This sounds simplistic, but it really is the basis of a successful auction. As we gather the items, we are ahead of the game if we can match the items to the guests we plan to invite to our event. It would make little sense to solicit fabulous trips if the guests are not people who can bid on fabulous trips! Likewise, soliciting items that are mismatched for your guests makes little sense. Imagine if you were raising money for your yacht club foundation, and the guests attending were all members of the yacht club. How well do you suppose rides on a yacht would sell? Correct! Not at all. So, when soliciting items, give strong consideration to the potential guest list, and do the matching in advance whenever possible.

The chairperson of the Procurement Committee should consider having a kickoff rally, as we discussed in Phase II, to get the volunteers and other members of their committee excited about going out into the community to get items donated. It should be as much a social event as it is a training and informational meeting. At the kickoff rally, the following should be accomplished:

1. Make the procurement cutoff date widely known to the members of your organization. Ending the procurement process at least one month before the auction gives enough time to print catalogs and organize items.
2. Brainstorm a list of items that will capture the interest of your bidders and potential bidders.
3. Train the committee on how to ask for donations, what to ask for, and where to ask.
4. Hand out procurement packets and describe how to fill out the procurement forms and where to return them when completed.

The most important part of the rally is getting the procurement forms in the hands of your committee members, volunteers, and other supporters.

Once they have the forms, they are able to go out, on their own or in groups, and solicit items. The Procurement Chair should monitor the progress and report periodically to the Steering Committee. Encourage people to acquire unique experience items and think about packages (e.g., plane tickets with a condo stay; a ball game and dinner). Remember, make this process a creative and enjoyable experience.

You will want to include the following in the procurement packet (this was also listed in Phase II when we talked about the kickoff rally):

- An envelope or folder to contain all materials
- Two letters to potential donors outlining your request for donations and highlighting the mission of your organization; let your solicitors make copies of letters
- Two procurement (donation) forms
- A one-page prompt sheet for solicitors that helps with sample "Ask" questions
  - Include information about the event such as date and theme.
  - Provide the tax ID number of the organization.
  - Be sure to ask if the donor would like an invitation to the event.
  - List the procurement due date.
  - Ask for backup marketing materials to use for displays.
- A list of sample auction items. You can use a copy of the ABCs of Procurement, a subset of which is included in the Resources section of this book (the entire document can be downloaded at www.auctionhelp.com).
- Optionally, a list of sponsorship and underwriting opportunities for donors who would prefer to make a cash contribution
- Instructions for returning the completed forms

You may also wish to include the following questions and answers to help clarify common issues that generally come up during the procurement process.

## Common Questions about Procurement

Q: I am supposed to procure $XXX worth of items for the auction. I don't know where to start! Any ideas?

A: Start with yourself. What can you donate? Then ask your friends, neighbors, and relatives. Also, existing clients and vendors of your organization are a good source, because they will want you to succeed. It is easier to ask others to help if you have started with yourself.

Q: I do know a lot of people, but I just don't feel right asking them for something. How do I approach them without imposing?

A: You are not imposing. Remember, your friends and associates want to help you. They just need to be shown how they can do that. Most work for companies that donate regularly as part of their philanthropic mission in the community. They just have to be shown where the need is. Make it easy for them by asking for something specific! You will be amazed at the success you will have when people can give you something specific and do not have to decide what would be appropriate. Most people will just say yes or offer an alternative idea.

Q: Most of my associates are attorneys, accountants, and other professionals. Should I be asking for legal assistance or tax help to be donated?

A: Typically, these services are not good sellers in an auction, because the process for selecting an attorney or accountant is most frequently through a referral. As an alternative, ask them what they do for fun. Do they have a condo, a boat, do they fish? These items can all be donated, or great packages can be made from them. Don't lock in on the profession; most good items come from what people do in their spare time. They may also wish to underwrite a consigned item or trip, or perhaps become a sponsor. Don't leave them off your "Ask" list. These individuals are also great resources for underwriting since they often only have cash to "give." Ask them to underwrite the valet, the bar, perhaps your flowers or a consigned item for which you'd otherwise have to pay.

Q: I have a friend who is offering a really great item for our event, but he is asking for $500 back if it sells for more than that at the auction. Is this a good idea?

A: This is called a *consignment* item. Using consigned items to fill your auction catalog can be a bad idea, but there may be times where *judicious* use of consigned items may be a very positive addition to your own procurement. (More information on how, when, and why to use consigned items can be found later in this chapter, in the section titled The Case for Consignments.)

Q: My next-door neighbor has a great lawn mower that is about 10 years old and would like to get rid of it. Should we take it for our auction?

A: Generally, you should accept only new merchandise for your auction. You don't want your guests feeling that they are attending a garage sale. Exceptions to this rule might include genuine antiques, sports memorabilia, and other such unique items. For these types of items, however, you may need to ask for or independently arrange a professional appraisal of the item for proof of authenticity and determination of fair market value.

Q: My mother wants to help, but doesn't know what she can donate. Any ideas?

A: Does she do any creative or craft work? A knitted sweater, gift basket, catered dinner, or other such creative ideas will all work well. Does she like to cook? Maybe she would be willing to prepare a gourmet dinner for eight to be delivered for a special occasion.

Q: I have an airplane. Would a ride in my airplane be a good item?

A: Absolutely! Anything like an airplane ride, picnic lunch, classic car ride, or anything else that people might not be able to go out and purchase are perfect items to have in your auction.

Q: Some of the people I talk to don't really want to donate any tangible items. Would we take a cash donation?

A: Absolutely. Cash is always good. You have costs for decorations, mailings, and other out-of-pocket expenses. Cash underwriting is an excellent donation. Also, cash can be used to purchase or under-write items for the auction, which will sell for more than the underwriting value.

Q: Some of the people I talk to want to know if they can write off their donation against their taxes. How do they do that?

A: They need to talk to their accountant. However, if they qualify, the fair market value of an item is generally the amount accepted for a write-off. In most cases, the value is what the item would sell for in a store. In the case of items not available in stores, the amount the item sold for at the auction may possibly determine the value. Be sure to advise your potential donors to check with an accountant, since all situations are different.

Q: I was going to get an item donated, but I found that someone else already procured that item. Should I just forget that getting that item?

A: No! Duplicate items are perfectly okay. Often, having more than one of the same thing will allow for some flexibility, since one of them could be combined with other items to create a unique package. You also have the ability to trade duplicate items with other organizations for one of their duplicates. Never turn down an item!

Q: I am going to go prospect for items at the mall. Any suggestions on how to I can get stores to give me items for the auction?

A: Generally, the people working in the stores have little authority to donate items. You will be able to procure a few small items, but finding the manager or owner and contacting him or her directly will bring better results.

Q: I don't have time to contact a bunch of people to get items, because I work all day and when I get home I am tired. How can I help?

A: You have more time than you think! It is best to contact potential donors as you go about your normal routine. Coworkers, vendors, clients, and so on are all great people to procure items from on your normal work schedule. You don't necessarily have to set aside specific time to get donations.

Q: I am new to the area and don't know many people. How do I get started?

A: Who do you know in the area from where you just moved? Start by making a list of everyone you know, regardless of whether they live locally. Include relatives, past employers, former neighbors, etc. Now see if any of them would be willing to help you by getting *two* items each. They could donate one item and get one more for you. This way just five of your contacts could net you twelve items (two from each contact, plus two yourself)! This is the multilevel procurement strategy, and it can be very effective and time-efficient.

When asking for items, it's a great idea to follow some general strategies to avoid hearing a negative answer and to reduce burnout. The following will help improve your chances of successfully hearing "Yes" more often than "No."

- Ask for something *specific.*
- Ask for big-ticket items first, but gratefully take whatever alternative is offered.
- Enlist help from your friends, neighbors, coworkers, and relatives. The more help you get, the easier it is to be successful.
- Don't cold call businesses. Ask businesses you know for maximum results.
- Remember, you are helping the donor get publicity for their product or service, or you are helping them get a possible tax deduction. You are not imposing. Most people want to help; they just need to know *how.*
- Set the example by donating something yourself *first.* Share your donation idea with other donors to help their thought process.

- Be creative. Think unique!
- Make a list of things *you* would like to buy at the auction, then go out and get those things donated.

Most importantly, ask for something specific that you know that person has the ability to give. If you go to your Uncle Robert and you know he has season tickets for the local professional baseball team, ask him if there are any games that he will not be attending for the coming season and whether he would like to donate the tickets. This way, you have done the work for him; he does not have to think of something to donate. Instead, you have suggested something so that all he has to say is "Yes" or "No," and chances are that if he says "No," he will suggest something else as an alternative.

## The Procurement Form

The procurement form is also frequently called the solicitation form, donation form, gift-gathering form, item contract, and many other names. The purpose of this form is to complete the transfer of title of a donated item from the donor to the soliciting organization. It also serves as a temporary receipt for the donor of the gift (they will receive an official receipt with the thank-you letter) and contains a detailed description of the donated item so that catalog preparation can be accomplished. Generally, this is a multipart form, so copying data or making copies of it becomes unnecessary. The top sheet serves as the master copy for the file; the second sheet goes to the data entry people; and the third part is a receipt for the donated item and is given to the donor. Some organizations will use four-part forms, allowing an additional copy to be retained by the solicitor in case there needs to be any follow-up activity.

### Designing the Form

The procurement form is a *contract* used to secure item donations. It actually transfers title to the item from the donor to the soliciting organization. Therefore, please stress to your committee how important it is that the information gathered on the form is accurate and complete and that the form is signed by the donor or donor representative. The form should contain a place to capture all essential information, including the following:

- Donor or business name (this will be included in the auction catalog), address, phone/fax numbers
- Contact name, direct phone number, job title

- Donor's signature with the procurement date and the name of the auction representative
- Fair market value for the item, conditions, restrictions, blackout periods, or other limitations (all of which will be included in the auction catalog)
- Accurate short title and long descriptions of item (both of which will appear in the auction catalog)
- Whether item is tangible or whether a certificate is provided
- Whether the donor has included any additional materials for publicity
- Whether the donor wishes to have an invitation to the event (but does not provide free entry)
- Any pictures of the item, if appropriate, to market the item in the Web-based catalog
- The Web site URL of the donor's business, to be hyperlinked from the auction Web site catalog

You will also want to include the following on the form:

- Your organization's logo
- Spaces for tracking, catalog, and code numbers
- Your organization's name, address, phone/fax number, and contact name
- Federal Tax ID Number
- Cutoff date for procurement
- Auction theme in your form header

Exhibit 8.1 is an example of a procurement form. Note how all the important elements we just described are included. Note also that this form is intended to be the four-copy version we described, in which the third copy stays with the auction representative, but copy four is for the donor. Again, just a variation of what we previously discussed.

### Preparing the Form

Since your committee and volunteers will be filling out these forms, please take time to review with them these instructions for how the forms should be prepared.

- Use a ballpoint pen, so the writing goes through clearly to all copies.
- Print neatly, since the second-sheet copy will be used to prepare the catalog.
- Fill in the donor's information completely. Make sure the address is correct and be sure to get a telephone number.

| 10th Annual Holiday Gala | | | | | |
|---|---|---|---|---|---|
| *Donor Information* | | | Please fill in with Ball Point Pen | | AUCTION MAESTRO PRO |
| Donor or Company Name (as it should appear in the catalog): | | Donor 2 or Company Name (as it should appear in the catalog): | | | |
| Donor Contact Person (not listed in the catalog): | | Donor 2 Contact Person (not listed in the catalog): | | | |
| Donor Address (include City and Zip): | | Donor 2 Address (include City and Zip): | | | |
| | | | | | Donor(s) Signature (Required): |
| Donor Phone #: | Donor FAX #: | Donor 2 Phone#: | Donor 2 FAX #: | | |
| Auction Representative: | Auction Rep Phone #: | Team Name: | Code/Category: | Donation Date: | Please send me an Invitation to the auction. ☐ |

| *Donated Item Information* | | | | Catalog Deadline: 12/4/2004 | |
|---|---|---|---|---|---|
| Tracking Number: | Catalog Item Name: | | Item Value (fair mkt value): | Minimum Bid: | Expiration Date: |
| Detailed Item Description: (Quantity, Size, Color, Restrictions, or other information to ensure proper understanding of the donated item:) | | | | | |
| | | | | Storage Location: | |

☐ Tangible Item – Displayed at Auction    ☐ Delivery by Donor    ☐ To be Picked Up by Auction Representative
☐       Not Displayed at Auction    ☐ Donor to Provide Promo Material    ☐ Auction Committee to Provide Gift Certificate
☐ Intangible Item    ☐ Donor to Provide Gift Certificate    ☐ Matching Funds

| Item Label | Brief Item Name: | Donor's Name(s) as it should appear in the catalog: | Donor Phone #: |
|---|---|---|---|
| Tracking Number: | Catalog Number: | Code/Category:    Package With: | |

| Please return forms to: | *Sample Procurement Form* | Fed Tax ID |
|---|---|---|
| Copy 1: Office<br>2: Catalog/Database<br>3: Auction Representative<br>4: Donor Receipt    (425) 688-0809   Fax: | 1200 112th Ave NE, Suite 250<br>Bellevue, WA 98004<br>EMail: support@maestrosoft.com | 95-1234567<br>Your Donation may be<br>Tax Deductible. Check<br>with your Tax Advisor. |

Copyright 1998 MaestroSoft, Inc.  Preprinted forms available from MaestroSoft (800) 438-6498

**Exhibit 8.1    Procurement Form**

- Make sure any restrictions or expiration dates are completely listed. This information is essential for the auction catalog. Bidders need to know this information during the auction so they can make educated decisions about their bidding.
- Determine whether the item is a tangible item or a certificate. Be sure to indicate that on the form. Also, if there is a certificate, pick it up at the time of preparing the form and be sure to include it when you return the form.
- If the item is tangible, determine who will deliver it to the storage location. If the donor will deliver it, make sure to get a time and date of delivery and remind the donor that it must be received by the catalog cutoff date to be included in the catalog. If the Auction Committee is to pick it up, please make arrangements for someone to do so and write on the form when pickup will occur.
- Make sure to get the signature of the donor and be sure to put the solicitor's name on the donor form as well. Be sure to include the solicitor's telephone number so he or she can be called for clarification if the catalog designer has any questions.

- Provide the donor with the last copy of the form. This is their receipt (for their records and possible tax deduction). Keep the next copy for the solicitor's records. Send the remaining copies to the person within your committee who is designated to receive the procurement forms. The address will be on the form.
- If any marketing literature is available for the item, please include that with the form. This will help with the table displays of the items.
- Have fun! Remember that donors want to help. They just need to know how. Ask for *specific things*, because the more specific the request, the better your opportunity for success.

## Once You've Received the Commitment

Once you are under way with the procurement process, you want to have a plan for what to do with the items as they are received. As previously mentioned, having auction management software will make your job much easier, because it handles the task of tracking the donations, donor information, thank-you letters, donation receipts, production of reports for decision making, Live and Silent Auction item distribution, catalog numbering, and of course the production of the catalog and the bidder forms. You will also find the software helpful in preparing the items' table easels and for creating certificates for those items donated without a tangible certificate. Should you wish to operate without specialty software for all of these tasks, you can do so, but these tasks will still need to be accomplished. Therefore, for simplicity and because we know you are dedicated to the Five-Year Plan approach, we will assume you have acquired auction software. If not, you can devise your own methodology to accomplish what lies ahead, using the software approach as a guide for what needs to be done.

### Receiving and Storing the Items

As the items are received, they should be stored in a safe, secure area that is clean and dry. Items should arrive with all but the donor's copy of the procurement form attached to the them. The back copy was used as a donor receipt and therefore will no longer be attached. The next-to-the-last copy goes to the auction representative, so there is a record of the procurement in case there is a question about the item. The top two copies are brought in with the item. One is sent to the Database Committee; the other serves as an item tag until the item is assigned a catalog number and receives an inventory label of its own. Once the item receives an inventory label, the form may be removed and placed in an office file for archiving.

The data entry staff will enter the item into the software, capturing all the data on the form. The donor's name, address, and other contact information will become a permanent record, so accuracy is a must. The title, description, value, and item category will be used in a variety of ways, from writing the description for the catalog; to producing the bid forms; to creating the tracking reports for the committee to use to check procurement progress; to producing table easels, inventory labels, thank-you letters, and ultimately the bidders' purchase statements. Therefore, it is essential that complete information be provided, because bidders are making a buying decision based on the accuracy of the description. It's a disaster for your organization when a successful bidder finds out after the event that the item or trip they purchased was not as it was described in the catalog. At best, this causes lost credibility; at worst, it results in a lost sale and a refund. You will therefore want to recruit dedicated people who are willing to shoulder the responsibility of accurately entering the donation form data. However, they are data *entry* people, not data *creation* people. They can only enter the information that they have been provided, and they must assume that information is accurate.

Some committees choose to have the procurement donation forms stop first at a small team of volunteers who first verify the accuracy and completeness of each form before it is delivered to the Database Committee. They will check for missing restrictions or blackout dates on trips, dinner donations that do not state how many people are included or expiration dates, tickets to ball games without a quantity stated, and other such errors of omission. They will also look for complete donor contact information so that the donor can be thanked and contacted for additional information if needed. While this detour in the data entry step is optional, you may find it a worthwhile addition to keep from succumbing to the garbage in, garbage out syndrome.

Once entered in the database, the software will generate a tracking number for each item. This number is not the catalog number, which will be created much later, after the items are packaged, divided into Live or Silent Auction sections, and placed in the sequence in which they are to be sold. The tracking number is a permanent identifier that never leaves that item, so it cannot be confused with any other item, no matter how similar. The tracking number, once assigned, should be affixed to the item with a label, then the item should be stored in a clean, safe, and dry location. Often this may be a volunteer's home or office, a room at the school, or some other secure location. Certificates and small valuables, such as watches, autographed cards and baseballs, and jewelry, should be stored in a safe, if possible.

Periodically, the data entry staff should prepare a tracking report listing all items and send that report to the Committee. This will provide needed visibility to aid in following up on the process of procurements and progress toward the goal. The data entry staff may also be asked, from time to time, to prepare special reports, such as descending dollar reports, reports by item category, or one report listing all donations by auction representative.

If the workload for data entry is to be shared, and your committee has decided to use the Internet to publicize your event and publish an online catalog, then you can easily accomplish all of these tasks using Web-based services, such as those mentioned in the Resources section of the book. With online services, data entry is performed through a Web browser by several data entry volunteers, and the online catalog is created automatically as items are entered. Committee members can use the same Web site to review reports at their leisure, so the data entry volunteers are not burdened by this task. As an added bonus of the online approach, links to donor Web sites can be inserted in the online catalog; solicitation of auction items becomes easier when you can offer greater visibility to potential donors for their generous items.

## The Case for Consignments

A consignment is an item that is provided for sale by a supplier with the intent that it will sell for higher than the cost paid to that supplier. Payment is always after the item has been sold at auction, and if the item does not sell, may be returned to the supplier at no cost and no risk. We often get asked about the wisdom of adding purchased items to the Live or Silent Auction. Our routine answer for nearly 20 years has been *no*. However, we have recently changed our position on this subject, with very specific conditions and with sound reasoning. First, let's cover some background.

The idea of buying something and then turning around and selling it at your auction has always offended us for several reasons: It risks selling the item for less than it cost (unless the minimum bid is higher than the cost), and it takes buying power out of the auction audience to secure only a fractional increase in income.

Suppose you can buy an item for $500 and it sells for $700. You took $700 of buying power—the budget your audience uses—out of the auction, and used that buying power to earn only $200. That is not sound logic, and it works against you. This is why we are generally not in favor of the buy-items-to-sell process. The worst of the bad situations is when a third party tries to get you to let them set up your Silent Auction for you and handle all the item procurement, forms, and cashiering. Why? Because you will find that after they deduct the cost of their items and their handling fee and commissions, you are left with relatively little profit to show for it. Meanwhile, they have used your audience to market their jewelry, their clothing, their memorabilia, or whatever else they have to offer. We have witnessed events that had gross sales of $50,000 and net sales of less than $10,000 after the items were all paid for. This simply is not fair to your audience, who expect most of their generous support to go to your cause, not to your vendors. You take all the risk and cover the marketing costs to fill your room, and the outside supplier benefits by being able to sell his items to a captive audience, paying you a fraction of the sales. You would be much better served by having fewer items, but all free of cost, so that 100% of your sales go to your bottom line. What is better, a $50,000 gross, and $10,000 net, or a $20,000 gross and net? The answer is obvious.

So what is the exception, and how do you let it work to your advantage? Start by visualizing a tent. It has a tent pole at its center, right? If you want to make a bigger tent, you first have to start with a taller tent pole. *This* is the case for having a few (emphasis on *few*) consignment items. There are some items you just cannot get without purchasing them, unless your committee has incredible connections. Most committees don't have the connections it takes to get Super Bowl tickets; golf at St. Andrews, Scotland; or an auto-graphed Rolling Stones guitar. However, often these items and many more similar and unique items are available through services at a fraction of the fair market value. Let us tell you right now that you should *never* pay retail for anything you plan to sell at your auction, because the chances of that item selling well over the fair market value are nil. However, if you can get a very unique, standout item at perhaps half price, you can certainly make a profit from it at nearly any auction. So, the case for consignment is made: *if* you can get a premier item, *if* you cannot get it any other way, and *if* you can make a decent profit from having it in your auction. As a bonus, the premier item or items help you establish a higher tent pole by setting the expectation higher for the items that are donated outright, plus you help draw bidders to your event by having the premier items available.

Now, another benefit to consigned items is that you can enlist the help of your supporters to minimize the cost impact to your organization. Many potential donors are left out of being asked to help because their business is not one that could donate an item appropriate for an auction. Doctors, lawyers, architects, financial planners, bankers, real estate sales people, mortgage companies, and other similar professions do not sell, manufac-ture, or provide a product or service that would be a good auction item. However, all of these professions can underwrite the cost of a fabulous trip, unique experience, or wonderful item of memorabilia. You can ask them to help prime the pump for your procurement process by agreeing to under-write the cost of one of the items available on consignment. As an example, you might have a local doctor or lawyer cover the cost of a weeklong stay in Bali at a fabulous 7,000-square-foot villa. The value is approximately $6,500, but it can be consigned for a cost of $3,500. If the underwriter is willing to cover the consigned cost, they get the visibility in the program, on your Web site, and in marketing materials for your event of having donated a trip worth more than $6,500, and it only cost them $3,500 to do it. When that item is sold at your event, you receive 100% of the selling price, because the cost is already covered. This is an excellent way to get fabulous items, raise the expectations for your event to a higher level, and keep your costs for items at a reasonable level.

Now, having discussed a lot of the *good* reasons for using consigned items, let's talk about a few of the potential negatives and where they can possibly hurt you. Potential problem #1: Sometimes, vendors ask for a place in your silent auction area to set up a display and sell numerous items in exchange for donating a percentage of their sales to your organization, or sharing all income over a certain amount, or similar "deals." Don't let yourself get talked into this. Your bidders will spend too much time looking at all the items but not bidding, and that is all wasted time that would have been used to bid on the items you have received at no cost. Limit your items with costs to just a handful, and then limit it to the premier items that will create buzz about your event.

Another possible trap is when the organization or person placing the item in your auction insists that payment for the trips or items be made to them, and then, subsequently, they will take the responsibility for paying the vendor. There can be a number of problems with this, including a risk that:

- The item you included in your auction actually had a much lower cost than what had been represented to you by the intermediary at the time you accepted the placement.
- You have no idea whether the trip or item came from a reputable source that will stand behind the placement, should there be any problem with an item or redemption of a trip or experience.
- In the worst case, the agent placing your trip may accept the money from your organization, but never pass it on to the trip or item supplier. If that agent or organization goes out of business, or disappears, you will have a host of unhappy winners who have paid for their auction items, with no way to fulfill their purchase.

While these may sound like extreme cases, they *do* happen, and it's important that you be aware of who is representing you for your consigned items. Make sure the agent has a good reputation and can provide references on request, and insist that your payment is made out directly to the *supplier* of the product or trip.

To maximize your effort and to take full advantage of the consignment exception, you should first pick your two, three, or four premier items from your supplier and use these items as examples of what you already have when talking to committee members, potential donors, and others who are trying to procure items. Starting your procurement process by first getting your big items (even if consigned) in hand can be a powerful motivator. What gets more attention? "We have a trip to Bali, a Disney Cruise for a family, tickets to the All-Star Game, and an Aerosmith autographed guitar so far, but of course we need many more items for our event" or "Well, so far, we have a dinner out, some car wash booklets, some wine, and a few children's items." Remember to try to get as many of the consignment items as possible underwritten, so you maximize the revenue to your organization, not to the auction company or item vendor. That's using consignments as a draw and as a multiplier, not as a drain on your fundraising efforts.

So, to briefly summarize this topic, remember these points:

- Use consignment items judiciously. Think of them as a seasoning to your own solicitation efforts, not the main course.
- Never overload your event with purchased items. Consignment items can help you get better donated items by setting the bar higher and encouraging your donors and committee to find donations that aspire to that level.
- Use consignment items than can legitimately double their cost when sold at your auction, have no up-front cost to you, and no risk if they are not sold.
- Finally, beware of using intermediaries who insist you pay *them* and say that they will be responsible for paying the vendor. While most people are honest and legitimate, there have been incidents where the intermediary was not performing in good faith.

By using a few strategic consignment items, you can build a bigger tent for your auction items to fill. It all starts with a taller tent pole, and *that* is the reason to use consignments.

CHAPTER

9

# Promoting Your Event

## Table Captain Process

Using table captains will help you fill your room with like-minded folks who are attending your event not only to have a good time, but also to support you, because of the way they were invited. The process works like this:

- Solicit at least 10 volunteers to be table captains—these are often board members, members of your Steering Committee, or influential members of the local business community.
- Have a table captain kickoff party—this is an informal, quick social event to introduce the captains to the expectations of their role and to give them their invitation packages.
- Provide at least six full invitations with return envelopes to each captain. They will hand-deliver these to the people they plan to invite.
- Instruct the captains that they should first call six close relatives, friends, associates, coworkers, members of their church or service club, or anyone else they believe would accept an invitation to attend the event, and sit at their table.
- Have the captain follow up with each of these people by physically handing them the invitation (not mailing it).
- Instruct the captain to follow up with these potential guests to see if the invitation RSVP has been filled in, and offer to pick it up to deliver to the committee.
- Offer to provide more invitations, should any captain need more.

This personal touch, including the one, two, three approach (call, hand out the invitation, follow up with a call) is the fastest way to hearing "Yes," and will fill 10 seats with strong support, because each person at those tables was handpicked by a supporter. If you need more than 10 seats filled in this manner, add more table captains.

Notice that the captains were *not* asked to buy the table, although they may choose to do so. By allowing the captains to fill the table with people who will pay their own way into the event, you are more likely to get real buying power, because these folks are opting in voluntarily, not just coming to fill a seat. The theory is, if they are willing to pay, they are more likely to be willing to spend money in other ways.

## Audience Development

We are going to focus our attention now on building the audience, a process called audience development. Early in the planning stages for the event, your committee determined a target number of people to invite based on the number of buying units needed to accomplish your auction income goal from items and other event-night revenue. Recall that one buying unit (a single person or couple sharing a common number) represents an available revenue amount of from $250 to $750, assuming you have provided enough procurement for them to spend their money. We will assume the procurement process currently under way will provide the needed items and value to allow that generosity to flow, so now let's turn our attention toward filling the room with bidders, not eaters. Remember that we want the room to be filled with people who are there for the cause or because they were invited by someone who cares about the cause. To accomplish this, we will be using two invitation methods. First, you will invite all known supporters of your cause by sending out an invitation with an RSVP. These would be the people on your mailing list and the mailing list of your support network, such as board members, vendors, and prior guests at other events. Second, you will want to organize your team of table captains, as described in greater detail in the preceding section, who will agree to fill half or more of the tables with friends and family who share their support for your cause, or at least share a willingness to help the table captain support his or her cause.

This two-pronged approach will allow you to relax, knowing that the buying power is in the room to make the auction a success. You will know this because in the first case, your prior supporters will be deciding to attend because of their desire to support your effort. In the second case, you will have tables filled with supporters who have been handpicked by the table captains because of their ability to bid and buy. Filling the room in this manner, rather than randomly, is the best way to assure you have a room full of bidders, not just eaters.

Let's stop for a minute and consider the opposite—a room full of eaters, rather than bidders, which is a great way to have your auction items liquidated well below their value. This situation happens when there is a disconnect between the motivation of the host (your organization) and the people who are sitting at the tables at the event—often, it a result of too much emphasis being placed on *selling tables to sponsors* rather than *filling tables with bidders.* Let us explain.

If your committee makes selling tables to corporate sponsors a priority, then this may result in tables that are paid for by a company sponsor, but the people actually sitting at the tables may be that company's employees, vendors, or customers. Rarely will company leaders attend the event and sit at the table their company paid for, unless they are specifically requested to be there by the host committee. Those attending might only be there because the company gave them a free entry to sit at the company table, and may only be there for the party, not to support the fundraising aspect of the event. Guests who get in free also, in many cases, drink too much, pay too little attention to what is going on around them, and do not take part in the bidding process. We call them "guests in borrowed evening gowns and rented tuxedos," which is not meant to be cruel or elitist, just stating the fact that many of these folks will not be able to be bidders in the Live Auction portion of your event. They are thrilled that you are feeding them, otherwise they would go home empty handed.

You can prevent company-paid tables from being filled with people who cannot bid, or at least offset their lack of buying power, by being specific at the time you sell the tables to the company. Explain that you are appreciative of the support you are receiving by their purchase of the table sponsorship, and you hope they will be equally supportive by inviting guests to sit at their table who will be able to be active bidders. By mentioning this at the time of the sale, you are making clear that while the price of the table is appreciated, you are expecting that they will take care to send employees and clients who can also participate in the bidding. If you sense any hesitation that they will be able to do this, offer to fill the table for them, so that their company table will be well represented with active bidders. Of course they would not like to have their table poorly represented or, worse, have empty seats. If they accept your offer, then place a few of your known supporters at the company tables to spread the bidding around the room and to ensure that no company is embarrassed by having an empty table or one that appears to not be participating.

Using the table captain approach will offset some of the eaters-not-bidders risks as well. If half of the room can be filled deliberately with hand-selected attendees, as the table captains will provide, then the randomness of the guests at the corporate tables can be mitigated.

In order to begin the audience development process, use the following checklist:

- Make a list of everyone the committee members can provide from their own mailing lists and support network. Have them include all relatives; coworkers; neighbors; college friends; service, social, and athletic club members; and former associates.

- Enter the information from this combined list into your software so invitations can be addressed.
- Precall a select list of contacts from this list to personally invite them to the auction. Let them know they will be receiving an invitation.
- Follow up with that select list after the invitations have been mailed to make sure each invitee has received an invitation. Offer to take their RSVP information over the phone, or direct them to your Web site to register for the event if you are using a Web site to promote it.
- In the invitation, plan to use a tiered pricing strategy to maximize your results.
- Use the "cause" and a sampling of the items available in the auction to rally support and build enthusiasm. Convey the message that this is a "must be there" type of event.

## Save-the-Date Cards

When you have prepared your list of people and entered their information into the software database, you are ready for your first mailing: the Save-the-Date card. This card provides a simple "Who, What, When, Where, and Why" snapshot of the event. Keep it jazzy but uncluttered. You are trying to get your invitees' attention, not tell the whole story. Costs to attend, auction items, and other information will follow later. You are merely creating curiosity and anticipation. The purpose of this card is to get the potential guest to hold the date. This approach is similar to the news station teaser during prime time: "Big asteroid threatens Earth—film at eleven!" You are priming your invitees to expect more information later.

### About Mailed Pieces

When designing mailing cards and invitations, make sure that the size is within the limits of presorted mailing sizes. Check your postal regulations so that you're not wasting money on off-size mailings, which require extra postage.

Once the Save-the-Date card is out, you can move on to designing the invitations. However, for those highly organized committees who really want to have their theme promoted on all materials, you could have both your Save the Date card and invitation created and printed at the same time. You may also wish to have your catalog cover designed and printed along with the invitations. By combining the Save-the-Date card, invitation, and catalog

**Sample Save-the-Date Cards**

cover in one printing, you are likely to save money on color set-up fees and perhaps even printing charges, because there may be enough room to also print the Save-the-Date card in the "waste area" of some invitations or catalog covers. Having a good print specialist who can work with your committee to help you make these decisions will be beneficial. Under no circumstances, however, should the Save-the-Date card be needlessly delayed just so it can be combined with the printing of the catalog cover and invitations. The card must go out soon after the date and location of the event is confirmed and locked in by contract.

## Web Site

In today's information-based world, often the most cost-effective way to give a potential supporter a lot of information about your contribution to society is to have a well-designed Web site. The Web site should contain information on how your organization was founded, the people who benefit from your existence, your mission, a calendar of events, and contact information so people can reach you.

Another integral part of your Web site should be a way for people to donate money to your organization online. In addition to making donations, you can provide information about your event. If they are able to access a page where they can donate an item or register, then you will have an excellent resource for promoting your event. In the Resources area in the back of this book, you will find vendors who can supply Web sites to promote your event, accept online contributions of items and money, allow viewing of your catalog, and allow invitees to register and pay to attend your event—and even bid on selected items if you wish them to do so.

Your organization's primary Web site can be linked to your event-specific site, too, so it is not necessary for your regular Web site to be modified or for a new Web site to be created. Keep it simple and cost effective by using the technology that already exists.

## E-mail

To curb the high costs of printing and postage, organizations are increasingly turning to the technology of e-mail to get the word out about their events and community outreach programs. An e-mail broadcast list can be a very powerful tool, and you can include attachments such as brochures that people can print out (at their expense, not yours!) and links to important Web sites where people can directly donate money, contribute items for your auction, and even register to attend the event. Supporters can even forward these e-mails to people in their spheres of influence, to increase awareness of your organization and its mission.

Using e-mail for a Save-the-Date announcement is all right, but it does not replace a physical card that comes through the mail, and for good reason. First, you have no confirmation that the e-mail was received, much less read, as many people have spam blockers that prevent general e-mails of this type from ever reaching the intended person. Second, with a physical mailing, a card or envelope will be returned to you if the address is incorrect, so you have the advantage of cleaning your mailing list using the Save-the-Date card mailing before you mail the more expensive invitation. No such confirmation of mailing address is possible if you only use the e-mail for your save the date.

E-mail is a great tool for internal communication among the committee and for augmenting your other contacts with potential guests, but it does not replace the physical card or invitation, which, like it or not, must be mailed or hand delivered. With that said, you can ask for an e-mail address on the RSVP card in your invitation, and if your guest registers for your event and adds the e-mail contact, you now have a great way to send updates about last-minute auction items added and to direct attention to the Web site to review the online catalog or for online bidding.

### Tiered Pricing

The idea behind tiered pricing is to provide individuals with a desire to attend the event at a premium price point above the standard pricing level. Yes, some people will actually wish to pay more! Often we find that people who want to support the beneficiary of the auction will wish to "overpay" so they can make a larger contribution to the cause as part of their entry price. If the budget has been properly set, the cost of attending the auction at the basic entry level (often called the "Friend of the Organization" level) will offset all of the cost of producing the auction on a per capita basis. Therefore, any admissions at levels above the friend level (often called patron and benefactor levels) will add additional revenue not anticipated in the general budgeting process. The additional revenue can be used to offset other costs of operating the auction. Also, it is common to offer a corporate-level table, which is a reserved table (between eight and ten guests) and will include similar recognition for guests as either patron or benefactor individuals, with the cost of their tickets being eight or ten times that of individual entries.

Tiered pricing affords several advantages for both the attendee and the sponsoring organization. The advantages to the organization are quite obvious:

- Adds additional revenue, which often is not part of the budget
- Creates the image of an upscale event, because there are guests attending in patron and benefactor status
- Helps to justify the friend-level pricing
- An event with patrons and benefactors is likely to draw people with the capacity to bid on higher-value items and be less likely to draw "bargain hunters."
- It helps set the tone for the event, making it a fundraiser, not merely an auction.

The guest who chooses to pay a higher entry price for the event accrues advantages as well:

- There are tax advantages to the patron and benefactor because of the additional cash component of their entry price. The difference between the fair market value of the event and the actual amount paid to attend is generally a deduction.
- Patrons and benefactors are provided with upgraded seating and special recognition in the auction program. They are also recognized at some point throughout the evening, and may wear some kind of recognizable marking (a medallion, corsage, boutonniere, etc.).
- Some auctions also provide auction scrip, a credit toward auction purchases, as an incentive for patrons and benefactors. The scrip is not refundable. The guest must use it for bid activity or it expires at the end of the evening. For a more detailed discussion of auction scrip, refer to Chapter 7 in Phase II of this book.

### Example of Tiered Pricing

Exhibit 9.1 shows suggestions for tiered pricing. Note that in the examples, the terms friend, patron, benefactor, and corporate are used to indicate various entry levels. If you have names that tie better into your theme (e.g., a Medieval theme might use "Duke & Duchess," "Prince & Princess," "King & Queen," etc.), feel free to use those instead. Many auctions will have additional levels as well, such as gold patron, silver patron, gold benefactor, and silver benefactor. Also note that the use of auction scrip will help justify the tier levels and make it easier to explain to guests the various levels of pricing.

### Exhibit 9.1   Tiered Pricing Chart–Example

Typical tiered pricing strategy: Values are shown to provide relative examples. Actual values for each level are set by the Auction Committee.

| Level | Entry Price | FMV* | Scrip Level | Potential Deduction |
| --- | --- | --- | --- | --- |
| Friend | $50.00 | $35.00 | $0.00 | $15.00 |
| Patron | $100.00 | $35.00 | $50.00 | $65.00 |
| Benefactor | $250.00 | $35.00 | $150.00 | $215.00 |
| Silver Corporate | $1,000.00 | $350.00 | $500.00 | $650.00 |
| Gold Corporate | $2,500.00 | $350.00 | $1,500.00 | $2,150.00 |

*FMV is fair market value of the event per person.

Note that the corporate levels are calculated for a table of 10 guests. Also, the potential tax deduction is listed as the difference between the fair market value and the amount charged. The actual tax deduction, however, depends on whether the corporation is classifying the deduction as a charitable donation or an entertainment expense.

In the preceding example, you will notice that the fair market value is less than the amount charged. The fair market value is generally the amount a person would pay for a comparable meal at a restaurant, plus other items of value provided as a guest. In almost all cases, the fair market value of an event is less than the level established as the Friend level to attend the event.

Notice, in the table on page 128, that the auction scrip is part of, but not all of, the difference between the fair market value and the amount charged. This is because scrip is, essentially, a prepaid auction purchase. It has no value unless it is spent on items at the event, so the amount of scrip is based on the level of the guest. It costs the auction nothing to offer the scrip because it never equals the difference between the friend level and the higher level selected (benefactor, patron, etc.). In addition, you may find that not all of the scrip (and sometimes, none of it!) is turned in for credit against auction purchases. Some guests don't make any purchases; some choose not to use the scrip and pay in cash. In this case, the scrip becomes a cash donation to the organization. Because guests entering at higher levels have received a tax deduction for the *entire* amount of their entry less the fair market value, the scrip appears to be a bonus to them for coming to the event at the higher level. For some, it is more of an incentive to be a patron or benefactor, rather than a friend.

The use of scrip at the corporate level is even greater. A company purchases the corporate table as either an entertainment expense or a charitable deduction. The table is generally hosted by the company president, owner, or general manager, who will invite key employees or clients to attend the event with their spouses. When the host of the table arrives, the auction scrip is in that person's registration packet and not divided up among all at that table. The host can either distribute the scrip or keep it for personal use. Because people sitting at a corporate table are generally hosted, they tend to bid more actively, since they believe it is part of the expectation for having been invited. The host, if still in possession of the scrip, will bid actively as well, since the scrip has no value unless a successful bid is made.

Tiered pricing allows supporters of your organization, or the beneficiary, to attend the event at a higher value than would be available with single-level pricing. The use of auction scrip further enhances the auction by adding bidding power to the audience, which must be spent to have value. Additional tax advantages may also be realized for some attendees. Be creative with your titles for higher-level entries. Use the theme as a starting place and add status to the entries. This way they will appeal to potential guests.

### About Auctions and Alcohol

We are often asked by our clients whether it's a good idea to offer alcohol at their event. There is a frequent misconception that, when it comes to alcohol, more is better—that people will lose their inhibitions the more they drink, which should translate to higher revenue. In reality, this is not the case, and too much alcohol can actually negatively impact your event in more than one way.

Rowdy, nearly drunk people are a distraction to other guests, and those sitting near them will find themselves focusing more on the drunken behavior than on the message you are trying to convey about your cause. People who have had too much to drink are no longer focused on why they are at the event; they are focused on themselves, so don't plan on their bidding any more, or at all. If they do become a successful bidder, they may have no recollection of winning, so the risk of buyer's remorse causing a lost sale after the event increases. If you decide to serve alcohol at your event—which is fine, if it is appropriate for your guests' expectations—you might consider limiting its free aspect in some fashion. For example, you might have a hosted bar for the first hour, then convert it to a nonhosted bar after that. When people spend their own money on drinks, they tend to drink less. If you provide wine with dinner, you might consider providing the first few bottles on the table, then allowing additional bottles to be purchased. Avoid situations where you have a hosted martini bar or similar excessive drinking opportunity that remains open all night. If you do have such a bar, shut it down early when the guests enter the dinner room.

Also, there is some debate about whether volunteers and staff should be allowed to drink during the event. While you do not want to deny your volunteers a good time—after all, they are donating their time and are working very hard to support your event and your cause—there are some cautions of which you should be aware:

• *Anyone* who is responsible for working with money should not be consuming alcohol. That includes registration volunteers taking cash or checks, processing credit cards, and so on. It also includes volunteers who are responsible for taking, closing out, or recording bids, since this function leads directly to downstream charges. While it is unlikely that staff might be caught mishandling money, you don't even want for the possibility of anyone inferring that there could be a problem, so it is best to make a "no drinks" policy for volunteers who are involved with money or charges.

- The amount of alcohol volunteers consume can become an issue. If you have volunteers who have stacked their "cocktail hour" drinks four deep at registration (don't laugh . . . we've seen it!), trying to consume as much as possible before the "real" party begins, you can imagine in what condition they'll be come checkout and cashiering time. Remember, the volunteers, even though they are not being paid, are there to do a *job*, and without their help your event can very quickly become disorganized and chaotic. Plan for extra volunteers to break up the duties during the evening, and allow them to drink once their "shift" is over. This is a better way to ensure that the volunteers can enjoy the party while still remaining focused on helping with a smooth and controlled event for your paying guests.
- Finally, drinks of *any* kind—especially those served in tippy wine stems or martini glasses—and computers do not mix. Many an event has had its computer systems fail due to one ill-timed spilled drink. Keep liquids of all kinds clearly away from any computer, printer, or keyboard.

## Invitations

The invitation process is the classiest way to fill a room. We do not recommend selling tickets but, rather, inviting people to a specific event. The "By Invitation Only" approach raises the event a notch above the come-one-come-all path that lesser events employ. You do not want an event that is fully open to the public, but rather one that solicits support for your cause and draws from known and new contacts that you want to become supporters. You will send out the invitations by mail or, ideally, have them delivered in person to all invitees. Inside the invitation, you will include an RSVP card so the guests can respond. For planning purposes, you really do want a response, even if the contact cannot make it to the event.

Your invitation should include the following information:

- On the invitation:
  - Date and time of event
  - Location

- ◆ Theme
- ◆ Organization hosting the event
- ◆ Organization's Tax ID number
- ◆ Fair market value of the event entry cost per person
- ◆ Organizations your event will benefit
- ◆ Auctioneer's name (optional)
- ◆ Cross-section of items available (most popular)
- ◆ Phone number for questions
- ◆ Web site address for event (to register online and view items)
- On the RSVP return card:
  - ◆ Places for guest name, phone, address
  - ◆ Menu choices
  - ◆ Tiered pricing levels
  - ◆ Place to indicate number of guests at price of entry desired
  - ◆ A place to indicate who they will bring as guests if they purchase a table
  - ◆ A "regrets" line, with an option to make a donation if the guest is unable to attend
  - ◆ A place to indicate whether their company has a matching fund program
  - ◆ A request for their e-mail address

Be sure to enclose a response envelope (postage paid if possible).

Notice that we did not ask for a credit card number for anyone wishing to pay with a card rather than a check. For security reasons, you should ask that anyone wishing to pay by credit card either register online through a secure connection on your event Web site or call the office to provide the card number by telephone. Having your guests place their name, credit card number, and signature on a card that is mailed back is a security breach you should avoid. Not only is there a risk of that card's being intercepted before it gets to your office, once you enter the credit card number to log in the payment, what do you do with the card? Most organizations will want to keep that card in a file folder "just in case" they need it again, which propagates and multiplies the risk. You are much safer if guests register themselves online, which will let them have the comfort of knowing that their credit card information is not floating around somewhere.

Once you have registered your guest in your auction software, we suggest sending the guest an acknowledgment that you have received their RSVP and payment, accompanied by directions to your Web site to preview the auction items. This can be done by e-mail, if they have provided an e-mail address, or by sending an acknowledgment card with the Web site address. The acknowledgment will also serve as a reminder of the date and location of the event and the time the doors open.

One word of caution: Do not provide a complete agenda for the evening, including details such as when dinner starts, as that will be an invitation to arrive late. People who are still driving to your event are *not* spending any money in your Silent Auctions!

The following invitation examples have all the essential elements and can be used as a general guide to help you design your own invitation.

Feel the Love

Medina Elementary
2006 PTA Auction

Saturday, February 11, 2006
5:30pm Westin Bellevue

Class Project Unveiling
Valentini Cocktails and Silent Auction
Dinner and Live Auction
Dancing to Follow

Please RSVP before January 20, 2006

*Per IRS Regulation 67-246, the fair market value of this event is $60.
Federal tax ID#91-1328998.*

**Sample Invitation with RSVP Card—Note the Different Levels and the Area for Regrets Donations and Corporate Matching Funds (Continued)**

○  I/We will be DELIGHTED to attend!
Please reserve _____ seats at $90 per person.
My seating requests are listed on the reverse.

○  I/We would LOVE to join the "Tickled Pink" Club.
Please reserve _____ seats at $150 per person.
The SWEET gift waiting at my table will ensure a charming evening

○  I/We ADORE our faculty/staff and wish to sponsor
_____ member(s) at $90 per person.

○  Regrets! I/We already have DELICIOUS plans for the evening,
but wish to support Medina PTA with a contribution of $_____

○  My employer, _____, will graciously
match my tax-deductible contribution. Please contact me.

**Please RSVP by January 20, 2006.**

**(Continued)**

Doors Open and Silent Auction Begins
at 5:00 p.m.

Live Auction
Dessert Dash
Restaurant Frenzy

A special appeal to support the
North Sound Student Scholarship Fund
will be offered during the evening.

*Menu*

Pan Seared Flat Iron Steak
with Dauphinoise Potatoes

Pan Seared Halibut Filet on Roasted
Vegetable CousCous

Vegetarian Entrée Also Available

Ron Hannon, Auctioneer

Per IRS regulation #67-246, the fair market value of this event is $40.

**North Sound Christian Schools**

**Invites You**

**to an Evening**

**of Spirited Bidding**

**and Fun**

**at the**

**1st Annual NSCS District**

**Gala Benefit Auction & Dinner**

**Saturday, April 28, 2007**

**5 p.m.**

**Lynnwood Convention Center**

**3711—196th Street SW**

**Lynnwood, WA  98036**

Please visit our Auction Website
and On-Line Catalog at
http://northsoundchristian.maestroweb.com

## Another Good Sample Invitation and RSVP Set (Continued)

# The 2007 Gala - Response Card

Reservation Deadline: **April 13, 2007**
Seating is limited to the first 400 guests

| | | | | |
|---|---|---|---|---|
| Guest | $50.00 per person | X _____ | = $ _____ | |
| Patron | $100.00 each | X _____ | = $ _____ | |
| | (includes $25 auction SCRIP*) | | | |
| Benefactor | $150.00 each | X _____ | = $ _____ | |
| | (includes $50 auction SCRIP*) | | | |
| | | | | |
| Table of 10 | $500.00 per table | X _____ | = $ _____ | |
| Patron Table | $1,000 | X _____ | = $ _____ | |
| | (includes $250 auction SCRIP*) | | | |
| Benefactor Table | $1,500 | X _____ | = $ _____ | |
| | (includes $500 auction SCRIP*) | | | |

I am unable to attend, but please accept my donation to support
excellence in education.                                                           $ _____

Total Payment Enclosed:                                                    $ _____

Name(s):_____

Address:_____

Phone Number:_____

E-Mail:_____

My employer matches charitable contributions:

Company:_____

Menu Selection: *(Please indicate numbers of meals)*
Steak _____    Halibut _____    Vegetarian _____

Please charge my:  VISA_____  MC_____  Exp. Date:_____
Card #:_____

**(Continued)**

# 10

# Event Preparation

In this chapter, we will cover the final preparations for your event before the actual day-of-event logistics. This will include planning the room layout at the event location with consideration for space allocations and the seating of your guests. We will also discuss the preparation of the auction catalog, what should and should not be included, and how to handle the distribution of auction item displays. We will also dicuss the Live Auction sequencing, which can affect your bid activity in a positive way if properly handled.

This chapter involves the last stage of preparation prior to the actual event-day logistics, so it will be beneficial for your committee to read this last part thoroughly to be sure all their responsibilities have been met. The part toward the end on Silent and Live Auction distribution will be of particular value to any of your committee members who are preparing the auction catalog or are involved in item display.

## Planning Your Event Space

All commercial venues can provide you with a room diagram so you can work on space allocation. If possible, have the room provider give you a diagram that includes the location of the dinner tables, bars, and entry and exit points. Fill in the chart with your own drawings for the Silent Auction tables and registration and cashiering areas. You will also want a separate room where volunteers can "hang out" when they are not on duty; this room should be stocked with food, snacks, water, and sodas for them. *No alcohol* should ever be permitted in the volunteer room. Period. Volunteers must be alert to their assigned tasks, and once they begin drinking, their reliability drops. Also, you may have some underage volunteers and they will be unsupervised in some cases, so you do not want the liability of having alcohol accessible to minors.

Included on the next page is a general seating chart for a Live Auction dinner. Silent Auction sections can vary; they can be "wings" off the Live

Auction room or completely separate rooms, depending on the location and size of the auction. Use this plan in setting up sound and staging areas, as well as deciding on a seating chart for your guests and premium entry sponsors (patrons, benefactors, corporate sponsors, and honored guests.)

### A Sample Seating Chart

To help you plan the ideal placement for your auction guests, we have provided you with a pattern-coded seating chart (see Exhibit 10.1). This seating arrangement we recommend is very important to ensure maximum participation from your strongest financial supporters. Strategic placement of guests whom you know will bid high and bid often is one of the keys to making a Live Auction successful. If you place those key guests in front of the stage, you achieve two important purposes. First, these important guests are easily seen and recognized by the auctioneer, and second, because they are in the front of the room, everyone *else* sees them bidding and will want to participate, too.

Here are the criteria for the different colored tables and how guests are assigned to them:

⊕ **Level One Tables**   These tables are for your guests who paid a premium entry fee (e.g., patrons, benefactors, corporate sponsors, etc.). These are guests with whom the auctioneer will be very familiar by the end of the evening. They will be bidding on the majority of the Live Auction items and will probably give a generous amount to your Fund-An-Item, should you choose to have one. It is not uncommon for organizations to spoil these tables with favors and premium wine and champagne.

○ **Level Two Tables**   These tables are for guests who will probably be successful bidders on several of the Live Auction items. They are in the auctioneer's direct line of sight and are able to see and compete with the other guests in the front of the room. Expect strong bidding to be in this area.

◉ **Level Three Tables**   This next category of table is for those guests who will likely bid on and win one or two Live Auction items. They are there to support the organization and paid to be a part of the event, but don't have the income to be highly active bidders in the Live Auction.

◎ **Guests-of-Honor Tables**   The final type of tables is reserved for your guests of honor. These are members and speakers in your organization who may not have paid to attend the auction and may not even be actively bidding. Placement in the front of the room allows them easy access to the stage for

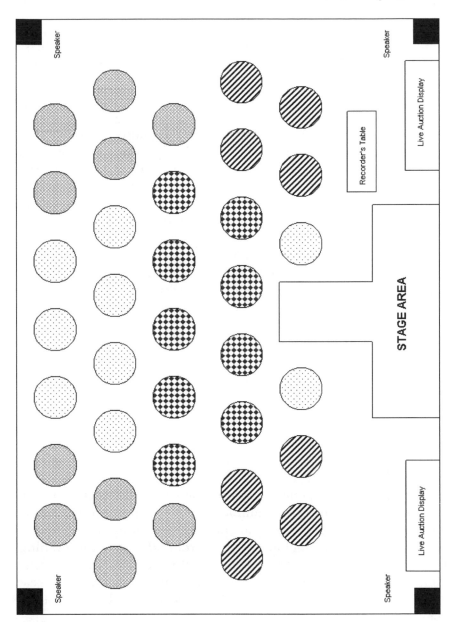

**Exhibit 10.1    Sample Seating Chart**

presentations and gives them high visibility for recognition, but keeps them out of the auctioneer's view so he or she can concentrate on active bidders.

Placement of these guests is imperative to ensure maximum results from your auctioneer. However, be careful, when you place guests, to be discreet. Don't offend your guests by purposefully placing them at the back of the room just because they don't have as much status as another guest. Always attempt to grant seating requests, even if they don't fit this mold. Guests will have a better time if they are seated at tables with people they know!

## Auction Catalogs

The auction catalog is an important tool for your guests; it ensures that they are adequately equipped to do their "job" of supporting your organization and its cause. Since every guest will receive a copy of the catalog, you will want to make sure that its quality properly represents and communicates the tone and expectations for your event. When creating your catalog, you will want to take into account the theme and location of your event, your guests' interests, the needs of your benefactors and donors, and your budget.

Auction catalogs can serve several purposes. Consequently, there are some key sections that you always need to include, and several others that you might consider including. Most good catalogs will contain these sections:

- A welcome letter from the committee Chair and/or the head of the organization
- Acknowledgments
- An agenda for the event
- Auction rules
- Item listings

### Welcome Letter

The Welcome Letter is generally written by either the Auction Chair or a high-ranking official in the organization. The purpose of the letter is to thank the guests for attending and showing their support for your cause. This is a great time to include a gentle reminder that the evening is a fundraiser; take the time to thank your guests in advance for their generous bidding throughout the evening. Although many guests will never read the letter, it is still an important part of the catalog and should always be included.

### Acknowledgments

While the Welcome Letter sometimes includes elements of the Acknowledgments page, ideally it should really be a separate component of the catalog. Many people have invested a great deal of time, energy, and effort in preparing for this event, so show your appreciation by dedicating one or more pages to communicate that sentiment. The Acknowledgments page typically recognizes Auction Committee chairs, organization administrators, any premium supporters (such as patron- and benefactor-level guests), underwriters (corporate and private), volunteers, and anyone who expended extra or noteworthy efforts.

Exhibit 10.2 is just one example of an Acknowledgments page you might see in an auction catalog.

## Let's Hear It for the VOLUNTEERS!!!

### Auction Committee Members

| | |
|---|---|
| John Simpson | Renee Johnson |
| Jennifer Walters | Barry Black |
| Mike Hessler | Kelli Reynolds |
| Julie Scaldina | Gerold Neuharth |
| Deb Misner | Natalie Christian |
| Roxie Wood | Fred Rogers |

### Auction Night Volunteers

| | |
|---|---|
| Travis Harrington | Kathy Rodriguez |
| Rachelle Erickson | Justin Root |
| Eugene Hardin | Jim Smith |
| Kate Neth | John Byrd |
| Martha Brewer | Nancy Drake |

### A Special Thanks to Our Auction Coordinators

| | |
|---|---|
| Auctioneer: | Jay Fleek |
| Auction Coordinator: | Terri Smith |

**Exhibit 10.2   Sample Acknowledgments Page**

### Agenda

You should include a schedule for the event's activities near the front of the catalog, so that guests know when each Silent Auction will close, when dinner is served, when the Live Auction begins, what other activities there will be and at what times, and an expected end time for the event. Frequently, the agenda also includes other elements, such as when cashiering opens and what the menu or meal choices are for the event. One note: Do *not* send out a detailed agenda for the event to guests in advance. Providing detailed information about the schedule of your event turns into a suggestion for guests to arrive late!

A sample Auction Day schedule appears later in this chapter. You may use this as a suggestion for your own event, but note that not all items in the actual schedule appear in the agenda printed in the catalog. Include in the catalog only those items that are directly relevant to your guests.

### Auction Rules

One section that you will absolutely need to have in your catalog is a section on the rules of the auction. This is critical, because your guests will make assumptions, often incorrectly, about the terms and conditions of your items for sale. Moreover, many of your guests may be unfamiliar with auctions, or perhaps have never attended a charity auction, although they may have attended art or commercial auctions. With potentially hundreds of items for sale, all with different descriptions, blackout periods, or delivery options, you need to have one backup set of conditions and terms that covers areas where the item descriptions may not be explicit. For example, it is a good idea to have a default expiration date of one year from the event date for any intangible items that do not have an explicit date stated in the description. Also, in the case of motor vehicles, it is a good idea to point out in the auction rules that vehicles are not to be delivered at the event, but after title transfer occurs at a dealer, bank, or motor vehicle office. You may also want to point out in the rules that extras, such as licensing fees, insurance, taxes, and change fees are the responsibility of the bidder. It is also a good idea to include in the rules that items are nonrefundable and, unless otherwise stated, cannot be exchanged.

Rules should be placed in the auction catalog, but do not need to be in the front, or necessarily in large font. Publishing the rules in the back of the catalog is acceptable, but your guests should be verbally advised that they are there by the auctioneer or emcee.

Following is a collection of rules commonly used at auctions. Since no two events are the same, you will want to tailor them to fit your situation.

**General Rules**

1. Upon entry, each guest will be given a bid card. To bid in the Silent Auction, simply write your bid number on the Silent Auction form corresponding to the desired item. The bid number next to the highest bid amount at the end of the Silent Auction will be declared the successful bidder of that item. To bid in the Live Auction, hold your bid card with the number toward the auctioneer so the auctioneer can clearly see it. By bidding in the Live or Silent Auction, each bidder agrees to these auction rules.

2. A bid acknowledgment by the Live Auctioneer is a legal contract to purchase the item. In the Silent Auction, the bid you have written on the form that is designated by the Silent Auction official as the top bid is a legal contract to purchase that Silent Auction item.

3. Top bidders must pay for their items at the cashiering tables, which will open at the *conclusion of the Live Auction.* It is not necessary to pay for each item after purchase. We prefer that you pay for all your purchases only once, at the end of the event. Payment in full, however, is mandatory at the auction.

4. Auction items will be awarded to one purchaser only. The bidder who has bid the top amount for an auction item will be responsible for full payment of the item. As a convenience, the auction committee may elect to allow for the splitting of final bid amounts among bidders who may have agreed to pay a portion of the top bid amount. Unless split bids are authorized, a purchaser who wishes to split the payment for an auction item must collect the individual payments from the other guests and either present those payments to the auction cashier at the time the purchaser pays for the top bidder's purchases, or accept those payments as a partial reimbursement for the total payment the purchaser has made.

5. All purchases are final and there will be no exchanges or refunds on items unless otherwise noted or warranted.

6. Bidders with auction scrip (credit toward auction purchases) must submit the scrip tickets at the time the bidder makes the payment. Scrip may be transferable, but it is not refundable or applicable to a prior payment. Scrip is applicable to Live and Silent Auction purchases only, and may not to be used for raffle, cash contributions, or other nonauction purchases.

7. Bidders who elect at registration to be served under the qCheck[TM] system do not have to stand in line to pay for their purchases. Instead, qChecked guests will have receipts for redeeming their purchases delivered to them during the course of the Live Auction or made

available at a qCheck will-call area. Please see a cashier or other registration personnel for information on this payment option.

8. The auctioneer's decision will be final, and he or she reserves the right to reject *any* bid that is a partial advance over the prior bid increment.

9. We will gladly accept your payment by currency, personal check, or credit cards and debit cards accepted by our credit card processor. Cards accepted should be displayed at the time of check-in. Please ask if you have a specific card or alternate payment request. Please make checks payable to (*enter auction name, organization, or appropriate payee*). In (*insert month and year your organization was granted tax-exempt status*), the Internal Revenue Service granted (*enter the name of your organization if appropriate*) charitable organization status. We are, thus, a 501(c)3 charitable organization, and your payments are tax deductible as a charitable contribution only to the extent provided by law.

10. Unless otherwise noted, all goods, services, or certificates must be claimed and used within one year of the auction date.

11. *<Insert auction or organization name>* reserves the right to add or withdraw, without notice, items to or from the auction.

12. The purchaser assumes the responsibility to locate and remove purchases from the auction premises. Purchasers may claim from the Certificate Table (if one is provided) or at the retrieval point, the certificates for services and tangible items not displayed. Just show your *paid* receipt, and you will receive the certificate. You will be asked to show your *paid* receipt for tangible items at the door when you depart.

13. All items not removed from the auction premises this evening:

    Will be stored for you at *<insert location>* and you may claim your item(s) between __:__ A.M. and __:__ P.M. on *<insert date>*.

    May be claimed on *<insert date>* between __:__ A.M. and __:__ P.M.

    Items not claimed by this date will be stored at the purchaser's expense.

14. Due to license and insurance regulations, all motor vehicles and other items requiring a title transfer or license may be claimed at: *<donor's place of business or auction office>* on *<insert date and time>*. Purchasers must pay for all transfer fees, license fees, and all taxes, as well as make arrangements for insurance coverage from the time of purchase.

15. Reservations for trips and vacation accommodations must be mutually arranged with the donor, unless otherwise noted. Tickets in travel packages are for coach-class service unless otherwise noted. No refunds will be allowed on travel packages for canceled tickets and/or accommodations.

16. Travel will be provided by donors as described, even if the prices increase above those stated. Because travel charges change, travel costs may decrease the values stated, but no refunds will be allowed.

17. *<Insert auction name or organization>* has attempted to describe and catalog all items correctly, but all items are offered "as is" and "where is." *<Insert auction name or organization>* neither warrants nor represents, and in no event shall be responsible for, the correctness of descriptions, genuineness, authorship, provenance, or condition of the items. No statement made in this catalog or made orally at the auction or elsewhere shall be deemed such a warranty, representation, or assumption of liability. The values listed are estimates only, and are not warranted for tax purposes or fair market value. Items have not been appraised unless specifically otherwise noted.

18. Each person issued a bid number (bidder) assumes all risks and hazards related to the auction and items obtained at the auction. Each bidder agrees to hold harmless from any liability arising therefrom *<insert auction or organization name>*, its elected and appointed officials, members and employees, the auctioneers, the auction company and its agents and employees, event organizers, sponsors, and/or volunteers connected with the auction.

### Item Listings

The catalog needs to contain information about the items you have up for bid. While we mentioned earlier that many organizations choose to leave Silent Auction items out of the catalog, at a very minimum the Live Auction items need to be included. Your guests will need to know several pieces of information about each item, and the information needs to be clear and sufficient so they can easily follow along. The information you need to include about each item is:

- The catalog number of the item
- The title of the item (e.g., "The Ultimate Golf Escape," "Breakfast at Tiffany's," etc.)
- A complete description of the item
- Any restrictions or special conditions, such as blackout dates, limited use, number of people, taxes and fees not included, etc.
- The fair market value of the item
- The donor

You may want to include some additional information, depending on the item. For example, if the item is a piece of art, providing a profile of the artist may be appropriate. If you have a special case of wine, you may want to include some information about the winery. Frequently, committees choose to include pictures in their catalog; this can often enhance the guests' readability and help keep their attention.

While we have mentioned this previously, be conscious of the font size and style you use in your item listings, just as you are in the rest of the catalog. Item descriptions should use an easily readable font with a minimum 12-point font size. Ideally, you will want to list one Live Auction item per page. If your guests can't easily read the catalog, they won't follow along, and that can directly equate to lost revenue.

### Catalog Size and Format

Auction catalogs can come in as many different sizes and formats as there are auctions. However, there are some formats that work better than others, and there are some common errors that committees may make that turn an otherwise effective catalog into one that works against them.

Shown are several different standard catalog format sizes.

Catalogs can be spiral bound, saddlestitched, or book bound. Generally, the type of binding you use will be dictated by the size of your catalog and your budget. Regardless of what type of binding you use, it's best if the catalog can be easily opened and will stay opened as your guests page through it.

In keeping with your event's theme, you should create an eye-catching cover and title page for your catalog. The images here give you some examples of auction catalogs. In addition to some appealing images that support your theme, your catalog cover should include the theme name or event title, name of organization, the location, the date, and any names/logos of presenting sponsors. The title page inside the catalog has more complete information on it, such as the auctioneer, master of ceremonies/announcer, and honorees (if any); the address of the auction location (if catalog is mailed to guests in advance); the major underwriters and sponsors;

8½ X 11    4¼ X 11    8½ X 5½

**Three Examples of Auction Catalog Sizes**

and the top administrator(s) in the organization. Many guests will keep their auction catalog as a souvenir or reminder of the event, so in addition to being functional, make it attractive. You may need to engage a professional graphics design group to handle some of the design elements or perhaps even lay out the entire catalog, but remember to keep your budget and goals in mind as you do so. Many catalogs can be made very appealing without breaking the bank.

### Note

Whatever you do, please resist the temptation to save money by writing or printing your bid numbers on the back page of the catalog. While it may seem like a great idea, by doing this you are actually ruining your guests' ability to bid. You want them to follow along in the catalog during the Live Auction so they know when the item on which they want to bid is coming up; when you put the bid number on the back of the card *you force them to close their catalog to hold up their bid number!* Then, when they put down their bid number because they want to confirm the details of the item on which they are bidding, they have completely lost their place in the catalog. They are now out of sync with the bidding action, and that can cost you bids. Let the catalog serve its purpose, and get a separate bid number.

One word of caution: As you work to make your catalog unique and attractive, be careful not to sacrifice function for the sake of form. It is possible to be *too* creative when designing your catalog and its contents.

First and foremost, your guests need to be able to easily read the content at any point during the event. Many people are reluctant to put on reading glasses in public, and small, flowery fonts can make the catalog nearly impossible to read, especially in the lower light used for ambience during dinner events. Also, resist the urge to get overly creative in how you lay out your text. Ergonomically, there are fonts and printing styles that are best for reading, and sometimes appearance and "novelty" will work against you. Take, as an example, the auction catalog that used all capital letters, randomly bolded, for the item description. Then the words in the description were arbitrarily split . . . not by syllables with standard hyphenation, but randomly, in an attempt to look "edgy" and "different." The result is shown in Exhibit 10.3.

```
┌─────────────────────────────────────────┐
│                                         │
│           TRIP: A WEEK IN P             │
│             ARIS FOR TWO                │
│                                         │
│         GOURMET DINNER COOK             │
│         ED IN YOUR HOME FOR 10          │
│                                         │
│          MONTANA FLY FISHING            │
│                       EXPERI            │
│          ENCE AT 'FISH 'EM UP'          │
│                    LODGE FOR            │
│                    TWO ANGLERS          │
│                                         │
└─────────────────────────────────────────┘
```

**Exhibit 10.3   Sample Catalog Ad**

Rather difficult to read, isn't it? It's unique, but guests will likely put the catalog aside quickly, because it's too hard to decipher and they won't follow along. Do your guests a favor, and make your text clear and large enough that they can read it by dim light; then your catalog will do its job. You may save a few dollars by using a small font that decreases your page count, but using a legible font—at a readable size—that attracts and retains just one extra bidder's attention in your Live Auction will more than pay for the extra ink and paper.

These days, many organizations are forgoing printing their Silent Auction items in the catalog. While it may seem like a good idea in principle to give your guests an idea of what's up for bid, in reality they won't generally read the catalog in advance to research their Silent Auction items. People enjoy wandering around the Silent Auction areas and doing their "shopping" in person, so including these items in the catalog isn't to anyone's advantage. Also, by excluding the Silent Auction items, your committee can cut down on the number of catalog pages and reduce the costs of production.

### A Sample Auction Day Schedule

Use this schedule as a guide to develop your own unique agenda. This is only a guide for planning your event. You will want to create your own agenda, based on this basic order of events but modified to match your schedule, expected times, and events based on your specific auction.

### Welcome to the (your auction name) Annual Auction!

| | |
|---|---|
| 5:30 P.M. | Doors open, registration begins |
| 5:30–6:00 P.M. | *Early arrival incentive period (complimentary wine/champagne, hors d'oeuvres, raffle, etc.)* |

| | |
|---|---|
| 5:30–7:00 P.M. | Silent Auction bidding/Live Auction viewing |
| 6:30 P.M. | Silent Auction #1 closes |
| 6:45 P.M. | Silent Auction #2 closes |
| 7:00 P.M. | Silent Auction #3 closes |
| 7:01 P.M. | Dining room opens |
| 7:15 P.M. | Welcome and introductions |
| 7:30 P.M. | Live Auction begins |
| 8:30 P.M. | Super Silent Auction closes (if used) |
| 8:30 P.M. | *Major Item(s) sold around this time* |
| 8:45 P.M. | *Fund-an-Item* |
| 9:00 P.M. | *Cashiering opens* |
| 9:30 P.M. | Live Auction ends |
| 9:30–10:00 P.M. | *Cashiering, checkout, and item pickup* |

This schedule assumes you have roughly 35–40 items in your Live Auction. While auctions of 30, 40, or more items were fairly common historically, today more charities choose to offer fewer items, but items that are more specifically selected for appeal and anticipated yield. You don't want an auction that is so long your audience is worn out at the end, so keep their schedules—and their interests—in mind as you plan the schedule of your event.

Feel free to use this template for modeling your own schedule of events. You will likely substitute the actual names or "color designations" of your Silent Auctions as they fit the theme of the evening. Anything on this list that is in italic lettering is just for your organizational reference, not to be included in your printed schedule prepared for your guests. The most important items to include are when the Silent Auctions close and when the dinner and Live Auction is expected to begin.

### Sample Silent Auction Page

As we mentioned in the section entitled Catalog Size and Format, many auction committees are deciding to skip listing the Silent Auction items in the catalog altogether. Because guests rarely use the catalog to preselect items in which they are interested, you can frequently save on your printing and production costs if you skip this section of the catalog. If you still want to include some information about your Silent Auctions items in the catalog, you may just want to list the catalog numbers by Silent Auction section, along with a title for the items and maybe the donor, rather than printing full descriptions. The item bid forms and table tents or easels used in setting up your auction displays (see Phase IV for more on effective displays and easels) will contain all the information about the particular items, including full

---

# Woodinville Rotary Foundation

### *Wine and shine gala*

### Red Silent Section #1

**100   CORDLESS TOOL SET**

Every guy needs multiples of every kind of power tool. Here's a complete power tool set that includes a 16-bit drill, sander, jigsaw, flashlight, and circular saw. They all use the same battery, and the set comes with two batteries and a wall charger.

Carston Reddy Construction

$ 200

---

**101   TEN HOURS OF BOOKKEEPING SERVICES**

Taxes coming up? If you own a business and need to have your taxes done, let a bookkeeper do it. They are up to date on all the IRS codes, restrictions, exemptions, and exaptions. Guaranteed to relieve stress.

Winfred R. Hatch Co.

$ 200

---

**102   TWO-PERSON TENT**

Head to the great outdoors in comfort with this two-person tent. Includes inflatable built-in mattresses, waterproof tarp cover, vented zipper openings, entrance mat to catch needles, dirt, rocks or whatever else might get on your shoes, and built in shoe racks and clothes cubbys.

Trekker's Travel

$ 150

---

Page 1

A Sample Silent Auction Catalog Page with Full Descriptions

**Exhibit 10.4   Catalog Pages for Silent Auction Items (Continued)**

descriptions of the item, its value, its donor(s), any restrictions, and other information that the guests need to know.

Exhibit 10.4 shows two catalog pages listing Silent Auction items; the first includes full descriptions. The second sample shows the same page without descriptions, offering a condensed format. Of course, there are many other

# Woodinville Rotary Foundation

*Wine and shine gala*

**Red Silent Section #1**

100   CORDLESS TOOL SET
        Carston Reddy Construction
        $ 200

101   TEN HOURS OF BOOKKEEPING SERVICES
        Winfred R. Hatch Co.
        $ 200

102   TWO-PERSON TENT
        Trekker's Travel
        $ 150

103   AUTOGRAPHED POSTER FROM "AMERICAN
        TREASURE"
        ??????????
      No Price for Stardom

104   DECORATED CHRISTMAS TREE, DELIVERED
        Cowboy Cola, Ima Cusak
        $ 200

105   UNDERWATER BASKET-WEAVING CLASSES
        Peggy & Donald Harrison
        $ 60

Page 1

A Sample Silent Auction Catalog Page—No Descriptions

**Exhibit 10.4   (Continued)**

sizes, formats, and styles, but this should serve as a suggestion. Your auction management software will help you quickly create and generate pages based a variety of formats, but even if you aren't using software to generate your catalog, this page can serve as a sample.

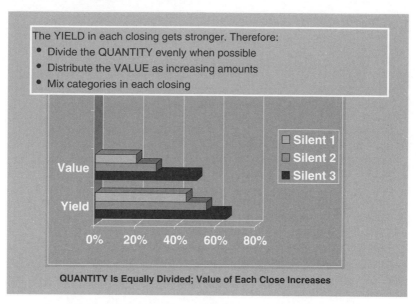

The YIELD in each closing gets stronger. Therefore:
• Divide the QUANTITY evenly when possible
• Distribute the VALUE as increasing amounts
• Mix categories in each closing

QUANTITY Is Equally Divided; Value of Each Close Increases

**Exhibit 10.5   Divide Silent Auction to Compress Bid Activity**

### Allocating Silent Auction Items to Sections

When making advance plans for your Silent Auction, and prior to including them in your catalog, plan your sections so that they have equal numbers of items, but with ever-increasing values. The logic here is that as you close out a section, eliminating those items from bidding, you compress the bid activity on the remaining higher-value items. Consider the chart in Exhibit 10.5.

Note that the quantity of items in each Silent Auction section is the same, but the value increases from the first closing to the last. The yield, as a percentage of value of the items, increases with each closing, which is why we do not want the values of the items equally divided. If the last closing is worth twice that of the first closing, and we make an additional 20% on the last closing, we would certainly want that extra 20% applied to a higher value of items.

Your auction management software will help you divide your Silent Auction items in this manner. By looking at the values relative to your proposed sections, you can move items around until you achieve the proper relationship. A typical relationship of values to sections might look like this:

| | | |
|---|---|---|
| Section A (first closing) | $10,000 Value | 50% yield = $5,000 net |
| Section B (second closing) | $20,000 Value | 60% yield = $12,000 net |
| Section C (third closing) | $30,000 Value | 70% yield = $21,000 net |
| Total Silent Auction | $60,000 Value | 64% yield |

If you're not using auction management software, you can still use these values and categories to manually come up with a division of items that will support similar ratios.

Many organizations like to divide their Silent Auction sections by item categories, assuming this makes it easier for their guests to "shop" for items in which they have interest. While there is some logic to this, how do you select which categories of items will close first and which will close last? More importantly, how do you analyze your results after your event (when you begin planning for next year, as part of your Five-Year Plan) to determine which categories were hot sellers and which were not? Could it be that a category that did not sell well was merely shortchanged because of the time allocated for bidding? Closing entire categories of items before other categories is not a great idea. If your committee wants to display auction items by category, then have these categories in areas within each Silent section. For example, you could have Silent Auction A (the first closing) set up with all artwork in one area, then children's things, then travel, then memorabilia, then home and hearth, and so on, until all categories of items are displayed. In section B, the same categories of items would be displayed in a similar relative location, again in groupings by category. In this manner, when we close a section, we only close out a portion of the entire category. This has the additional benefit of allowing bidders who have particular interest in a category to not be taken out of the bidding just because that category was closed early. They can now merely move on to the next section and continue their bidding.

### Sequencing Your Live Auction Items

Before you produce your catalog, you will need to decide in what order you will present and sell your Live Auction items. However, before you sequence the Live Auction items, you will need to determine which items you wish to include in the Live Auction. This is a whole separate topic for discussion, but for the sake of brevity, here are a few tips to guide you when selecting the items you wish to sell in your Live Auction:

- Select items that have emotional appeal and are higher in value.
- Put in items that will have wide interest and create bidding wars.
- Leave out items with very limited appeal, where there may be only one or two potential bidders, regardless of the value of the item.
- Leave out items that will cause embarrassment for the potential bidders (no tummy tucks, face lifts, vasectomies, tax consultation, or divorce mediation!).
- Include anything that will create a positive buzz.

- Leave out anything that is too complex to explain quickly.
- Leave out anything with too many restrictions or with a narrow window of availability.
- Include items for kids that parents and grandparents can fight over.
- Look for items that can be sold more than once to more than one successful bidder.
- Always start with a lower-value and tangible item—never start with a certificate item.
- Have something for everyone to bid on—don't make the Live Auction just for the rich folks.

The order of the items as they are listed in the catalog needs to match the order in which these items will be sold. This is so your guests can easily follow along in the catalog, are aware of what item is being sold at any given time, and can quickly determine how soon an item in which they are interested in placing a bid will appear in the auction.

While to some it may appear that items in the Live Auction appear in an unpredictable or arbitrary order, auctions that raise the most money take particular care to arrange their Live Auction items in a very deliberate way.

Your auctioneer will most likely want to work with you to arrange the sequence of sale, but in the absence of that help, we offer some suggestions. The best way of sequencing your Live Auction items is to arrange them so that the values resemble a bell curve, as illustrated in Exhibit 10.6.

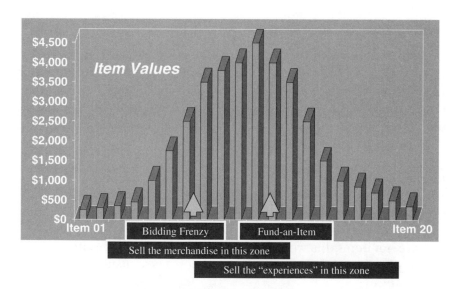

**Exhibit 10.6   Live Auction Catalog Sequencing**

*When* you sell items in the Live Auction is often as important as *what* you are selling. Here are some guidelines to follow when sequencing your Live Auction items for your catalog:

- Start with a tangible item whenever possible (to focus the attention of the audience)—the more emotional appeal, the better. Something for kids is always good (a wagon of toys, a big stuffed animal, an assortment of video games and a player). A fresh, hot apple pie is a good alternative, or an "instant romance" package (roses, champagne, flutes, dinner for two at a romantic place).
- Place your premier item about 50–60% of the way through your list—never save the best for last! The second high bidder needs to have some good items to bid on after the high bidder of the premier item wins.
- Do your Fund-an-Item (also called Raise the Paddle or Emotional Appeal) right after you sell the premier item, while your audience is still thinking big numbers.
- Ramp your values up to the premier item whenever possible, although it is more important to ensure similar items aren't placed back-to-back (e.g., don't sell two dinners, two trips, or two pieces of memorabilia in a row). Mix the categories of items whenever possible, but also avoid jumping from a low-value item to a very high-value item; it's hard for the audience to shift from a $500-item bid mentality to a $10,000-item bid mentality. That is why it is best to ramp up the value, whenever possible.
- Merchandise sells best early in the Live Auction; experiences (trips, dinners, golf outings, etc.) sell best later on. Avoid selling tangible items at the end of the auction; that is the experience zone. People tend to think more in terms of purchasing tangibles early in the auction, whereas later they are more interested in spending their available budget on unique experiences or event-based items, hence the term "experience zone."

# PHASE III

# CONCLUSION

Can you feel it? You are getting close to the big event! In Phase III, we brought you through all the major steps required to build your audience and secure your auction items. We logged the items into your auction software, securely stored them until auction day, and built your auction catalog. We sent out invitations, organized your table captains, handled the RSVPs, and began promoting the items using your event Web site. All that remains to do now is get ready for the event with auction preparation logistics, and then sit back and have an auction!

So now it's time for Phase IV, Event Execution, where we will set up the displays, prepare your guest registration packets, and print all your collateral materials needed for a successful event. Hang in there, it is almost *showtime*!

# PHASE IV

# EVENT EXECUTION

**Phase IV
Event Execution**

Y ou have been planning and working for six months, and now it is showtime! Whatever happens in the next 24 to 48 hours, *please* remember one very important thing: You are much more knowledgeable about what's been done during the planning stages and what's going on behind the scenes than any of your guests will be. They will see the *results* of your effort. You will see the *process*. It's like watching ducks on a pond—while we see the grace with which they glide across the water, the ducks know they are paddling like heck below the surface!

Your event will be very much like that. Your guests will see a flawlessly orchestrated event that will bring excitement and energy and generosity out of your audience. They will not know, or care, what has been going on for six months to bring it all together. They will be impressed, and you will be rewarded, so don't be too critical of the last stages as they unfold—you are bound to have some bumps and bruises as a result of unforeseen issues; they cannot be avoided. Do not let them consume you. Delegate the details to others on your committee so you don't have to shoulder all of the last-minute crisis management. Put others in charge and let them handle the details and fix the issues. Your job is to manage the big picture, not to micromanage the details.

One of the best ways to reduce last-minute issues is to avoid leaving until the last minute anything that does not need to be done at the last minute. In fact, anything that can be done ahead of time should be done as soon as possible. You do not want to print bid forms on the day of the event; you have known about the items for months and probably had catalog numbers assigned to them for more than a week. Print your forms the day you create your final catalog, because there is no value in waiting. If you get additional items after that, then create an addendum for those items and print just the forms needed for these additional items. Delaying printing of all auction forms until the last minute just adds unnecessary stress to an already stressed-out committee.

Think about what else can be handled before the day of the event, and make sure none of these tasks drift into that day. It is far better to be all set up and ready to go early, with nothing to do except wait for your guests, than to be scrambling as doors open to get the last-minute items completed.

With this important advice in mind, we now come to the final preparation and execution of your event-day materials and processes.

# 11

# Preparing for Your Day-of-Event Needs

Each of your auction guests will need some type of welcome packet to guide them on the day of the event. At a minimum, they will need a bidder number and a listing of the Live Auction items. What follows are some suggestions for preparing to welcome your guests, and what you need to provide to them so they can enter the event and begin bidding.

Although we talk about registration packets and discuss the use of envelopes, you might want to consider an alternate approach that has been successfully employed by many committees. Since a bid number and an assigned table for dinner are technically all the guest needs to be able to enter the event and begin bidding, you could bypass the step of handing out packets altogether and just give each guest a business card–size label with the guest's name, bid number, and table number printed on it. They can use this number for bidding in the Silent Auction, and then use the table number to find their table in the main room for dinner. At the guest tables, volunteers would have placed the actual Live Auction bid card for each bidder seated at that table, along with the catalog of Live Auction items. In this system, guests do not need to carry anything during the Silent Auction and cocktail reception. Keeping their hands free will allow them to hold a drink and still be able to pick up a pen to bid. Obviously, this approach works only if you are using assigned tables for guest seating, but if you do, it's a good alternative to the standard practice.

## Registration Packets

When guests arrive at your event, it's important for you to give them all the information they will need to successfully do their jobs (i.e., having a good time and bidding generously) at the auction. Typically, this information comes in the form of a registration packet.

The contents of registration packets vary, but in general they usually include:

- One or more bid cards (more specifics about bid cards follow)
- One or two copies of the item catalog—Live Auction items at a minimum, Silent Auction items optional
- Event agenda
- Addendum for any last-minute items or updates
- Preaddressed business-size envelope

Other items that may be included in the packets, depending on your event are:

- Name badges
- Drink tickets
- Tickets indicating menu choices for the dinner (beef, fish, vegetarian, etc.)
- Map of venue with auctions drawn out, if the flow of the rooms is not intuitive or obvious
- All reserved auction scrip
- Any other promotional materials your organization thinks is necessary, such as a tribute book or materials from key sponsors

Registration packets should be in one or more boxes at the registration desk so that preregistered guests can check in with the registration staff as quickly as possible. For preregistered guests, packets should be labeled with guest's full name, bid number, table number, and entry level (e.g., sponsor, benefactor, etc.), if there are different levels. Registration packets should be filed in alphabetical order by guest's last name, not by bid number. This is because guests may not know their bid number at the time of registration, but they always know their last name! If you have many guests attending (100 or more unique buying units), you'll want to divide the registration packets into multiple boxes across the alphabet (e.g., Box 1 contains last names starting with A-M, Box 2 holds N-Z), for ease in getting to individual packets during the registration flurry.

Depending on your event, you may be faced with the situation in which not every guest that arrives has preregistered. These types of attendees usually fall into the following categories:

1. Attendee is a guest of another registered attendee.
2. Attendee is a walk-up guest who heard about the event and decided at the last minute to attend.
3. Attendee was invited, but did not register prior to event.

4. Attendee was invited and believes he or she had preregistered but the registration staff and database have no record of his/her registration.
5. Attendee is replacing a guest who previously registered.

Each of these situations is handled in a slightly different way, so let's take a look at the processes for each.

**Case 1: Attendee Is a Guest of Another Attendee** Sometimes you have the situation where a guest (either a couple or individual) registers and pays for one or more guests besides themselves. One typical example is an individual or corporation who buys or sponsors an entire table. At the time the table is purchased, they may indicate that they intend to fill it with three or four other couples. Yet, as late as the day of the event, you don't know the actual identities of the hosts' guests.

The way you handle this at registration is to make up the appropriate number of registration packets to serve the number of people who are guests of the hosts at the same table. This means you will also create placeholder records in your database, so that there are preset bid numbers and records for those couples or individuals ready for the day of your event. Since you don't know their actual names, however, you will create these as "Guest of" records. In other words, let's say that Mr. Michael Jacobsen and his wife are hosting a table for 10. They haven't provided the names of their guests seated with them, but you know it will be four other couples. You know the couples are coming, so you will create four records with a last name of Jacobsen (to associate them with the host), and first name of "Guest One," "Guest Two," "Guest Three," and so forth. When the labels for the bid packets are printed, they appear as "Jacobsen, Guest One," which allows you to file them under Jacobsen—their host. When the guests finally arrive, they may give their own name, but you won't have a record of that. Instead, you'll ask them, "Are you with someone this evening or part of a group?" When they respond that, yes, indeed they are the guests of the Jacobsens, then you know where to find their bid packet—filed under Jacobsen.

The final step of this process is to make a note of the guest's real last name so you can update that in your auction software. When it comes time for the auctioneer to recognize and thank the winning bidder, you'd prefer he say "Thank you to the generous bidders, Mr. and Mrs. Andreas" instead of thanking "Guest One of Jacobsen."

**Case 2: Attendee Is a Walk-up Guest** This case is handled in a manner fairly similar to the preceding one. Instead of "Guest of" packets, however, you will create a number of "walk-up" packets. These packets contain all the same elements of a regular registration packet, except that you have no name or table assignment associated with the bid number until the guest actually arrives.

In your auction software, create temporary records for the expected number of walk-ups. As a general rule, if you create temporary records for about 10% over your currently registered guests, you should be fine. Adjust that number if your event historically has had a higher rate of walk-up guests. Your temporary records will be named "Walk-up #1," "Walk-up #2," and so forth. Each of these temporary records will receive a bid number, and, if you already know where you have seats available at tables, you can give each one a table assignment. Store these walk-up packets in a special place with your other registration packets, this time filing these special packets by bid number.

When the walk-up guest arrives you will hand them the first available walk-up packet you created. During the registration process, collect any fees due for the event and capture actual name/address information with which to update the database later.

Continue using this process for any subsequent walk-up guests, always choosing the next available bid packet so the bid numbers remain, ideally, in sequential order without gaps in the number sequence. If they get out of sync, it's not a crisis, but it simply makes it easier for the auctioneer to quickly scan a list of numbers while thanking the successful bidder when there aren't gaps in the numbers.

**Case 3: Attendee Was Invited, but Did Not Preregister**   In this case, you probably have a record of the guest in your auction software, but you didn't assign them a bid number, because you didn't know they were actually coming. Also, they don't have a "real" bid packet prepared for them, again, because you weren't expecting them. From the perspective of giving them a bid packet and number, you'll handle this in the exact way you would handle a walk-up (previous case), giving them the next sequential walk-up registration packet. The only significant difference is that, before you add the guest's name, you will need to first check in your auction database to see if there is already a record of the person, so you don't add them a second time. Once you have found them or added them, if necessary, associate the bid number you just gave them with their name record in the software.

If they haven't preregistered, you probably haven't collected any monies for event tickets or the dinner, so ideally you'll need to take care of that, either by collecting the money at registration or getting a card on file so you can charge them later as part of their evening's purchases.

**Case 4: Attendee Was Invited, and Believes They Have Preregistered, but You Have No Record of the Registration**   If you have no record of a guest preregistering, you probably didn't assign them a bid number, nor did you generate a specific registration packet for them. This case is similar to Case 3, because you likely have the guest's name record in the database, so you won't need to add them again. What you don't have is a bid number associated with that guest. Again, handle this type of guest just like you would a walk-up guest—give them the next sequential walk-up packet after apologizing for not having them on file.

How you handle dinner tickets or entry costs at this point is largely up to you. It's possible that this guest simply mailed their RSVP late and it has arrived in the mail over the weekend or will arrive in the next day or so. If they place a card on file, you can take their word that the "check's in the mail" and worry about how to settle their dinner charges after the event. If you are unsure about who the guest is or how reliable their word is, you can ask for some form of payment at time of registration. Our recommendation is to assume the guest has truly paid, give them their registration packet, and wish them a good time so they leave registration impressed by your customer service and in a happy and, hopefully, generous mood. Sort out the dinner charges and invoice them after the event if it turns out they haven't paid.

**Case 5: Attendee Is Replacing a Guest Who Previously Registered**   This happens all the time. You may have the Morrises on file as attending the event and have prepared their registration packet, which is waiting for them. Yet, the attendees before you are Mr. and Mrs. Lee, who have indicated they are taking the place of the Morrises, who were unexpectedly called out of town. The temptation might be to just give the Lees the Morrises' packet and call it good, but you don't want to do that. Even though the Morrises didn't show up, you really want to retain the information that they did accept your invitation and they did support your organization by paying for their event tickets. If you simply changed the name of the attendee record associated with the bid number from Morris to Lee, you've potentially lost that history.

Instead, treat the Lees as a walk-up, but assign them to the Morrises' table, rather than giving them a new table assignment. Add the Lees as new attendees, corresponding to the bid number on the walk-up packet, and the Lees are on their way to enjoy the evening, to be generous, and to bid heartily. They do not need to pay for the dinner, since the Morrises already paid for theirs and have sent the Lees in their place. The Morrises' packet will remain unclaimed and they will simply be a "no-show" at the event. Any purchases or donations the Lees make that evening will be recorded on their own unique bid number, so you have a record of their generosity and can invite them to attend your event next year.

### About Bid Cards

Bid cards are readily available for sale from many auction companies. Generally, bid cards consist of a piece of cardstock with a number printed on one or both sides. The best format for the bid card is black, bold print on white card stock to enhance visibility. Standard bid card packets come in packs of 100 numbers, two cards per number. The size of the bid card can vary, from a *full-sheet*, typically $8\frac{1}{2}'' \times 11''$, to half-sheet cards, which are, as you might imagine, half that size. There are also pocket bid cards, which are the size of a standard business envelope and are intended to fit inside a gentleman's shirt or jacket pocket. There are also special holders available for pocket cards that can be printed with your organization's or sponsor's logo, which are not only nice for freeing up a guests' hands during the cocktail hour or silent auction, but have additional utility after your event to continue to publicize your message.

When choosing what size bid cards to order, keep this in mind: Pocket bid cards work best in smaller, intimate settings with roughly 150 or fewer guests, such as cocktail parties or golf tournaments. Half-sheet bid cards will work in a medium-sized venue, with guest counts up to about 250. If you have a large space, or more than 250–300 guests, you'll need to go with full-sized bid cards to ensure good visibility of bid numbers during the Live Auction.

**Pocket-Size Bid Cards with Holder**

Another mantra to remember about bid cards: "cards good, handles bad." You may be familiar with the variation of bid cards that include handles—they are generally called bid paddles. While they may work great at a commercial or art auction, they are not great for charity auctions. When you put a handle on a bid card you've just unintentionally added functionality that has nothing to do with bidding! Your paddle can now serve as a handy fan in hot weather, can be used to summon wait-staff for more coffee, or drive away an annoying fly. When you use paddles, your auctioneer may not be able to quickly determine whether a guest is genuinely bidding or just waving to a friend! Keep the format of the tool consistent with the purpose.

Bid numbers can be assigned to every number from 1 to 9999, depending on how many guests are attending your event. It's best to use three-digit number sequences, if you can, starting with "101." If you mix single-, double-, and triple-digit bid numbers, not only is it harder for your auctioneer and recorders to track bid numbers during the Live Auction, but also some guests may be upset because Mr. Anderson was assigned bid number 1 while the Zook family—who are major supporters of your event—were assigned bid number 205. There may have been nothing more driving

**Comparison of Bid Card and Bid Paddle**

**Handwritten Bid Paddles. Very Difficult to Read in Large Audiences—and the Handle Is Still a Bad Idea!**

the number assignment than the first letter of their last name, but lower-order numbers carry with them a subconscious message of priority or importance. Using consistent three-digit numbers also avoids potential confusion when guests inadvertently bid using a one- or two-digit table number instead of their bid numbers.

Another caution: Some committees believe that it's a good idea to match table numbers to bid numbers. For example, assigning all bid numbers starting with 1 (e.g., 1, 11, 12, 13, etc.) to Table 1, or those starting with 10 (e.g., 101, 102, 103, etc.) to Table 10, and so forth. Worse yet, some people will try to get really clever, mixing numeric table numbers with alphabetic bidder designations to come up with bid numbers such as 12A through 12H. This is a nightmare, because not only have you created "numbers" that are really difficult to read from the stage—from a distance it can be very hard to differentiate a *C* from a *D*—but you've now made it unnecessarily difficult to move guests among tables, because of the link between bid numbers and table assignment. Good auction software will allow you to easily manage guests and table assignments, providing you with several flavors of cross-reference seating reports, so do yourselves a favor and avoid this troublesome practice.

When assigning bid numbers, best practice dictates that you assign one bid number to a couple, and then provide them each with an individual bid card using that number. You certainly can assign each member of the couple a unique bid number, but this can cause unnecessary complications when they want to cash out with one combined total at the end of the evening. Single guests, of course, are assigned one bid number, if you know they are attending solo; otherwise, include the second bid card in case they bring a guest.

There are many variations you can select to customize your bid cards, but keep within the parameters of the standards we've discussed. Some alternatives implemented in the name of creativity or frugality can actually work against you, such as printing dark numbers on a colored background, or printing or writing the bid number on the back of the catalog, as discussed in Phase III. Others, such as using the back of the bid card as a portable billboard (see Phase II), are great and can add to your event's bottom line. The point is, bid cards are an inexpensive but highly valuable tool. Any and all customization is possible, but before making major design changes, be sure that your variations support the purpose of the bid card and its function and don't degrade its usability. If you don't know where to go for bid cards and what options are right for your event, you can use the Resources section of this book as one place to start.

**Bid Number Handwritten on Back Cover of Catalog—for an Auction of 1000 Guests!**

**The Back of the Catalog Is a Bad Place for the Bid Number. It's Hard to See, and If the Bidder Follows Along in the Catalog, the Number Is Hidden**

## Printing Other Guest-Related Collateral

To properly prepare for your guests and to minimize labor during the auction, we suggest that you prepare as many of the required printed materials as possible in advance. If you attempt to print materials that could have been prepared in advance while guests are arriving or during the event, you are merely adding to your volunteers' stress and workload. Some of the materials you will need that should be prepared before event day are:

- Bidder packet labels (includes guest name, table number, and bidder number)
- Cashiering folder labels in bidder number order
- File folders for cashiering, one for each buying unit
- Table seating chart (several)
- Bidder number-to-table cross-reference chart (several)
- Alphabetical check-in list (one per guest registration volunteer)
- Walk-up registration packets for unknown guests (more than you think you will need)

**White Letters on Red Backing—Creative, But Very Difficult to See in a Dark Room**

- Auction addendum with last-minute donations or corrections to auction item descriptions
- Raffle sales tracking sheets, with continuous numbers to track remaining available tickets (one per volunteer sale person)
- Live Auction bid forms
- Silent Auction bid forms
- Fund-an-Item recorders' tracking sheet (at least three)
- Recorders' tracking sheets for Live Auction sweeps
- Extra bid forms for last-minute donations

While much of the preceding list may appear to be simple to produce (and it really is with software), leaving it to the last minute increases the risk that one or more items on this list will be forgotten. Starting the Live Auction only to discover that you do not have the forms or the other recording sheets is embarrassing and will delay the auction while you track down or print the forms. There is little value in delaying these print jobs once the data is ready.

One caution has to do with assigning bidder numbers to your guests. As you may suspect, the bidder number is the key to all the accounting, and it is very important that bidders are accurately charged for their purchases and donations at the event. Do not make the mistake of changing bid numbers once they have been assigned because, as you can see from the list, the bid number appears on the cross-reference list, the check-in list, the cashiering folder label, the guest bidder packet label, the alphabetical list, and the table seating chart. One change can skew all the numbers, so once you assign numbers and start printing materials, never change bid numbers. If a guest calls and says they are not coming to the event, then leave their number as a no show. Never reuse it.

## Bid Forms, Table Tents, and Auction Display Considerations

When it comes to merchandizing your Silent and Live Auction items, it is best to think Nordstrom's, not Walmart. If you plan carefully, and you have selected an auction location that has not restricted your space, organizing the displays will really allow the creativity to flow. You will want to let each item or package have its own visual space, meaning that it is an absolute no-no to stack one item behind another on the tables. Items placed behind others are reduced to second-class status and do not get the attention from bidders that they deserve. As you face the Silent Auction tables, you will want to "see daylight" between the items, meaning that each item gets its own place. For planning purposes, you could start with two feet per item, but of course larger items may require more space. Optimally, you want to end up with one foot between each item.

You will also want to build "skylines" with the displays, so that all of the items are not at the same visual level, but rise and fall, like the skyline of a city, to provide an interesting dimension. The bid forms should be placed directly in front of the item being sold, and there should also be a descriptive table easel (sometimes called a table tent) for each item. The printing of the descriptions on the easels should be in a 16- or even 18-point font size so that the descriptions can be read easily from eight feet away. This is important because you do not want your guests to have to queue up at the edge of the tables and bend over to read small print on bid forms to learn what you are selling. When guests can read a description from eight feet away, they are drawn in to the table to bid if the item interests them. Large font on table easels allows potential bidders, several people deep, to be interested in the item, not just the person closest to the table.

One final note: Many guests will either not bring their reading glasses or will choose to not wear them, so the easier you can make it for them to read your descriptions, the greater the chances of their bidding and the more money you make.

Now let's discuss some other considerations that will help you get the most out of your Silent Auction. Lighting is first and foremost, because if your guests

**Silent Auction with Good Display and Ample Room**

cannot see the items or read the descriptions, you will not be making any sales. While a candlelight dinner might be excellent to set a romantic mood, you want the Silent Auction to have the lights all the way up. The combination of low light and small print on forms and easels is deadly to your bid activity. You have come so far in your planning process, don't let it all slip away because you did not provide adequate lighting. If you need to bring in extra lights, do it. You do not need to rent expensive lights. In fact, what works really well for Silent Auction rooms are torchière lamps, which are available at any lighting or hardware store for about $15 each. Placing one of these lamps about every eight feet around the Silent Auction tables will provide wonderful indirect lighting while making it easy to read the bid forms and table easels. At the end of the night, you can place these lights at the check-out area and allow guests to buy one on their way out for $20 each—you will sell out!

From the standpoint of space consideration, your tables should be set to take advantage of the largest dimensions of the room. Typically, this means you'll line the outside walls of the room with tables, then build islands of tables in the center of the room. When building those islands, be sure to allow at least eight feet from the edge of one island to the edge of the nearest other island. In other words, any pathways you create in and around the tables must be at least eight feet wide to allow for adequate guest access and flow.

**Before (of course!)**

**After (naturally!)**

Look at the sample pictures on page 174 to see the contrast between a well-thought-out Silent Auction and one that is too cluttered and difficult to navigate. Both are from a charity wine auction, and both pictures were taken in the same location, at the same event, one year apart. This is a true "before" and "after" situation. Which do you think had more active bidding?

Even though this event has similar numbers of items with similar values, the After auction made considerably more money for the client than the Before auction. This was accomplished by packaging groupings of the wines, rather than selling each bottle as an individual item. Note that by doing this, several positive things were accomplished: The groupings were placed in skylines, making wonderful displays. There was plenty of room for bidders to get to the tables, and the displays themselves were attractive and drew the bidders in. Observe the spacing between items and the bid forms set on colorful backings. Finally, notice the large signage describing the section and announcing the closing time for the section. Well done all the way!

### Bid Forms

Your auction will be conducted throughout the evening in a variety of ways, beginning with the Silent Auction, then perhaps a Mini-Live Auction, then on to the Live Auction, with the Fund-an-Item, a sweep or two, and perhaps one or more raffles. There may also be a few sign-up opportunities to underwrite special programs. Each of these will require bid forms or tracking forms. With auction software, printing these is quite simple, but even if you don't use specialty software, you can create forms to serve these purposes.

The Live Auction form is very basic. It contains a place to list the item number, the description, the donor, and a blank space to write the successful bidder number and the final bid amount. The recorder merely writes the final bid amount and bid number on the form and sends it back to the cashiering area for data entry.

The Fund-an-Item form is used to list bid numbers that are held high in the air when the auctioneer asks for pledges at a specified dollar amount. As an example, should the expected levels be $1,000, $500, $250, and $100, then the recording sheet would have columns with each of these denominations at the top. As the auctioneer calls the bid numbers at each level, the recorders write the bid number down in the corresponding column. When completed, the recording sheet is delivered to the cashiering area for data entry.

A sweep is a process where multiple bidders each get to win the listed item. The recorder merely writes down the bid numbers as they are called by the auctioneer and records the final bid amount that each bidder will pay.

Silent Auction forms come in a variety of sizes and shapes, and have a number of processes that can be followed to achieve the final bid amount. A complete discussion of the Silent Auction process is listed below, as well as several sample forms and their uses.

Samples of many of these forms are provided for you in the Resources section.

**Silent Auction Bid Forms**   Silent Auction bid forms are the vehicle by which bidders will tell you how much they are willing to pay for any given item. Generally, it is printed as a multipart carbonless form—white, yellow, and pink. The white is used as a master audit copy, the yellow is a guest receipt, and the pink is used to track the item until it is redeemed. Each item has its own form, which contains the name of the item, a description of the item, any restrictions, the catalog number, and the name of the donor. Depending on the system in use for bidding, the form will often have the minimum bid and minimum raise amounts, and places for the bidder to write their bidder number and the amount they wish to bid. Some organizations also ask for bidders to list their name and even their telephone number—*no!* See the sidebar, which explains why this is a bad idea.

### Personal Information and Bid Forms

You may have seen bid forms used at other auctions where guests are expected to write in their names and/or their telephone numbers instead of using just a bid number. This is a really bad idea for several reasons, ranging from merely benign to potentially risky. On the benign end of the spectrum, consider that when you write a name on a bid form, everyone else at the event knows you've bid on a particular item. This can result in lower yields on your Silent Auction items for two reasons: 1) People may not want others to know that they are bidding on the IRS tax attorney services or liposuction, or 2) Mary may not want to outbid her friend Sally on a child's gift basket out of respect for their friendship. On the ``risky'' end of the spectrum, consider that many people feel uncomfortable listing their phone number, especially people who are famous and/or have a high net worth. Also, while it is unlikely this would happen, single guests may be reluctant to list a phone number because of the potential of someone's picking it up off the bid forms as they follow the guest around the room. You get the idea. Bid numbers are anonymous and safe, and really are the only thing a guest should need to place a bid. All other information is unnecessary and doesn't gain you a thing.

If you are using an auction management software system, the preparation of the bid forms is extremely easy. We suggest you use a system that preprints the actual bid steps on the form, rather than using a format where the guests write in each step as they go. Think of the logic here: If you are having your guests do mental math and then expect them to write legibly in the proper place on the form, not only are you slowing down the bidding process considerably, but you run the risk that some of your hundreds of guests might not perform these instructions perfectly. Why take the risk when you can expedite the bidding and ensure all the bid steps are correct by allowing the auction software to produce clean and professional bid forms with each bid step accurately printed? Now all your guests have to do is place their bid number in the space next to the amount they wish to pay for the item. No mistakes allowed.

Exhibits 11.1 and 11.2 show some sample Silent Auction forms.

In Exhibit 11.2, note that the bid steps were prepared by the auction software so the guests did not have to do the math. Also notice that there is a Guaranteed Purchase feature to let bidders win instantly. More on Guaranteed Purchase follows a little later in this section.

Here are some tips to enhance your Silent Auction forms:

- Choose preprinted forms and type or print your information on the forms. Handwritten forms look unprofessional and can be hard to read at a glance.
- The form should include a clear description of the item and any exclusions, blackout dates, expiration dates, restrictions, etc.
- For added professionalism, mounting the invoices on construction paper always adds a nice touch. If you choose a color scheme for your Silent Auctions, be sure the color of the paper on which you mount the bid form matches the color of the auction. When mounting the form, be careful that you attach it by the bottom (pink) copy of the form. This procedure makes closing easy, as the top two copies are free to be separated from the mounting. Double-sided tape makes this mounting job easy.
- Choose auction bid forms with a place for a preselected bid step amount.
- The less people need to write in order to bid, the more time they will have for bidding. We recommend that people bid using only their three-digit bid number. If these three numbers are all people need to write for bidding, they will be more inclined to bid and will bid more often.

There are two methods used for bidding in a Silent Auction, each of which uses a specific type of bid form. There is the traditional Silent Auction

| B-207 | Value: $900 |
|---|---|

**One week's stay at the Happiness Hotel**

Get away from it all. This hotel is only two hours from downtown, but you will feel like you are a world away. Just on the other side of the sand dunes from the beach, this quaint little hotel includes a common area with fireplace, full kitchen in each unit, indoor pool and hot tub, and free continental breakfast in the morning. Includes a six night, seven day stay in a deluxe room with either two double beds, or one King sized bed.

Donor(s)  Happiness Hotel

| Bid # | Telephone # | Amount Bid |
|---|---|---|
| | | $270 |
| | | |
| | | |
| | | |
| | | |
| | | |
| | | |
| | | |
| | | |
| | | |
| | | |

‡ This Item Requires a Certificate          Expires: 2/12/2006

Organization Legal Name:
Federal Tax Id #

*MaestroSoft, Inc. - Copyright 2008*

*Note on the form above that there are no predetermined bid steps. Also, private information, such as a telephone number, should never be exposed in a public way, so avoid using it on your bid form.

**Exhibit 11.1   Good Example of a Bad Form**

system, then the Guaranteed Purchase system. Both are successful, and guests will be able to readily understand both types.

The traditional bidding system consists of a preprinted bid form that lists the item's catalog number, description, fair market value, opening bid, minimum raise amount, and a series of 10 to 30 lines where the bidder writes a name, bid number, and bid amount. When a new bidder wishes to bid, they can write their bid number and any amount they choose above the minimum raise on the next available line. The benefits to this system are that the amount can go as high as people are willing to spend on any given item, and people aren't constrained to bid specific dollar amounts. The downside is that this form of bidding is time consuming, mistakes are more likely to

White Silent Section # 2                                             Value
## B-207                                                             $900

**Item:** One week's stay at the Happiness Hotel

Get away from it all. This hotel is only two hours from downtown, but you will feel like you are a world away. Just on the other side of the sand dunes from the beach, this quaint little hotel includes a common area with fireplace, full kitchen in each unit, indoor pool and hot tub, and free continental breakfast in the morning. Includes a six night, seven day stay in a deluxe room with **Donor(s)** Happiness Hotel

| Bidder Number | | Bidder Number | | Bidder Number | |
|---|---|---|---|---|---|
| _____ | $270 | _____ | $685 | _____ | $1,101 |
| _____ | $353 | _____ | $768 | _____ | $1,184 |
| _____ | $436 | _____ | $852 | _____ | $1,267 |
| _____ | $519 | _____ | $935 | **Guaranteed Purchase** | |
| _____ | $602 | _____ | $1,018 | **$1,350** | |

Organization Legal Name:
Federal Employer Identification #:              *MaestroSoft, Inc. © 2008*      * **This Item Requires a Certificate**

## Exhibit 11.2   Good Example of a Good Form

occur, and guests will generally raise the bid only by the minimum required raise. This also presents a problem for those guests who would purchase more than one item in the Silent Auction. If they have to hover around one item, they can only guarantee a win on that one item.

In contrast, the Guaranteed Purchase bidding system uses a preprinted bid form that includes similar information as the standard bid form, but with two major differences. The dollar amounts for bids are already filled in for the bidder, and there is a Guaranteed Purchase facility. Bidders need to only write their bid number next to the amount they want to bid and they have the option to use the Guaranteed Purchase facility. This immediate purchase facility generally requires the bidder to pay a premium to win the item instantly, typically 150% of the fair market value. Think of this as similar to eBay's "Buy It Now" option. If the bidder absolutely wants to win this item, entry of the bid number in the Guaranteed Purchase box next to the amount ensures that sale. This system allows the more popular items to be purchased right away, allowing bidders to concentrate their bidding on the remaining items.

Some committees prefer to avoid using the Guaranteed Purchase option on one or more of their Silent Auction items, and this is fine. The preprinted bid steps, even without the use of the Guaranteed Purchase facility, still have benefits because they simplify the process of bidding on an item to one step: writing in the bidder's number. Again, guests do not have to perform the mental math of adding the previous bid to the minimum raise, as it is already written for them on the form. Experience and statistics will show that the Guaranteed Purchase system will result in a 10% to 20% higher yield in the Silent Auctions. Sample Guaranteed Purchase bid forms are available for your reference in the Resources section.

*Some Great Examples of Silent Auction Forms and Display*

**Establishing Bid Steps for Silent Auction Items**    If you are using an auction management system, establishing the bid steps and printing the forms is straightforward. The software offers several format options and allows you to decide on what percentage to set for the Guaranteed Purchase amount for your items. Once you select your format for the bid forms and the amount you wish for the Guaranteed Purchase point, you merely print the forms. If you are not using software and wish to design your own forms, then you can use the chart in Exhibit 11.3 as a guide for bid steps. It is designed for a 14-step form, with a 150% Guaranteed Purchase option. Note that the bid steps are approximately 10% of the value of the item. Use this percentage as a guide if you design a form with more steps. Bear in mind, however, that the more steps you create, the longer it is going to take to get to the full value of the item. Assuming you have approximately the same number of items as buying units, then the 14-step form is ideal. If you have a significant seller's market in which the number of bidders is considerably more than the number of items, then you could use a form with 24 or even 36 steps, and a Guaranteed Purchase amount of 200% or more. Try to select a combination of steps and Guaranteed Purchase percentage that maintains bid steps of approximately 10% of the fair market or expected value of the items.

| FMV* | Opening Bid | Next Bid | Next Bid | Next Bid | Next Bid | Next Bid | Next Bid | Next Bid | Next Bid | Next Bid | Next Bid | Next Bid | Next Bid | Guaranteed Purchase |
|---|---|---|---|---|---|---|---|---|---|---|---|---|---|---|
| $10 | $2 | $3 | $4 | $5 | $6 | $7 | $8 | $9 | $10 | $11 | $12 | $13 | $14 | $15 |
| $15 | $3 | $5 | $6 | $8 | $9 | $11 | $12 | $14 | $15 | $17 | $18 | $20 | $21 | $23 |
| $20 | $4 | $5 | $8 | $10 | $12 | $14 | $16 | $18 | $20 | $22 | $24 | $26 | $28 | $30 |
| $25 | $5 | $6 | $10 | $13 | $15 | $18 | $20 | $23 | $25 | $28 | $30 | $33 | $35 | $38 |
| $30 | $6 | $8 | $12 | $15 | $18 | $21 | $24 | $27 | $30 | $33 | $36 | $39 | $42 | $45 |
| $35 | $7 | $9 | $14 | $18 | $21 | $25 | $28 | $32 | $35 | $39 | $42 | $46 | $49 | $53 |
| $40 | $8 | $11 | $16 | $20 | $24 | $28 | $32 | $36 | $40 | $44 | $48 | $52 | $56 | $60 |
| $45 | $9 | $12 | $18 | $23 | $27 | $32 | $36 | $41 | $45 | $50 | $54 | $59 | $65 | $68 |
| $50 | $10 | $14 | $20 | $25 | $30 | $35 | $40 | $45 | $50 | $55 | $60 | $65 | $70 | $75 |
| $55 | $11 | $15 | $22 | $28 | $33 | $39 | $44 | $50 | $55 | $61 | $66 | $72 | $77 | $83 |
| $60 | $12 | $17 | $24 | $30 | $36 | $42 | $48 | $54 | $60 | $66 | $72 | $78 | $84 | $90 |
| $65 | $13 | $18 | $26 | $33 | $39 | $46 | $62 | $59 | $65 | $72 | $78 | $85 | $91 | $98 |
| $70 | $14 | $21 | $28 | $35 | $42 | $49 | $56 | $63 | $70 | $77 | $84 | $91 | $98 | $105 |
| $75 | $15 | $23 | $30 | $38 | $45 | $53 | $60 | $68 | $75 | $83 | $90 | $98 | $105 | $113 |
| $80 | $16 | $24 | $32 | $40 | $48 | $56 | $64 | $72 | $80 | $88 | $96 | $104 | $112 | $120 |
| $85 | $17 | $26 | $34 | $43 | $51 | $60 | $68 | $77 | $85 | $94 | $102 | $111 | $119 | $128 |
| $90 | $18 | $27 | $36 | $45 | $54 | $63 | $72 | $81 | $90 | $99 | $108 | $117 | $126 | $135 |
| $95 | $19 | $29 | $38 | $48 | $57 | $67 | $76 | $86 | $95 | $105 | $114 | $124 | $133 | $143 |
| $100 | $20 | $30 | $40 | $50 | $60 | $70 | $80 | $90 | $100 | $110 | $120 | $130 | $140 | $150 |
| $125 | $25 | $38 | $50 | $63 | $75 | $88 | 100 | $113 | $125 | $138 | $150 | $163 | $175 | $188 |
| $150 | $30 | $45 | $60 | $75 | $90 | $105 | $120 | $135 | $150 | $165 | $180 | $195 | $210 | $225 |
| $175 | $35 | $53 | $70 | $88 | $105 | $123 | $140 | $158 | $175 | $193 | $210 | $228 | $245 | $263 |
| $200 | $40 | $60 | $80 | $100 | $120 | $140 | $160 | $180 | $200 | $220 | $240 | $260 | $280 | $300 |
| $225 | $45 | $68 | $90 | $113 | $135 | $158 | $180 | $203 | $225 | $248 | $270 | $293 | $315 | $338 |
| $250 | $50 | $75 | $100 | $125 | $150 | $175 | $200 | $225 | $250 | $275 | $300 | $335 | $350 | $375 |
| $275 | $55 | $83 | $110 | $138 | $165 | $193 | $220 | $248 | $275 | $303 | $330 | $358 | $385 | $413 |
| $300 | $60 | $90 | $120 | $150 | $180 | $210 | $240 | $270 | $300 | $330 | $360 | $390 | $420 | $450 |
| $325 | $65 | $98 | $130 | $163 | $195 | $228 | $260 | $293 | $325 | $358 | $390 | $423 | $455 | $488 |
| $350 | $70 | $105 | $140 | $175 | $210 | $245 | $280 | $315 | $350 | $385 | $420 | $455 | $490 | $525 |
| $375 | $75 | $113 | $150 | $188 | $225 | $263 | $300 | $338 | $375 | $413 | $450 | $488 | $525 | $563 |
| $400 | $80 | $120 | $160 | $200 | $240 | $280 | $320 | $360 | $400 | $440 | $480 | $520 | $560 | $600 |
| $425 | $85 | $128 | $170 | $213 | $255 | $293 | $340 | $383 | $425 | $468 | $510 | $553 | $595 | $638 |
| $450 | $90 | $135 | $180 | $225 | $270 | $315 | $360 | $405 | $450 | $495 | $540 | $585 | $630 | $675 |
| $475 | $91 | $143 | $190 | $238 | $285 | $333 | $380 | $428 | $475 | $523 | $570 | $618 | $665 | $713 |
| $500 | $92 | $150 | $200 | $250 | $300 | $350 | $400 | $450 | $500 | $550 | $600 | $650 | $700 | $750 |
| $525 | $94 | $158 | $210 | $263 | $315 | $368 | $420 | $473 | $525 | $578 | $630 | $683 | $735 | $788 |
| $550 | $97 | $165 | $220 | $275 | $330 | $385 | $440 | $495 | $550 | $605 | $660 | $715 | $770 | $825 |

**Exhibit 11.3   Silent Auction Bid Increments**

**Live Auction Bid Forms**  The Live Auction form is used to record the successful bidder number and the final bid amount when called by the auctioneer. As with the Silent Auction bid form, it is printed as a multipart carbonless form where the white is the original, the yellow is the guest receipt, and the pink is for tracking the item. Exhibit 11.4 shows a sample Live Auction form.

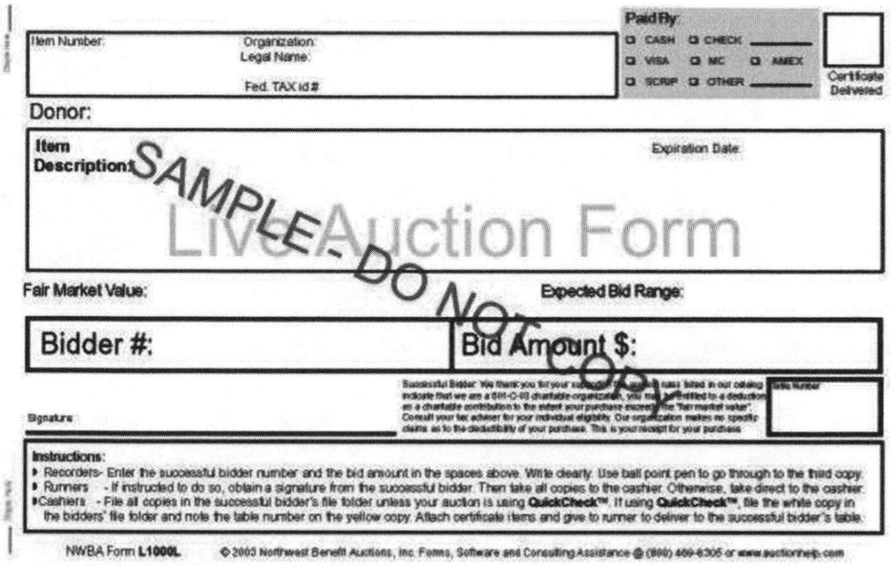

**Exhibit 11.4   Sample Live Auction Form**

### Table Tents or Easels

A table tent or table easel is one of the best ways to market your auction items in the Silent and the Live Auctions. It's just not possible to print the detailed descriptions for auction items on the bid forms in a large enough font to be readable. The easel provides a place where descriptions can be printed and displayed for better viewing at a distance. It makes little sense to require bidders to bend over to read small print on bid forms in the Silent Auction. It's uncomfortable, it's not graceful, and it does not draw in other bidders who may be several steps behind the bidders at the table edge. An easel can list the descriptions in 14- to 18-point font, making them readable from many feet away. This allows considerably more potential bidders than just those close to the tables to see the item descriptions.

The table easels can be made of a variety of materials, with sizes typically around 10 inches by 13 inches. Often the easels are made of artists' foam core or matting material and come in colors to match the color code of the Silent Auction sections. When the description of the item is printed on standard paper and mounted on the easel, the color of the easel makes a very nice frame around the description sheet. Look at some examples of auction displays with the easels describing the items:

**Examples of Auction Displays with Table Easels**

### Other Auction Display Considerations

And now, a final note on display of the auction items. Your guests will have many distractions during your event. They will be mingling with other guests, listening to music, having a drink and an appetizer, all while trying to move through the crowd of people in your Silent Auction. You are vying for their attention, so make it easy for them to bid. Have an emcee or your auctioneer announce the table closing times, and highlight popular items. Avoid crowding items together, and of course have plenty of lighting. Use clear, bullet-point descriptions of the items, because lengthy descriptions simply will not get read. Use color codes to differentiate the Silent Auction sections, and stick to primary colors that are easily recognizable. Red, white, and blue sections, or green, yellow, and purple sections are all good. Avoid colors that men don't recognize, like mauve, peach, teal, chartreuse, avocado, or champagne. Keep it simple!

Finally, be sure that you have a good sound system that will reach through the entire Silent Auction area, so that when it is time to start the closing countdown, your bidders will feel the sense of urgency to get those bids on the forms.

**Some Examples of Good Live Auction Displays and Preview Sections**

## Cashiering Requirements

One thing you will certainly need to do at your event is have some process for handling payments. By *payments*, we mean *any* form of payment, whether that is a personal or corporate check, a credit card payment, or cash. As a general rule, we advise against taking cash for any part of your evening. Ideally, you'll set up your event so that attendees can use their bid number for any charges at the event, including raffles, balloons or other favors, merchandise, even drinks, if your caterer or venue can keep a tab open for a guest by their bid number. Handling cash brings with it a myriad of possible risks, including that of loss or theft, the challenges of making change, issues with accounting for guests' charges against cash payments (which you'll want to do for your guests' potential tax purposes), and more.

If you do decide to accept cash at your event, we'll cover a best-practices process for managing it, along with other payment types, in Chapter 12. Most events can be run just as well accepting only credit cards and checks as payment for auction purchases and donations. While you may feel that the percentage your bank or processor will charge you is an unnecessary cost, in reality, using credit cards at your event can actually be a major benefit to your event revenue, especially if you are able to take cards with no preset credit limits, because guests will tend to be more generous when they use credit cards than when they know they are writing a check that evening to cover their generosity. To get the most out of your payment processing function, you also want to make sure your processor doesn't charge more for credit cards entered online or for other nonswiped transactions. This will allow you to take guests' RSVP charges in advance and begin processing those payments to your bank.

In general, know that technology has made it easier to take payments, match those against guests' charges, and account for it all after the event. In the next section, we'll discuss bank card payment processing—credit cards—in somewhat more detail. Later, we'll cover the actual processes you'll use to ensure your guests' purchases are properly recorded, to enter payment information and match it to those charges, and to know how it all adds up when the evening is done. Although we will be talking about how technology is used to aid in this work, technology won't do it all for you, so we'll be discussing the behind-the-scenes activities that take place to manage your event easily and efficiently.

### Bank Card Payment Processing

As we discussed earlier in this Phase, it's important that the first impression your guests have of your event is a positive one. The other thing that they will remember is the *last* impression, and for most guests, the last thing they do at your event is pay for their purchases or donations. We're about to discuss a way that will kill two birds with the same stone, making sure both the first and last impressions your guests get of your event involve no lines at the beginning of the evening and no lines at the end, either.

The way to accomplish this task is to have your guests preauthorize their payments at the beginning of the evening. This method of express checkout (sometimes called by other names like qCheck™, QuickCheck, or Express Pay), uses commercial payment processing software to take a swipe of the guest's credit card during registration. By offering this option to your guests, you accomplish the following:

- Since you already have their payment information on file, there is no need for them to come to cashiering at the end of the evening to cash out.
- Guests who are typically reluctant to bid or donate because of the fear of having to stand in a cashiering line are more likely to be generous when they know their "card is already on file" and they won't be penalized for their generosity.
- Guests who have bought nothing but are now being asked to raise their paddle and make a cash donation during the Live Auction are more likely to do so if they are assured that this act of support won't force them to stand in a long line.
- If guests have preauthorized payment for their items and donations, they don't even necessarily have to stand in a line to pick up their guest receipts—those can be brought to them at their table during the Live Auction. That's another convenience that shows your appreciation for the guests' comfort. All they then have to do is pick up their actual items and go home!

While there are many different commercial solutions out there to accomplish this task, the process is supposed to work like this:

1. When the guest arrives at the event, they are told that, as a convenience to them so they do not have to stand in a cashiering line at the end of the evening, you are taking a swipe of their credit cards at registration. (Note: We're using the word "swipe" here intentionally. In some events, committees are still taking either manual imprints of credit cards or using credit card processing terminals that record and print credit card information. In the section that follows, we'll explain the differences and not only why some methods are better than others, but also why some can open you up to potentially serious risk and possible liability.)

**Auction Attendee qChecks at Registration**

2. When you swipe the card, you will associate that card with the guest's bidder number.
3. Return the card to the guest, give them their registration packet, and they're on their way to enjoy your event.
4. Using either a built-in interface within the payment processing software or manually, you'll indicate in the auction software (if using) or manually that this person's payment is on file (i.e., they are qChecked).
5. As your event progresses and you close out auction sections, you can take qChecked bidders their guest receipts at their tables. If you're not using this process, when your guests get ready to leave your event, prepaid guests can come to a separate checkout area to pick up their guest receipts and redeem their items, bypassing cashiering entirely.
6. While you can prepare temporary statements for qChecked guests to give to them at the end of the evening, a full and final receipt will be mailed to them a few days after the event. Again, no reason for them to stand in a line!

If a guest qChecks but does not make any purchases or donations, no charges or holds are put on their swiped card. Again, there's no reason for them to stand in a line to pick up a blank check they may have left at the beginning of the evening, and nothing to void out.

Now, as alluded to at the beginning of this section, there are several payment processing solutions on the market that have differing processes and differing features. While many of them will work fine for your event, there are some critical differences involving secure handling and processing of credit card and personal data.

### Compliance with Data Security Requirements

Many of the features most commercial payment processors use are relatively similar. Most will record, in some fashion, the cardholder's card information. Processors used at auctions will generally allow you to tie a bid number to the card information, because that is how you'll need to track charges later. While many of these are features of function and convenience, and can be interchangeable to a degree, there is one area in which you cannot afford to be casual, and that relates to credit card and personal information security.

In Fall 2008, the first of the Payment Card Industry Data Security Standards (PCI DSS) went into effect. PCI DSS is a set of requirements developed by the major credit card companies to enhance the security of credit and debit card data. All organizations that process, store, or transmit payment card data—like the payment processors you may be considering using at your auctions and fundraisers—must follow the PCI DSS requirements or risk losing their ability to process credit card payments. After October 2008, any organization that requires a new merchant ID from the credit card companies must be PCI DSS compliant. By October 2009, all organizations must be PCI DSS compliant to process credit cards.

Why does this matter to you?

According to the Payment Card Industry standard, there are strict regulations about what information from a cardholder's card may be read, stored, and displayed. In the following sections, PAN stands for Primary Account Number—in other words, the account number on the credit card. While some of the details about the standard may seem a bit cryptic, here are sections 3.3 and 3.4 of the DSS, as stated on PCI's Web site. For more specific information about PCI, its standards and compliance requirements, visit their Web site, at www.pcisecuritystandards.org.

> **3.3** Mask PAN when displayed (the first six and last four digits are the maximum number of digits to be displayed).
>
> *Note: This requirement does not apply to employees and other parties with a specific need to see the full PAN; nor does the requirement supersede stricter*

*requirements in place for displays of cardholder data (for example, for point of sale [POS] receipts).*

**3.4** Render PAN, at minimum, unreadable anywhere it is stored (including data on portable digital media, backup media, in logs, and data received from or stored by wireless networks) by using any of the following approaches:

- Strong one-way hash functions (hashed indexes)
- Truncation
- Index tokens and pads (pads must be securely stored)
- Strong cryptography with associated key management processes and procedures.

*The MINIMUM account information that must be rendered unreadable is the PAN.*

Now you may be asking yourself, why do you need to know this, and what does it matter to you? It matters a great deal, and the following scenario should help explain why.

If someone asked you to store a hand grenade in your house, chances are you would refuse. If you were asked to store 250 of them, you would think the person asking was making a joke. However, figuratively speaking, many charities routinely do something similarly dangerous: They store credit card numbers in hard copy, complete with the expiration dates and names of the card holders, in a "secure place." The reason given to the charity is so it can have ready access to the card number should charges need to be modified, or in case they make periodic charges. Each of these card numbers is a potential bomb, should it accidentally or intentionally fall into the hands of an identity thief. If you use a payment processing terminal system to check people in at your event, use "knuckle-busters" to manually record card information, or ask patrons to fill out registration cards with their credit card information, it is quite possible you are storing hand grenades in your file cabinet at this very moment.

Consider this: The phones rings and you are told by a coworker a file folder is missing from your file cabinet. You know that inside that file folder is a paper tape (from your event check-in terminal) containing the complete credit card number, expiration date, and name of each of the attendees from your last event, or all the registration cards that contain credit card information. There are more than 250 of them. In the wrong hands, each one of these 250 credit card numbers represents a huge identity theft problem, a bomb waiting to go off. What is your next move?

Of course you will launch a search for the file and hope it was just temporarily misplaced, but what if it was deliberately removed by an employee or a volunteer? At what point do you call off the search, and begin calling your 250 patrons to advise them their credit card information has been compromised? What if the theft included not just the credit card numbers from your last event, but from all events for the last four years? A thousand stolen credit card numbers from your custody (or even one number) represent a huge liability to your organization. The next time you host an event, your patrons are going to be very reluctant to trust you with their information. This will directly cost your organization, reducing your ability to sell your auction items or receive donations. Further, should any of these credit card numbers fall into the hands of criminals, the liability to your organization (and you) is enormous. Board members would also be quite nervous if they were aware you were storing so many bombs in your file cabinet.

In this age of identify theft and credit card fraud, organizations have had to become increasingly knowledgeable and careful about how they take and record payment information. Until recently, it was common practice for guests to be asked for an imprint of their credit card at check-in. Generally, this involved carbon copy charge slips and a "knuckle-buster" imprinter. As guests became nervous about identity theft and having a carbon copy image of their credit card on file, several vendors came up with a swiped-card approach. Some vendors use a terminal for check-in, swiping the credit card and producing a paper tape containing credit cardholder and card number data for signature. Terminal approaches usually store credit card data within the terminal, and because printing a paper tape exposes those numbers, terminals are not secure. Guests may feel better about the check-in process because they see their card being swiped rather than imprinted, but from a security standpoint, there is little difference. In fact, it is easier to make a paper tape printout of card numbers from a terminal than to make a photo copy of a stack of imprinted slips, so in this regard terminals my be *less* secure than the old knuckle-buster methods used in prior years!

Storing credit card information in any manner where that information could fall into less-than-honorable hands is just bad policy. Surprisingly, not only is it easy to do, and routinely done, it is actually a recommended practice by some payment processors! Their advice is to "print a paper tape of all of the credit card numbers and store in a safe place." With some credit card check-in terminals, it is very simple to do this by selecting a menu choice, then pressing the print button. Out comes a full listing of all the stored credit card numbers, names, and expiration dates for each card that has been swiped that night. The process takes just seconds and can be done without requiring any password. Since many events use volunteers extensively at check-in, and any of these volunteers could easily print one of these tapes, it is simple to see that this sensitive credit card information could disappear immediately at the event. Unless someone from the organization continuously monitors the volunteers, you would never know a list of credit card numbers was even printed. Criminals could be stealing the identity of your constituents before you even process their credit card charges.

So, how can you defuse these bombs? The easiest way is to avoid creating them in the first place. The best credit card systems take a swipe of a credit card, which immediately inputs sensitive information into an encrypted data file. There is no paper tape printer, and no printout can be made of the full, unencrypted card number. At some point after the event, this encrypted file is uploaded through an Internet or telephone connection to a secure and certified processor, which is the only source that can decrypt the file. The processor will then provide the client (the charity) with a method by which to identify the payment information—but not the credit card—for the guest against which to process charges. At no time does the charity ever have access to (or need) their patrons' full, unencrypted credit card numbers. Corrections, additions, and credits are all handled using a payment key assigned to each guest.

This may sound complex, but the questions you need to ask your possible solutions vendors are pretty simple. As you evaluate your payment processing providers, ask them:

- Are they presently PCI DSS compliant, and if not, when do they expect to be?
- Are credit card information, guest names, expiration dates, and other personal information stored in encrypted files or in clear-text?
- Does the system have the ability to capture and hold the information securely prior to purchase? Real-time retail payment processing may be PCI compliant, but is rarely feasible for use at charity auctions. In the industry, the capability to take payment information in advance is called "store and forward" and is the best system to use for auctions, where "sales" are made throughout the evening, but charges are consolidated and generally processed after the fact.
- What method is used to make changes to charges, if necessary, after the event? Do you need to have the guest's credit card information, or is there a unique, separate payment key you'll use?
- Is there any way to print or generate a paper copy of one or more guests' credit card data or personal information? Is there a way to print a duplicate receipt with full credit card information? Hopefully, the answer to both of these questions is "no."

While you may feel it is statistically unlikely that *your* event will be hit with identity theft or suffer credit card fraud, you can't afford to take that chance. Should something even potentially damaging occur, your organization can be open to significant liability. Your patrons want to help you with your cause. They have a level of trust in you and your organization, and they assume you are looking out for their best interests as they support your event. When they trust you with their sensitive information, you should repay them by protecting that information. Making sure your payment processor is compliant with the necessary data standards is the best protection you have when you handle credit cards.

## Arranging for Volunteer Help

Volunteers are truly the great unsung heroes of any fundraising event. A volunteer is defined in the Glossary at the end of this book (and for our purposes here) as an individual who donates his or her time and energy, without expectation of pay, to be involved in your event in a supporting role. Typically, volunteers are part of your organization either directly or indirectly, such as employees, parents, or other supporters. Sometimes, volunteers can come from outside your group—either from another organization with whom you've agreed to exchange volunteers to work at each other's events, or from service organizations such as Rotary or Kiwanis.

Volunteers have such a critical role in making sure events come off smoothly that you literally can't live without them. In recognition of their efforts, be generous in your appreciation. You can never thank a volunteer too much or too often. Remember that they are doing what they do because they believe in your organization and its cause. They don't have to be there; they *choose* to be. And they frequently perform those jobs that are the least glamorous or visible, so they rarely get all the credit due them. The better you treat your volunteers and the more you let them know how important they are to you personally and to your event, the easier time you'll have recruiting them to help with the next event, so *never* take a volunteer for granted!

### The Volunteer Coordinator

With all the volunteers who are likely to be working your event, you'll need to have one central person whose job it is to manage these folks as they go about their various activities. The Volunteer Coordinator has the responsibility for getting all of the nonpaid volunteers organized to work effectively as a group. The Volunteer Coordinator generally knows many or all of the volunteers, is aware of their abilities, and can assign them to jobs that best use their skills. While you may have hired a professional event coordinator to help you manage your event, you still need a Volunteer

Coordinator who functions as the primary point of contact between your professional staff and your volunteer staff. This coordinator also typically trains and supervises all volunteers during move-in, setup, and throughout the event.

### Volunteer Job Descriptions

Here are detailed descriptions of the duties for which each volunteer is responsible. Again, depending on the size of the event, you may not need to fill all of these positions, or you may be able to "double up" on staff for some of them. You may wish to engage professional help or take recommendations from someone with experience in this area if you are unsure about your staffing needs.

- *Registration.* Registration tables should be located at the obvious entrance to your event. Registration volunteers take care of checking in guests and preprocessing credit cards through payment processing software, if used. Registration volunteers are generally trained to handle the majority of regular guest cases, but any guests that need special attention or don't conform to the standard process are sent to the troubleshooter. *(Used during registration.)*
- *Troubleshooter.* The troubleshooter stays close to the registration tables; frequently, he or she has a separate spot at one of the ends of the registration table. This volunteer helps all the guests who have special needs (e.g., they are seated at the incorrect table, there's a problem with their event payment, etc.). Having a troubleshooter keeps the regular registration staff focused on helping preregistered guests and regular cases. *(Primarily used during registration, sometimes throughout event.)*
- *Expediter.* Since registration packets are set up on one or more tables behind the registration volunteers, it's more efficient and expedient to have extra staff on hand to pull the registration packets for the registration volunteers than to have the registration staff get up to get the packets themselves. The expediter's job is make sure that when a guest comes up to register, the volunteer at the registration table can stay seated and begin to ask preliminary questions and preprocess credit card payments while the expediter finds the guest's registration packet. *(Used during registration and cashiering.)*
- *Silent Table Closers.* Silent Auction table closers are responsible for *closing out* items at the conclusion of each Silent Auction. Closing out an item means clearly circling the winning bid number and corresponding amount on a Silent Auction bid form. This can occur

either at the end of the Silent Auction section or while the Silent Auction is still open, if guests have entered a Guaranteed Bid amount. More about how Silent Auction table closers perform their function will be covered in the section Managing your Silent Auction, in Chapter 12. *(Used during silent auction.)*

- *Live Auction Display.* These volunteers hold up, carry around through the venue, or otherwise show off each Live Auction item as it is auctioned. Not to sound sexist, but these volunteers are sometimes referred to, in the industry, as "Vannas" (in recognition of Vanna White's letter-turning role in the *Wheel of Fortune* game show). Sometimes special props—such as models of a boat for a cruise, or platters of toy food and wineglasses for an exclusive chef's dinner—can be used to help showcase the item, especially if the item is intangible or large. The better the Live Auction items are displayed and featured, the more money the item is likely to raise, and the more memorable your event will be. Choose people for this job who have lots of imagination and energy, give them early information about which items will be in the Live Auction and in what order, and tell them that they are limited only by their creativity. *(Used during Live Auction and sometimes during cocktail hour/Silent Auction to showcase upcoming Live Auction items.)*

- *Spotters/Floor Auctioneers.* The job of a spotter is to identify bidders who may be out of the auctioneer's line of sight and to encourage and engage bidders in the auction process. They may also be called upon to identify the successful bidder at the end of the bidding system, so the runners can find that bidder and give them a gift or get a signature on the Live Auction form.

  The room is divided into sections—typically four sections, or quadrants—and a spotter watches his or her section for bids. If the auctioneer is looking the other way and a guest bids in the spotter's quadrant, the spotter shouts, "Here!" or "Bid!" to alert the auctioneer to the bid in that quadrant. Spotters may also raise their hands at this point in an *L* shape—with one arm raised over the head to indicate which spotter called the bid and the other hand pointed toward the active bidder. Spotting bids is particularly important as each bidding sequence draws to a close, because each bid at the end of the bidding sequence raises an extra increment of additional money for your organization. As the bidding sequence gets closer to its end, it is helpful if the spotters help the auctioneer indicate for the auction guests which bidder has the current high bid. This is usually done by raising a hand or prop (pompom, flashlight, etc.) to signify that the bidder either has or wants the bid. Since no two of these props can be raised at the same time, as soon as a new one goes up the guests know that a new bidder has taken the bid. This requires very close coordination among spotters in concert with the auctioneer, but with a little training, spotters catch on quickly and really enjoy helping raise the money.

Spotters may encourage guests to bid again, but must never interfere with the auctioneer's line of sight or with the communication between the auctioneer and the guests. Also, after the bidding is complete on the one item, there may a moment of confusion as the other guests congratulate the successful bidder. At the same time, the auctioneer is attempting to obtain the correct bid number from the successful bidder for the recorder. The spotters can be of *great* assistance in reminding the successful bidder to hold up his or her bid card. They must, however, never touch the bid card themselves so they don't inadvertently hold up the wrong one. Spotters need to be energetic and outgoing individuals who aren't afraid to yell when they see a bid. Because of the potential importance of this job, many organizations choose to hire professionals for this function instead of relying on volunteers. *(Used during Live Auction.)*

- *Runner.* Runners are a group of volunteers that work with the Live Auction recorders. When an item is sold in the Live Auction, a runner comes up to the recorder's table and picks up the Live Auction bid form for that particular item. If you've decided to get winners' signatures on the bid form, that runner goes to the successful bidder and obtains his or her signature. The runner takes the time to thank the guest for their successful bid, but does not get into a conversation with them. If the guest declines to sign the invoice, the runner does not attempt to discuss the matter with the guest but instead refers the matter to the person designated to handle that situation. Once the form is signed, the runner delivers it to the data entry area, where the information is entered into the database. After delivering the bid form, the runner goes back to the group of runners to wait for the next item, and the cycle repeats.

    Runners also have the job of taking guest receipts for items won to the successful bidders, if they have prepaid for their purchases via qCheck or a similar payment process. Runners will take the group of bid form copies to the winning bidder's table and, after confirming that the guest's bid number matches the bid number on the form, gives the guest receipts to the winner. The winner will then use these receipts later for picking up items or certificates that he or she won. *(Used from the end of the Silent Auctions through the Live Auction.)*

    Note: Some auctions choose to skip the step of obtaining the guest's signature on the invoices. Historically, many committees felt that if the guest signed the invoice, they would be more aware of and committed to the sale. However, this isn't really the case. If your auctioneer is recognizing and thanking the successful bidder after the item is sold, the winner (and the rest of the audience) is already aware of the win. The actual transaction (per your Auction Rules in Phase III) occurs when the auctioneer says "Sold!," not when the guest signs the bid form. If a guest truly has buyer's remorse and wants to be let out of the sale of the item, you would certainly honor that request, so getting a signature is generally an extra and unnecessary step that merely consumes time and resources. If your committee decides to skip this step, delivering invoices to data entry only needs to be done every 5 or 10 items. You may, however, still need a full complement of runners to deliver invoices, distribute top bidder recognition (balloons, medallions, etc.), or deliver a copy of the Live Auction invoices to those guests who have prepaid with a credit card through qCheck or other similar process.

- *Number Turner.* Auction guests like to look up to the stage and see a display that shows the number of the item currently up for bid, so they can keep track of current activity and plan for how soon their favorite item will appear. Volunteers can operate any system, from a tripod with numbers on poster board to a fully electronic slideshow presentation. Which method you use isn't terribly important, but the convenience and service to your auction guests is. With the general availability of technology, projectors, and screens, most events now do this function through slideshow presentations, so your number turner is the person responsible for advancing the display at the appropriate time. *(Used during Live Auction.)*

- *Recorder.* Located at a small table next to the auction stage, the recorders write down the final bid amount and bid number on the Live Auction bid form and, separately, in a catalog so there are two independent records of the top bid amount and number. Also, recorders can keep a cumulative total of the Live Auction, so the auctioneer can announce to the guests the total raised as the auction proceeds. If you are using auction management software, you may not need to have the recorders keep a total, because the software will do that for you, and you only need to print an occasional report and deliver that to the auctioneer for an update.

Ideally, you will want two or three recorders working during the Live Auction. We suggest a minimum of three during the Fund-an-Item portion of the evening, because redundancy will help avoid human error issues. During Fund-an-Item, the auctioneer calls the bid numbers fairly quickly, and sometimes one recorder will miss a bid or transpose a bid number (e.g., 167 is written as 176). If you have only two recorders during this process, it's impossible to determine which recorder has the correct information and which one missed the bid. A third recorder serves as a tie-breaker, because the chance of all three recorders missing the same bid or making the same transposition is pretty much impossible. If two out of the three recorders has a bid number on their recording sheet, you can trust that this number is accurate. Many committees will choose to have the three recorders on duty throughout the Live Auction, and this is fine, but it's really only critical to have three people recording during the Fund-an-Item. *(Used during Live Auction and Mini-Live Auction, if using.)*

- *Data Entry.* Most organizations today use some form of auction software to automate their event. This helps expedite the process of creating a catalog, tracking donors, registering attendees, recording guests' winning bids, and tracking money at the end of the night. You will need to have one or more individuals dedicated to data entry during your event to ensure that bid activity is entered accurately and in a timely manner, so that bidder invoices and totals will be accurate throughout the event and at the end of the evening for the cashiering process.

   It's often best to assign two individuals to this task, even if the workload appears to be manageable by one. First, if you have two people, they can work at the computer in shifts, giving each other an occasional break. Second, the person currently not at the keyboard can help make the data entry process easier and less strenuous for the person at the computer by reading the information from the bid forms to the person at the keyboard. This way, the data entry person doesn't need to look from the computer screen to the form and back again, reducing confusion and eyestrain, and increasing the efficiency and speed of data entry. *(Used throughout event.)*

- *Cashier.* Volunteers who sign up to be cashiers are stationed at the cashiering table, or ''bank.'' Their job is to accept payment from auction guests for their purchases and donations in the Live and Silent Auctions.

   Further detail about the cashier's duties and the cashiering process comes later in this Phase. *(Used predominantly at end of event, during cashiering process, but one or more should be on standby to serve any guests leaving early.)*

- *Cashier Assistants.* Much like the expediters at registration, these assistants retrieve the bidder folders at the end of the auction so the cashiers can complete the payment process for each guest at cashiering. Most organizations will train all their cashiering volunteers in the entire process, so the position of cashier assistant is really a technicality. Whichever cashier is not actively working with a guest can perform the job of retrieving the next guest's bid folder. *(Used predominantly at end of event, during cashiering process, but one or more should be on standby to serve any guests leaving early.)*

- *Filers.* As the various Silent Auction sections are closed and as the Live Auction proceeds, filers are responsible for separating and filing the bid forms in the guest's bid folders. Having adequate volunteers for filing is important to keep up with the work. Filers help ensure that the guest receipts that are delivered to guests who have prepaid are ready for the runners to take to tables, and folders with invoices are ready for each guest when they come to cashiering to pay. *(Used throughout the event, but usually beginning shortly after the close of the first Silent Auction section through end of the event.)*

- *Emcee or Announcer.* The emcee (for MC, master or mistress of ceremonies) or announcer is on stage with the auctioneer during and sometimes before the Live Auction. The emcee's primary duty is to announce the next item for bidding, providing the item number, title, donor, and a brief description. Then the auctioneer sells the item, and the process is repeated for the next item. Because this is a critical position, some committees recruit or hire a celebrity announcer or trained professional, instead of using a volunteer from the organization. The announcer must be a person who is comfortable on stage and is capable of marketing each item as it comes up. He or she usually prepares prior to the auction by carefully reviewing the Live Auction sequence and descriptions with the auctioneer.

    Since the guests already have the catalog with the Live Auction item descriptions in them, the announcer must avoid simply reading the description to the guests. He or she includes the basic information and a brief description, possibly highlighting something special about the item that makes it different or unique. The announcer uses personality and humor to make the presentation fun and exciting. Brevity is highly desired over lengthy descriptions. As a general rule, the announcer's descriptions should not exceed 8 to 10 seconds per item before turning the floor back over to the auctioneer. *(Used primarily through Live Auction; may be used during Silent Auction as well.)*

- *Master of Ceremonies.* Some auctions have a separate master or mistress of ceremonies. This person is usually a person of some influence in the organization or community, or in the group the event is benefiting. The master/mistress of ceremonies welcomes guests, thanks them for coming to the auction, and is in charge of managing the program flow, including introductions, door prizes, raffles; communicating important information; thanking guests of honor and sponsors; and so on.

- *Greeter.* Located at the main entrance to the auction, greeters welcome guests (by name if possible), direct them to the registration tables and coat check area, and answer questions about the first Silent section to close and the locations of bars or refreshment tables. Greeters may also be asked to help with controlling the flow at registration, directing any guests standing in line to the next available registration volunteer. *(Used primarily during registration, but may also be used at cashiering/ redemption to help with traffic flow.)*

### Volunteer Staffing Levels

The number of volunteers involved in your event is directly dependent upon the size of your event. Generally, you can scale the numbers of volunteers you'll need on the day of the event based on the number of attendees you expect. The primary role of the volunteer is to serve the guests and perform support functions in varying capacities. The numbers in Exhibit 11.5 are

**Exhibit 11.5   Sample Volunteer Staffing Levels**

| Volunteer Job | # of Volunteers Needed (per 100 bid units) |
|---|---|
| Volunteer Coordinator | 1 (can be more if assistant coordinators are required due to large number of guests/volunteers) |
| Reception/Registration | 2 (depending on if using qCheck™) |
| Expediters | 1 |
| Troubleshooter/Customer Service | 1 (total) |
| Silent Auction Table Closers | 2–3 (may use the same for each Silent Auction; depends upon number of items) |
| Live Auction Display Assistants | 2 |
| Live Auction Floor Auctioneers/Spotters | 2 |
| Live Auction Runners | 2–3 (depending on if using qCheck™) |
| Number Turner | 1 total |
| Recorders | 2 total (3 if using Bidder Recognition; ideally 3 for Fund-an-Item) |
| Data Entry (computers) | 1 |
| Cashiers | 2 |
| Cashier Assistants | 1 |
| Auction Filers | 2–3 (may be the same as cashiers) |
| Emcee or Announcer | 1 total |

## Optional Jobs

Greeters _____ 1

Salespeople (raffle, rose, diamond bar, balloon) 2–4 (per revenue generator)

Item Packaging/Pickup _____ 3–4

Coat Check _____ 1

Photographer _____ 1

Slides/Video Presentation_____ 1

Miscellaneous_____ 2

designed to help you gauge the number of volunteers based on the number of buying units you have attending. Remember that we defined a buying unit as either a single guest with a bid number or a couple sharing a number.

Use the numbers in Exhibit 11.5 as a general guideline; you'll tailor your actual volunteer staffing levels based on the activities you will have at your event and on any professional help you'll already have, such as professional event staff or data entry support. Also, if you are in doubt as to how many volunteers you should have in any area, err on the side of more, rather than less. It's always better to have more volunteers than you need. That way, you have the luxury of a pool of people you can move around or repurpose as conditions change, or you can allow volunteers to work in shifts, giving each of them breaks during the event. It's always better to have a volunteer who is looking for something to do than have guests standing in line because you don't have enough staff to manage the flow.

Not all of these volunteer counts have to correspond to a single individual. Many of these jobs can be doubled up. For example, the greeters and reception volunteers can also be a part of the cashiering team, or part of the Live Auction staff. Likewise, volunteers working in the Silent Auction as closers can also work as Live Auction recorders, spotters, or runners later in the event. How much you can repurpose people will depend on the size of your event, your available volunteer pool, and the volunteers' willingness to keep busy throughout the event or preference to work in shifts.

CHAPTER

# 12

# Conducting the Event

After months of planning and organizing, you've arrived: It's auction time! Now you need to put those processes in place that will help you manage the flow of the event as smoothly and efficiently as possible.

The processes we'll describe and recommend here are ones that have been tested literally thousands of times, at a large variety of events, from quite small to extremely large. While some variations are possible and acceptable, as a general rule you should not try to improvise, but go with what's been proven to work. If you do so, you should come to the end of the evening feeling successful and happy that your guests were treated well, arrived in good spirits, and will not only return, but will also recommend your event to others next year!

## Managing Registration

The process of managing your registration function is more than just making sure your guests arrive, get their packets, and start spending money. It's the very first impression your guests have of your event, so you want to make that impression a good one. If registration appears to be barely controlled chaos, with volunteers flying around looking confused and harried and a long line of folks waiting to get into the venue, many of your attendees are likely to opt out of standing in a horrendous line, will head straight for the bar, and will just bypass registration altogether, figuring they'll come back later.

And what has that done? Well, your guests are now in the Silent Auction area, where you're hoping they will be generous and support your cause, but they do not have the tool they need to do their job—they have no bid numbers. So, as they walk around the Silent Auction, looking at the displays you've spent so much time putting together and the terrific items you've assembled, they'll be lookers, not shoppers, and will just wander by without placing a bid. Even if they plan to return once they have their bid number, something may occur that prevents them from coming back.

For those guests who elect to remain in line, the effect on your auction is equally bad, if not worse. Guests who are standing in long lines at the beginning of the evening are already mentally calculating *how long the line will be at the end of the evening.* They are getting grouchy at having this kind of start to the event and thinking that if things are so disorganized at the start, how much more disorganized they will be as the night progresses. They'd like to get into the venue, get a drink, see the items, and socialize with friends, but instead, they are standing in a long line that doesn't appear to be moving very quickly.

**Guests Arriving for Registration**

This poorly managed registration process has several potential effects:

- Your guests may make a conscious decision to leave the event early so that they don't get caught in another long line at the end of the evening. That can cost you revenue, because people who are not in their seats are no longer supporting your event by bidding or raising their paddle.
- Guests may decide to show up later next year "to avoid the crush." That means you'll have fewer buying units available to bid during the Silent Auction, which directly affects your Silent Auction yield.
- They may decide not to return at all next year because of the hassles they encountered this time. And the negative impression may carry over to other people they know who are either guests now or might be in the future. In some circles, the "regular" guests at fundraisers are a tightly knit group who talk about the events they attend. You don't want to be known as the event that doesn't have its act together!

The processes and procedures that follow in these sections will help you avoid these lines, handle guest interaction efficiently and smoothly, and show you how your event can be legendary for its organization and flow, ensuring that your guests get in, get their stuff, and get bidding as quickly as possible—and in a great frame of mind to be generous!

### Guest Check-In

When a couple or individual arrives at your event, they fit into one of three general categories:

- Preregistered guest
- Registering guest
- Volunteer working for your organization

It is the job of the volunteers working at the registration table to determine the category to which the new arrival belongs and to handle their registration and check-in appropriately, so the guests can start bidding on items as soon as possible. In the following sections, we'll discuss how each type of guest differs, and then we'll continue with a discussion about how to continue once the unique handling of each type of guest is complete.

**Preregistered Guests** Earlier, in the discussion on registration packets, we covered a part of the process involved in handling preregistered guests. As a quick recap, however, remember that preregistered guests have sent in their

RSVP cards for the event already and have generally paid any entry fees. As a result, their bid packets have been preassembled and should be filed by their last name, waiting for their arrival at registration.

When the guests arrive, their registration packets are pulled by the expediter and handed to the registration volunteer. If any money is due for entry fees at this time, the registration volunteer informs the guest, who can choose to pay this fee at this time via a check, or, if your auction software has this capability, can request to have the entry fee added to their other day-of-event charges.

**Registering Guests**   Registering guests are those people who come to the event wishing to support your cause who either did not receive an invitation or received it and didn't have time to send it in. Generally speaking, both kinds of guests are considered walk-ups because you will not have specific registration packets ready for them. If the guest is an invited guest, chances are he or she will be in your event database. All other walk-ups are likely new to the organization, and their information needs to be added to your system.

In both cases, you will give these types of guests the next sequential walk-up packet that you prepared in advance. You will also need to get a payment from them for the event entry fee—again, you can accept a check for the amount now, or add it to the day-of-event charges if they prefer and if you have that ability.

**Volunteers**   One of the benefits of being a volunteer for the event is that all volunteers can be assigned bidder numbers without having to pay for entry into the auction. Volunteers will not need to get a full bid packet as would other types of attendees, but you will assign them a bid number and associate that with their name at registration, if you haven't already done that as part of your pre-event logistics. Volunteers can pick up a catalog at registration along with their bid cards, which they will need if they want to bid in the Live Auction.

Once you know which type of guest you are working with and have the right type of bid packet, you can continue with the registration process.

### Verifying Guests' Addresses

As part of your ongoing process of developing relationships with guests, donors, sponsors, and anyone connected with your organization, you will want to make sure you always have current information for them in your database. A great time to check with your guests for any address changes is when they come to your event.

It's simple and quick to do this at registration if you're properly prepared. If this is a step you want to include in registration, then as part of the bid packet you created for your guest, you should make sure to have a regular business-sized envelope preprinted with the guest's name, current address, and bid number. You can either print this information on the envelopes or simply use mailing labels you can preprint from your computer.

When the guest arrives at registration, pull this envelope from their bid packet and ask the guest, "Are you still at 123 Elm Avenue?" For privacy reasons, you probably don't want to read the entire address; the street address will generally be sufficient. If the guest confirms that this is still their address, you're done. If they let you know that the address has changed, give them the envelope and ask them to write their new address on it. You can drop the envelope in a basket at registration for later pickup to take to the filing/data entry area. Any address changes can be put into the database directly from this envelope so that the thank-you letters you'll be sending to your guests will go to the right place.

### Preauthorizing Payments

As the guest is waiting to receive a registration packet, the registration volunteer should let them know about prepayment options available so the guest can avoid the cashiering line at the end of the evening. Most of the time, this prepayment authorization involves credit card processing, but this also works if you get a check from the guest in advance.

**Guest Using qCheck™ Option at Registration**

The key message that guests need to know about prepayment authorization is that

- If they take care of this during registration, there's no need to come back to cashiering to settle up at the end of the evening. No more waiting in line.
- If you have selected to use the receipt delivery process, the guests will have their guest receipts delivered to them at their table during the Live Auction. Again, no line at checkout.
- They will be mailed a final statement of their charges at the end of the event. No reason to stand in a line waiting for that this evening, either.
- If they don't buy anything during the event, no amount is charged to their card.

With this approach, nearly every attendee will opt for the preauthorized payment option. It's important that you allow this to remain an option, however, and don't force it on the guests. For varying reasons (such as concerns about the security of the bank card processor, personal policy about use of credit cards, preference to pay by check at the end of the evening), the guest may decline the prepayment opportunity. That's fine. If they don't want to use this option, thank them and just continue completing their registration.

If they choose to preauthorize their payment, at this point you would take a swipe of the credit card per your bank card processor's procedures. If you are accepting checks for prepayment authorization, you'll have the guest fill out a check payable to your organization, but with no amount indicated. When you receive the check from the guest, be sure to write their bid number on it for tracking purposes. Once you've completed the guest's registration, take this check and make sure it is either placed in the business-sized envelope you are using for address corrections (as discussed earlier) and then is filed in the guest's bid folder, or staple it directly into the guest's bid folder if you are not using business-sized envelopes. This way, you can be sure this blank check doesn't slip out of the guest's folder.

Once your guest has qChecked$^{TM}$, you need to indicate somehow that they've done this. Depending on your bank card processing software and its integration to your auction software, the software may do this automatically for you. But if you don't have this capability, and as a backup in case there's a rare problem with the technology (or other conditions that prevent you from using this automatic feature, like a problem with electricity where you are set up), you'll want to have a paper backup that tells you your guest has preauthorized. If you're using #10 envelopes, this is easy; simply mark a *Y* or *Q* on the front of the envelope, right where the stamp would normally go.

You can use this same approach if you are collecting RSVP cards or registration cards at the event.

### Filing Registration Materials

Once the guest has left registration, there are just a few behind-the-scenes actions you will take to make sure their presence at your event is properly noted. You'll want to be sure that someone at registration has the duty to regularly pick up the business-sized envelopes that are placed in the filing baskets or boxes after guests have been registered. Those envelopes need to go to data entry if you need to manually note which guests have selected Express Checkout. If you don't need this step, then the envelopes go directly to the filing area, where they are filed in guests' bid folders, by bid number. If a guest has qChecked, it's not a bad idea, as another manual backup process, to indicate this on their bid file by making a quick mark on the tab with a bright highlighter. This gives anyone working with filing and delivery of guest receipts an instant visual cue that this guest has prepaid and can be given their guest receipts immediately.

## Managing Your Silent Auction

As we discussed earlier in this book, most auctions have a Silent Auction, divided into one or more sections, that precedes the Live Auction. Because Silent Auctions typically have many more items than Live Auctions, there's quite a bit of work to be done as the sections close to make sure that items are properly tracked to winning bidders, the amount raised by these items is recorded, and guests are correctly charged for their purposes. This section will cover all those processes to help ensure your Silent Auctions are handled efficiently and easily.

### Bidding in the Silent Auction

As your event progresses, guests will begin bidding on items in your Silent Auction sections. To make sure they can do this easily, check to see that the following conditions are in place:

- Does each item have a pen next to the form? Ideally, remove the caps from any pens. This will help ensure pens stay with the items, because people generally won't pick up and hold onto a pen that doesn't have a cap. Avoid using click-type pens or twist pens for this reason. Halfway through your Silent Auction, you may find that a good number of pens have disappeared.

- Make sure each item has the correct corresponding form. Guests can't bid on an item if there's no form, and the form needs to belong to the item and be obviously linked to it. Don't stack items and clutter forms near each other, or they could get mixed up.
- Have volunteers available to monitor the Silent Auction. As the volunteers patrol the sections, have them check forms to see if any Guaranteed Purchase boxes (if you're using this method) are filled in. If so, have them close out the item and deliver the completed bid forms to data entry. Removing the forms as soon as Guaranteed Purchases are completed will help the flow of item management, because you'll have fewer items left to enter and file at the close of each Silent Auction section. Also, when guests see that several items are selling as Guaranteed Purchases, it helps build a sense of urgency that they had better "buy" the items that interest them or those items may not be available.
- Have volunteers who are on patrol also check forms to see if any bid steps have been skipped. If so, have them draw a line between the two bids that bracket any empty bid steps. This prevents guests from accidentally entering a lower bid than the present high bid and helps eliminate confusion.

### Closing Your Silent Auction

Closing your Silent Auction section refers to ending the auction for that section per a defined schedule and making the items in that section unavailable for further bidding. The procedures for closing the Silent Auction are fairly simple, but it's important to do them in an organized fashion as a matter of efficiency, to minimize confusion and double work.

As described in the previous section on bidding, while the Silent Auction is open, table closers walk around the Silent Auction and close out any Guaranteed Purchase bids to avoid confusing guests who might think that any forms remaining on the tables while the Silent Auction is open means those items are still available for bidding. The auctioneer (or announcer) will begin a preliminary countdown from roughly 10 minutes before the scheduled closing time for that section until the actual closing time, periodically reminding the guests of the remaining time for that section. For example, the auctioneer might say, "There's only five minutes left to bid in the green section of the Silent Auction. This is a great opportunity to check your bids and make sure you are still the successful bidder on the items you want to go home with tonight!"

As the countdown to the closing of a section commences, the table closers—ideally, in teams of two individuals each for the actual closing—distribute themselves evenly around that section. All table closers need to be in position no later than two minutes before the actual close to be ready for the close and to hear any last-minute instructions that may come from the auctioneer. Once the auctioneer announces the section is closed, the first person in each team picks up the pens by each form. This prevents guests from "sneaking" in a final bid after the close, but this problem can be avoided by using the soft close technique (see the sidebar). The second person quickly progresses down the line of Silent Auction forms, circling the highest bid amount (checking the Guaranteed Purchase box first) and associated bid number. To avoid circling the wrong bid, we recommend you train your volunteers to start looking at the last bid on the form (typically the Guaranteed Purchase box) and scanning in reverse order across the bids until they come to the first one—that's the highest bid. If you start from lowest to highest, there's a tendency to miss the Guaranteed Purchase entirely and circle an incorrect winning bid.

The first person can now follow the second closer, tearing off the top two copies of the bid form (if you are using three-part NCR forms as we've recommended), leaving the third copy on the table with the item. The top two copies of the form are then brought to data entry, where they are logged in and filed. The third copy of the form is attached to the item, becoming the item tag.

## About the Soft Close for Silent Auctions

There are two philosophies about how to close Silent Auctions. The first way, which is most traditional, is to close based on the clock. That means that when the auctioneer counts down the time remaining for bidding on that section, when he or she reaches zero, that section is closed—no more bidding is allowed in that section. The benefits are that the section is closed at one designated time and all forms can be picked up right away. The potential negative is that, if two or more people are really interested in an item, they may resort to shenanigans to ensure they get that item, even if the section is closed. These tricks include adding a last, final bid, after the auctioneer has closed the auction, at an amount higher than the real one on the form at the time of the close, or crossing out someone's previous bid and substituting the new bid number for the original. Or they may suddenly be motivated to put a bid in the Guaranteed Purchase box and circle that amount and bid number as though the form was "closed" before the real table closers had a chance to circle the actual winning bid.

The soft close gets around most of these problems because it allows bidding to remain open on items that are very popular and have active bidding, even though the auctioneer has called that section closed. If two or more guests are actively bidding on an item, the table closers bypass that item, allowing the guests to ``bid out'' that item until they are done. If someone puts their number in the Guaranteed Purchase box, the item is closed. If other bidders drop out and only one remains, the item is finished and the table closers can close out the form.

The soft close is really much more civilized than the traditional time-based hard close, in that it does not force a guest to stop bidding just because the clock has run down on that section. There's no arguing about who was the last bidder or whether the last bid was put in the box when the auctioneer drawled out ``Clo-'' or ``-osed.'' Also, if you allow your guests to bid on the item until *they* are done, your yield on that particular item will likely be higher than if you'd just arbitrarily ended the bidding when the clock ran out.

### Filing and Backroom Procedures

Filing Silent and Live Auction forms and other paperwork is probably one of the most menial, yet critical, activities of the whole event. Even if you are using auction software, it is imperative that you have and use a paper backup system. The process we recommend is what we call an "automated manual system," one that uses technology and tools to their maximum advantage, but that is designed on a paper-based system that enables you to continue to manage the auction smoothly in the unlikely event that some of your automated processes can't be completed because of a problem. While it may sound redundant, we've been able to use this system and recover without guests knowing there's a problem when drinks were spilled on a computer, crashing it; during power outages, even in the midst of a rare summer thunderstorm in Southern California where the committee made *no* provision for dealing with inclement weather. There's nothing to beat a good insurance policy, and when it comes to auctions, preparing for the worst case is your best insurance policy.

When bid forms come from either the Silent or Live Auction area, the top two copies of the forms typically are brought to data entry. Note here that the process we are describing assumes you are using a three-part NCR-type (white/yellow/pink) bid form, as we recommended in Chapter 11. At that point, the information on the bid forms is entered into the computer. As each form is entered, the form is placed in an out-basket or -box, ready for the filing staff. Filing then continues using this process:

1. The copies are separated into the original (white) copy, and the yellow copy. The original copy is placed into a file folder labeled "Silent Auction Originals." If you have a large number of items or several Silent Auction sections, you may want to make a separate folder for each section. These original bid forms will be put in order by catalog (item) number once all forms for that section have been collected and split. Be sure you store these originals in a safe, but easily accessible, place in case guests have questions about their bids later. By filing them in numeric order, you can very quickly look up the original form, and by keeping them separate, you have a backup in case the winner's folder is lost or guest receipts are misplaced.

2. A second volunteer takes the guest copy of the bid form (yellow) to a second station, where gift certificates should be filed in a box, in numeric order by catalog number. The volunteer filer looks to see if there is a gift certificate in the file for the item. If there is, the volunteer staples the certificate to the yellow copy of the invoice.

3. The bid form, with gift certificate attached, is ready for filing into guest bid folders. The yellow bid forms—the guest receipts—are now filed into the bidder's folder by additional volunteers. The process continues until all Silent Auction sections are closed and all bid forms have been entered and filed.

These first three steps occur regardless of whether any follow-on processes, like guest receipt delivery, occur. We'll discuss how to handle those optional procedures in a moment. After you've completed Steps 1–3, you have all your forms filed. Live Auction bid forms are handled the same way you would handle Silent Auction forms. There are a couple of exceptions that, while guests are being charged, you may not have an actual "form" to file for that charge. These exceptions are:

- *Cash donations.* Fund-an-Item donations are recorded on an original recording sheet, but generally, there are no duplicate receipts for donations that need to be filed in the guests' folders. Fund-an-Item donations will appear on their final receipt, so usually that is sufficient. If you choose to create one for each bid, that's fine, but understand that these forms will need to be created (ideally, you should create them in advance when you generate your other forms, and have the donation amount—$5,000, $2,500, and so forth—indicated on the

## Filing Silent and Live Auction Forms

form so a volunteer only has to check a donation level and enter the bid number when transcribing these bids from the recording sheet to the guest's Fund-an-Item "receipt." Then these receipts can be filed in the guest's folder, just like any other bid form. Raffles are generally handled the same way.

- *Bar tabs.* If you allow guests to pay for any nonhosted drinks at the event using their bid number, there usually isn't a paper receipt for those drinks. The charges will appear on their final receipt and for most purposes, this is fine.
- *Sweeps.* If you have items that are sold by the couple—like a margarita party for 20 couples, or a custom art class for up to 30 children—these items are generally not sold off one at a time. Instead, they are "swept" off in the Live Auction, where the top 20 bids are recorded and each one wins a slot at the party. Alternatively, they can be sold off during the Silent Auction using sweep bid forms, as discussed earlier in this chapter. While there *may* be individual certificates for the winning bidders, sometimes there aren't preprinted bid forms for each slot. The sweep sheet is the original recording sheet, and data entry is done using this sheet. While the winner may receive a certificate, which is filed in the bid folder, there may be no separate bid form to file as well.

Before we leave the topic of filing, let's quickly discuss two potential variations that committees sometimes use. As you are evaluating whether you want to use these variations, consider the pros/cons of each.

- *Alternative to Step 1.* Instead of separating whites (originals) from the yellows (guest receipts), some organizations choose to file both copies directly in the guest's bid folder, after attaching the gift certificate to the yellow copy. The idea is to keep the full sets of forms in the bidder's folder, and, after guest receipts have been picked up or delivered to the table, the white copies still remain in the guest's folder as backup to the guest's receipts. This approach is fine, but there is a risk that the guest's folder might be misplaced or lost (yes, it sounds unlikely, but when many people are working in those folders in various capacities through the event, and with all the paper handling that occurs, it *does* happen). If so, you will have to rely on the pink copy of the bid form as your backup if you need to research bid information. Keeping the whites with the yellows can also cause problems for your audit if the whites are misplaced, because generally, after the event, all your pink copies of bid forms will have gone home with the item (remember the pink copy becomes the item tag after the Silent Auction is closed).

- *Alternative to Step 2.* One practice is to keep all gift certificates in the filing area until guests come to pick up their items, instead of delivering them to tables. The concern is that the gift certificates will be lost somewhere between the filing area and where guests are seated. This concern can be minimized by training runners to verify guests' bid numbers before they hand them their package of guest receipts. Runners are told that they must *never* simply leave the guest receipts on the table, regardless of whether certificates are attached. If a guest is away from the table at the time receipts are delivered, the runner simply takes them back to the filing area to either try delivery again in a subsequent pass through the Live Auction area or to be filed in the guest's bid folder for pickup.

Now, once you've accounted for these possible exceptions, it's time to discuss your next steps. If you are delivering guest receipts to qChecked winning bidders, continue with this step.

### Delivering Guest Receipts

One of the nicest things you can do for your guests is to make sure they stand in as few lines as possible during your event. By delivering guest receipts to any attendees that have qChecked, you are helping them avoid a line at cashiering or checkout. Once winning bidders have their guest receipts in hand, they can go directly to item redemption once the Live Auction is over; or, if they have only items with gift certificates, they don't even need to stop at redemption—they are done and can head home without going anywhere *near* a line. That's good customer service and will leave a favorable last impression on your guests.

Since the process of delivering guests' receipts is really just a continuation of the processes we started in the previous section, we'll continue the sequential number of steps for clarity. There are some alternate procedures, which will we cover once the primary process has been introduced.

4. Receipt Delivery
   a. When the majority or all of the Silent Auction bid forms are filed into bidders' folders, you can begin preparing for receipt delivery by grouping together those receipts for qChecked bidders. Keep all their guest receipts (yellow copies) together using a paper clip, rubber band, or staple. Now, determine at which table the guest is sitting, and place the grouped guest receipts in a folder labeled by the table number. Continue through qChecked guests' folders, repeating the process and adding them to the appropriate table folder. An alternate method for this process is to use a table/bidder cross-reference list and look for all bid numbers seated at Table 1. Pull those bidders' guest receipts, still aggregating by bidder number, for any guests who are qChecked, and place them in the Table 1 folder.
   b. Once a table's folder is complete with bidders' guest receipts, give the folder to a runner, who then takes the guest receipts to the appropriate table. When at the correct table, the runner verifies the guest's bidder number against the bidder number on the packet of guest receipts and then hands the guest receipts to the correct guest. As we mentioned previously in the alternatives to attaching gift certificates, if the guest is not at the table, the runner does *not* leave the guest receipts at the table. Instead, the runner takes those guest receipts back to the filing area to make another pass at delivery later. Alternately, the guest receipts are filed back in the bid folder for pickup later.

      This process continues for the remaining tables and the corresponding qChecked guests. Live Auction guest receipts can also be delivered in this way once the Live Auction has started, but there comes a point toward the end of the evening where it is no longer feasible to get receipts out to the guests before the end of the Live Auction. Also, some guests have a tendency to table hop so they can socialize with friends once the Live Auction wears down. At that point, you will want to stop receipt delivery, file the remaining bid forms at cashiering/pickup, and simply wait for the guest to come to pick up their last remaining guest receipts. Since there will only be a very few of these, this process tends to have a negligible impact on the cashiering or pickup lines.

c. Guests who have not qChecked do not have receipts delivered to them. Instead, their receipts remain filed in the bid folders until the guest is ready to leave, at which point cashiers will get a payment for the event charges before giving guest receipts to the winning bidder.

If you choose to bypass delivery of guest receipts to tables, that's okay. There are times and events where it's simply not practical or feasible to do so, such as during a small auction in conjunction with a golf tournament. Also, delivering guest receipts obviously requires extra volunteers to serve as runners, and your event may simply not have enough bodies for this extra service.

If you *can* do it, it's a great convenience to your guests. If you can't, then the process of preparing bid folders for pickup and cashiering can continue in one of two ways, usually dictated by the number of guests at your event and the proportion of which you believe—or find during the event—to have qChecked.

5. If you are able to have a separate area to allow people who have qChecked to come to retrieve their guest receipts without standing in the same line as those guests who still have to pay, pull the bid folders for qChecked guests out of the general filing boxes and put them in a separate box, still filed in numerical bid number order. Move this box away to the pickup area. When qChecked guests arrive to get their guest receipts, you can just give them their receipts and they proceed to where items are to be picked up.

You're now ready to start generating temporary statements for your guests. At the very minimum, you'll need to print statements for those who have not qChecked and file those statements in the bid folders, so you know how much they'll need to pay at the end of the event, but if you would like to do so and have the time and staff to accomplish it, you can print and file the statements for your qChecked guests as a convenience.

The process now continues with the cashiering and checkout functions.

## Managing Your Live Auction

While the actual tasks involved in managing your Live Auction are relatively small compared to managing the Silent Auction, registration, and cashiering, these activities are still very important to handle well, since they involve how you deal with the bulk of your event revenue. The following sections will discuss various aspects of your Live Auction. Note that your committee may decide that your event won't make use of all of them, but we describe them here for your information, as well as provide recommendations for how to handle them.

### Bidder Recognition

Recognizing the generosity of the successful bidders is always in good taste. Some organizations that have a volunteer auctioneer or even a professional auctioneer make the mistake of making a big deal over the generosity of some bidders because they're well known, while they fail to equally recognize less-known bidders. Familiarity can be a trap if acknowledgment is not evenly offered for equal deeds. Imagine the following scenario:

> Mr. and Mrs. Jones are well known to the auctioneer and have been supporting the school for many years. During the auction, they successfully win an auction item valued at $5,000. The auctioneer is effusive in his praise: "Wow, how about that! Thank you, thank you to Bob and Mary Jones for that wonderful bid! You folks are the greatest and always so supportive!" Of course, the audience cheers and applauds. On the next item, a bidder unfamiliar to the auctioneer also pays $5,000 for an item, but since the auctioneer doesn't recognize this bidder he merely says, "Thank you to Bidder 148 for your generous bid and support!" Bidder 148 now feels like chopped liver, so to speak. They paid the same amount, but the recognition afforded the Joneses far surpassed that of Bidder 148.

Often organizations like to hire auctioneers who "know the crowd." Unfortunately, no auctioneer can *always* know everyone, and those who are good at their jobs realize that the guests with whom they are familiar are not the only successful bidders. Having a bidder recognition system is a great equalizer. It allows the auctioneer to be able to treat all guests fairly and with equal respect, regardless of his or her familiarity with the audience.

There are several approaches a bidder recognition system can take, from a basic "cheat sheet" cross-reference list, with bidders listed in numerical order by bid number, to high-tech computerized systems that can show the winning bidder on a display screen for all the audience to see. The former—the printed report—is easily produced by your auction management software, which can also handle the computerized system in most cases. If you don't have auction management software, you can still produce this cross-reference list, but it may involve more work. With the computerized system, an assistant sitting next to the auction stage types the winning bid number on a laptop computer and the display screen pops up the corresponding name or names assigned to that number. Additional information, such as the winner's entry level to event (patron, benefactor, or corporate sponsor) can also be displayed. It's also possible to display the hometown of the bidders, so the auctioneer can really appear to know everyone in the room even if this is the first time he has worked this event. The decision to display this information on a small computer monitor that just the auctioneer can see, or to display it on a large screen for the entire audience, is the choice of the committee.

Even the low-tech printed report of bidder numbers and names enables the auctioneer to be knowledgeable about the audience and recognize each successful bidder by name, which is the proper thing to do in nearly all cases.

As an additional expression of recognition and appreciation, some organizations will send a volunteer out to the successful bidder with a small gift. This can be anything from a flower to a chocolate wreath on a ribbon (which might be related to the auction theme), a medallion with the year and organization name on it, or some other small token of appreciation from the committee for the bidder's generosity. Some groups also send a bottle of wine or champagne to a successful bidder's table, if appropriate.

## Bidder Recognition Gifts to Avoid

Some committees like the idea of sending out helium-filled balloons or something similar to recognize successful bidders. While this may seem like a good idea, there are several drawbacks to this plan. First, consider what happens when you have 400 guests in the room and you have 30 Live Auction items to be won. You now have 30 medium-sized objects—bigger than the centerpieces we warned you about previously—that can potentially block the auctioneer's and other guests' sight lines. This can cause a problem identifying bid cards as the event progresses and may keep other guests from viewing competitive bidding.

Another problem is that if, on average, one-third of your guests are successful bidders, some of them will be amassing a very noticeable collection of balloons. Most people don't want to be that obvious about their generosity and bidding history. If you're going to go with balloons, it's more diplomatic to instruct your runners to stop sending balloons to a winning bidder once two or three balloons have been ``awarded.''

> For these and other reasons, we suggest that you select a relatively inexpensive, but decent bottle of champagne or wine—or similarly desirable gift—to send to your winning bidders. Not only is it subtler, but the winner can choose to share it amongst the whole table or discreetly take it home.

A bidder recognition system will place all bidders on an equal footing for their generosity. It's important that you say "Thank you" as early and as often as you can to those who support your efforts. The auctioneer's thanking the bidder by name is the first step, a gift is the second, and, of course, a thank-you letter will follow the event.

### Staffing the Live Auction

Staffing your Live Auction requires fewer people than you needed for your Silent Auction. In general, you will need the following types of volunteers or staff to manage the Live Auction portion of your event:

- Recorders
- Spotters, if using
- Runners—in this case, runners who take the forms from the recorders' table to data entry after an item is sold. Also, if you are giving special recognition gifts to successful bidders, you'll need extra runners who can take these gifts to the winner's table.
- An emcee or announcer, if using, to assist the auctioneer
- Live Auction display helpers

Job descriptions for each of these positions appeared in Chapter 11.

Although this is not a strictly staffing issue, one topic that is worth pointing out here is that Live Auction recorders should always be prepared with extra supplies, including blank multipart bid forms, pens, blank paper, and a calculator, if desired. Frequently, the auctioneer may double up an item at the last minute, or sell something unexpected, if the audience is really into the spirit of the event and wanting to play. When a cake is sold during a Dessert Dash, then later one remaining slice of cake is auctioned off, *then* the frosting and remaining crumbs on the cake platter are also sold—well, there's no way to anticipate those items in advance, but it's the recorder's job to be prepared to keep up with these bids and the revenue they represent. (And, yes, this has been done in an event!)

*Filing and Backroom Procedures*

Live Auction filing is exactly the same as Silent Auction filing, except that invoices usually come in to data entry at a slower rate. The only time it is necessary to have a full staff filing during the Live Auction is if duplicate receipts for Fund-an-Item and sweep forms need to be generated and filed. After the runners have made the first pass on delivering guest receipts and certificates to the qChecked guests, deliveries then will slow to sending individual invoices and certificates out to guests. Some of the filers can now be transitioned into the role of becoming cashiers. Usually there is a group of attendees who finish dinner early and will want to check out about one-third of the way through the Live Auction. Although you try to encourage them to check out later to allow for greater accuracy in totaling and filing, guests do need to have the option to leave whenever they choose, so provide for some cashiering support at all times.

Other filers and volunteers may become responsible for generating guest receipts for revenue enhancers like the Fund-an-Item, but as we discussed previously, this is usually a step that isn't necessary and frequently is bypassed.

## End-of-Evening Cashiering

Generally speaking, the overriding objective guiding your management of cashiering at an auction is to keep in mind that your guests want to leave the auction venue as quickly as possible. By now, your guests have been at your event for many hours, and they have been very generous with their money and support during that time, so don't "reward" that generosity by inconveniencing them with long lines at the end of the event. Recall that the last impression can be a long-standing one, so it's important to know how a well-managed cashiering process runs and to keep lines to a minimum.

The first detail in ensuring cashiering goes smoothly is to make sure there are plenty of volunteers filing throughout the evening so you aren't scrambling at the last minute to finish up while people are trying to check out. If everything is filed in a timely manner, guests' folders will be ready by the time they wish to check out. Not having a guest's folder ready when they want to check out gives the impression that you are disorganized and unprepared.

Being properly staffed and equipped is very important when cashing people out at the end of the evening. Depending on the size of your auction, there should be at least one cashier for every 50 buying units. This assumes you are not using some form of prepayment authorization method (e.g., qCheck). If you have used a qCheck process, you can probably manage adequately with one cashier for every 80–85 buying units because many guests are likely to take advantage of the qCheck option, which dramatically reduces your cashiering load. In addition to these volunteers, one extra person for every two cashiers should be responsible for pulling the guests' bid folders—expediting—when they are needed.

If you have made use of the option to deliver guest receipts to qChecked attendees, you will likely have very few guests in a cashiering line at the end of the event. However, to help streamline flow, you may want to have one or more of your volunteers—the greeters or runners—who are currently not assigned to a job be in the cashiering area to help remind qChecked guests that they do not need to stand in line at cashiering. This will help flow control and shorten the line for any remaining guests who did not qCheck or who have special cashiering needs.

### The Cashiering Process

The standard process we recommend for cashiering is one that has been proven to work in many different auctions of many different sizes. Just as we set up for registration, we use a method that makes use of one primary line that feeds to "any available cashier." In the process that follows, we're assuming that the only people that are coming to cashiering are those who genuinely need to settle up their charges, since the other guests have already received their guest receipts or have gone to the checkout area to pick up their guest receipts.

When the guest approaches the cashier to settle up, the following takes place:

1. The volunteer asks for the guest's bidder number. The cashier, or an expediter, will get the bid folder for that guest from the filing box. Once the cashier has the file, the guest can be told how much to pay based on the printed statement in the folder. If you aren't using auction software, you will need to tally (carefully) all the guest receipts and receipts for cash donations and such on a calculator, and give the guest that total.

2. Your guest can now settle up using a credit card, by writing a check, or by paying cash for the auction charges. If the guest writes a check, remember to write the bid number on the check for reference. Then, staple the check, along with a copy of the statement or a sheet showing the total, inside the front flap of the bid folder. If the guest pays with cash, make sure you take cash for the exact amount and staple that cash into the bidder's folder just as you would a check.

3. You can now give the guest their guest receipts (yellow copies), with gift certificates attached if you've used that part of the filing process. The guest is now free to pick up any tangible items and head home.

## About Cash Payments

As we discussed previously, we strongly discourage using cash at your auction and recommend that you allow your guests to pay for their event charges using their bid number. Some guests may choose to settle up their event charges with cash, and if they have given you the exact amount due on their statement, that's terrific. However, if you need to make change, you have a challenge. You should not allow each cashier to have a separate cash box for change, because trying to reconcile that at the end of the evening will be a nightmare. Also, because of the potential risks of theft or loss whenever cash is present, you want to be doubly and triply sure that there isn't even the semblance of potential impropriety. As we mentioned before in a previous sidebar, any volunteer who is involved with cashiering, especially if handling cash, should not be consuming alcohol during the event.

If you have to make change, the safest way to do this is to designate *one* cashier supervisor who is personally responsible for the cash and has enough change to break large bills. You'll have to estimate how much change you are likely to need and carefully account for how much has gone in and how much change has been made so you can balance the cash box at the end of the event. Cash can be tricky, so if you can possibly avoid using it at your event, accepting only checks and credit cards for payments, that's the ideal case. You may even want to make your guests aware of your payment policy in advance by putting it on the invitation and RSVP card, so there are no surprises when the guest comes to cashiering.

4. Remember to thank the guest liberally for their generosity and wish them a good remainder of the day or evening before the guest leaves the cashiering table.

5. The bidder's file folder can now be put back into the filing box, if you want to keep all file folders together, or you can place them in a separate area for filing in an area you designate as *paid and picked up*. This can be one of your earlier registration boxes that has been repurposed for this use, or it can be the front or back section of the bid folder box, with a tab or cardboard that you use to indicate these are already *paid and picked up*. It's also not a bad practice to write "PAID—check inside" as a visual reminder that this bidder has paid and guest receipts have been turned over to the guest.

In summary, this is the general process you'll need for cashiering. Ideally, you'll have enough people to staff this function, and many guests will have chosen to use your express payment option, which will cut down on the workload—and lines—dramatically. No doubt you will encounter several questions from guests and volunteers during the cashiering process, and the following section will provide you with some of the most typical and the answers to them.

### Common Cashiering Questions

As auction consultants, we are often called up to answer questions that bidders or committee members ask at the end of the event or deal with situations that come up. For your convenience, here are some of the more common questions that bidders will have and the answers to those questions.

> Q: This guest has come to checkout and they are a qChecked guest; what do I do?

> A: If there is nobody to filter qChecked guests out of the cashiering line, kindly let them know that they are free to pick up their items and go home if they have received all their guest receipts and gift certificates. If the guest has not received all the guest receipts for items they were expecting, check inside their bid folder—there may be one or more last-minute items that you weren't able to take to their table (if you are delivering receipts), or perhaps they weren't at the table when the receipts were brought out. And make sure it matches what they think they bought.

> Q: The guest is sure they were the successful bidder on this item, but it isn't in their folder—what should we do?

> A: In this situation, using auction software can help you answer this quickly. The program makes it possible for you to go review the items sold to see which bidder number is shown as the winner for this item. If this still doesn't answer the question, you will need to go back to the original bid form for the item to see what bid number is listed as the winning bidder. Most of the time, the guest will see that someone else actually won the item after they placed the last bid, but if it turns out the guest *is* the high-bidder, you know it's just a clerical problem and the form may have ended up in the wrong folder, so you know where to look for it.

> Q: There was supposed to be a gift certificate with my item, but it's not attached to my guest receipt. What should I do to get it?

> A: This situation can occur for a few different reasons, but the solution and the answer are generally the same in any case. The most obvious

first step is to check your folder or filing box where gift certificates were originally stored; perhaps someone merely forgot to attach it to the guest receipt before filing. Another possibility is that if your committee didn't do a complete inventory to match specific certificates to items before the day of the auction, the gift certificate was not received as part of the donation. It's also possible that the item was doubled up during the event, and only one gift certificate was available at the auction. Finally, it's possible that the gift certificate was inadvertently attached to a different guest receipt, and that this error will be discovered by the guest with the unmatched certificate. Unless it's the first case, this isn't a situation that can be resolved at the event. The easiest way to handle this is to provide the guest with a form letter (we call this an ''oops'' letter) you have available at cashiering that tells the guest what to do in a case where a certificate is either not available or missing. Generally, the ''oops'' letter apologizes for the inconvenience and lets the guest know that he or she will need to call your office or the Chair responsible for procurement on the first business day after the event to get any missing certificate or item.

Q: The item I won is too big to take home tonight; how can I get it home?

A: Ideally, if you have overly large or cumbersome items in your auction, you should have made contingency plans to handle this situation. Cashiers should have detailed information on delivery of oversized items or where they can be picked up after the event is over. This should be the responsibility of the Inventory/Storage Chair. As we mentioned in Phase I, providing delivery service to guests' locations within a reasonable distance from the event the next day or within a few days is a really nice touch and shows appreciation for your guests. Having this service available may increase your yield on these items, because your guests will tend to be reluctant to bid on large items if they are worried about how they'll get them home in their two-seater sports car, for example. Prearranged delivery removes that barrier to bidding.

Q: I qChecked at the beginning of the evening, and I know I'll get a final receipt in a few days. Can I still get a total of my charges?

A: Any guest, whether they qChecked or not, should be able to get an accounting of their auction purchases and donations. At the end of the evening, what we provide guests is not called a *receipt*; it is referred to as a *statement*. Receipts imply finality; they are what guests typically take to their tax preparer to account for potential tax deductions. Since you have not yet performed an audit of event charges and sales, you are not 100% sure that all charges are completely accurate. All non-qChecked guests also need to receive some form of statement at the end of the event, because this is what you use to settle their charges. qChecked guests may receive a statement if they request one, or if your committee has decided to generate a statement for all guests, regardless of payment status. If you are using auction software, this step should be relatively easy. When you print a statement on demand, point out to your guest that this is not yet a final receipt, but a temporary statement of charges. But do let your guests know that they will be receiving a final receipt in the mail within seven to ten days after your event.

Q: While not strictly a cashiering function, cashiering often gets asked if there are boxes that a guest can put items in for easy carry out.

A: It's a good idea to have boxes, paper bags, shopping bags, or other supplies available for guests to consolidate their items so they can carry them more easily out to their car. Any Silent Auction items that are breakable, or came in their own packaging, should be repackaged before the guests come looking for them. That way, they get their item and go home. Even more convenient for guests is to have their items already gathered and arranged by bid number, so when they come to item pickup, all they have to do is pick up their bag (or bags) of items and walk out the door.

## Item Redemption

The final step in your day-of-event processes is to make sure your guests pick up the items they won during the Silent and Live Auctions. Again, keep in mind that the goal of this activity—as with all the other activities that touch the guests—is to make sure guests get the proper items as quickly and efficiently as possible.

The ideal process is one usually referred to as *secure redemption*. This process assumes that you have an area that can be secured in some way against guest access. Perhaps the redemption area is one where you can place a table across the entrance, with volunteers serving guests from the private side and guests waiting for their items on the public side of the table. Other alternatives are to cordon or rope off the area in which items are kept, or to have the area sectioned off in some similar way. Essentially, the idea is that the guests will not be getting their own items; you will have volunteers and event staff available to perform that function for the guest and deliver the items to the guest once collected.

The process for secure redemption is as follows:

1. When the guest comes to the redemption area, they present their guest receipts (yellow copies of bid forms) to the volunteer who is available to help.
2. The volunteer picks the items corresponding to the guest receipts from the redemption area and matches the catalog (item) number on each guest receipt to the item tag.
3. When items are collected and checked off, they are brought to and turned over to the guest.
4. As the guest receives each item, the item tag is removed from the item and initialed by the guest. The signoff on the pink copy is there to show that the guest did receive the item. The volunteer then takes the pink copy back and puts it in a box or basket for later filing, in numeric order, by catalog number.
5. The guest is ready to go home with all their terrific items, and the volunteer is ready to help the next guest.

Now, one thing to note: The process described above is the purest form of secure redemption. Step 4 is technically an option; most organizations do not require a positive control process that "proves" the item has been picked up by the guest. Most organizations will keep the pink copy attached to the item, and when the guest receives the item, both the guest receipt and the pink item tag go home with the guest. If you are concerned about proving that items were picked up by the guest, then you will want to use Step 4 as described.

Secure redemption also works if you've already collected and aggregated the items by bidder number. In this case, the volunteer only has to retrieve the collection of items, verify the item tags against yellow guest receipts, and the guest is ready to go!

As you can imagine, this process does require quite a few volunteers to get items for guests. This may not be feasible for your event, or perhaps your venue doesn't lend itself to securing the redemption area. In that case, you may want to try a variation of the secure process in which guests are allowed to collect their own items, but before they leave the area, their item tags are compared to their guest receipts and checked off by a volunteer near the exit. Other volunteers are standing by to help guests locate their items if they need help. This method requires fewer volunteers for redemption and still fulfills the original objective of making sure guests have the proper items, and only those items for which they have guest receipts.

Many events will bypass any type of secure redemption whatsoever and will simply allow guests to retrieve their own items. This isn't a method we would recommend, because you can see it's open to many different potential problems. But there are times where secure redemption just isn't feasible and you have to trust your guests to find the items they have bought, collect them up, and get home with all the pieces—but only the pieces that truly are theirs. After a long event, which may have involved a fair amount of drinking, you can quickly see why it's not only efficient but also a good practice to try to plan for some form of secure redemption at your event.

## Summary of Day-of-Event Logistics

Pat yourself on the back: At this point, you've successfully come through the day of your event and managed many different processes that all had to work together to work well. If you've implemented our recommended processes, you should have gotten all your guest and item collateral printed and organized well in advance. Your guests had complete packets preassembled and waiting for them when they came to registration. Guests were quickly and efficiently checked in, with minimal, if any, lines for them to endure. You were able to get the great majority of guests to preauthorize payments for auction purchases by taking a swipe of their credit card; this substantially reduced the number of guests who needed to come to cashiering at the end of the event.

During the auction itself, Silent Auction sections were closed in an orderly and quick manner. Data entry was able to keep up with recording winning bids, and the filers made sure all bid forms were matched to gift certificates and filed in bid folders. Guests who had preauthorized payments had their guest receipts delivered to their tables—again, no need to punish the guests for their generosity by imposing long lines on them! The few guests who did need to pay at the end of the event also had an easier time of it, as there were plenty of cashiers available to help them.

Finally, item redemption was set up in such a way that guests were able to quickly and conveniently get their items and head home, and your commit-tees were assured that the items that had been purchased by any given bidder actually went home with that bidder.

# PHASE IV

# CONCLUSION

Event day has come and gone, and you made it! Your guests were impressed by the atmosphere and energy at the auction, they were generous, they arrived and left happy because they had a good time with nothing to dampen their enjoyment. Your volunteers know they've done a great job that left a terrific impression on the attendees. Your committee can be proud of not only how organized things were, but also how smoothly everything ran. You were actually able to have some *fun* at the event, not just feel completely stressed out.

A lot of work led up to this day, and a lot of people were involved. Yes, the actual event is over, but there are still a few things left to do before you can breathe that huge sigh of relief and turn the reins over to the next committee and volunteers.

Phase V will guide you through those final steps, help you close the books on this year, and show you what steps you need to take now, while the memory of *this* event are still fresh so that you can not only celebrate this success, but plan for even better success for the next event.

# PHASE V

## POST-EVENT ACTIVITIES AND PLANNING FOR THE NEXT EVENT

*Phase V*
*Post Event Wrapup, Next Event Pre-Planning*

As we enter Phase V, there will be a tendency for your committee as well as the Chair to shrug their collective shoulders, exhale deeply, and say, "Whew! We did it! We are so glad that's *over*!" Not so fast. If the legacy you want to leave is one that will keep on living and rewarding generations of auction chairs and committees that will come after you, then your work is not quite done. You are almost done, but not yet.

Now that you did all that hard work planning, building the Steering Committee, structuring a successful event, putting all the pieces together,

231

and then watching the "magic" happen on auction day, wouldn't you really like to pass along all that you learned and save your replacement from having to start over once again? Of course you would. So, in Phase V we wrap up the prior event *and* begin planning for the next event. Like we said back in Phase I, auctions are a business that should never go out of business, but instead should operate on a continuum. The greatest gift you can give your organization is a formula for success, a plan that can be passed along to future committees, and a successful process that now merely needs to be managed, once you have put it all together.

By the way, successful implementation of Phase V will also mean that you will be able to "retire" from your duties without guilt and without continuous calls from your successor trying to figure out what to do, how to do it, and where to start, because you will have effected an orderly transition—a changing of the guard of which you can be proud, one that will not come back to haunt you when you least expect it! Remember, change is a good thing, but it must be gradual, happening over a long period of time to be most effective and for the change to stick. By properly fulfilling Phase V, you will ensure a gradual change, not force your successors to reinvent all the processes you learned, and the change will be evolutionary, not revolutionary—because, as we know, people get shot in revolutions! Your willingness to stay on past the event date to ensure an orderly and measured changing of the guard will be a lasting gift for which your organization will certainly be grateful.

In this last Phase, we will focus on wrapping up the current event by covering the following important areas:

1. The Post-Event Audit Process
2. Hosting the Post-Event Wrap-Up Meeting
3. Sending Out the Final Thank-You Letters
4. The Volunteer Party
5. Advance Planning for the Next Event

# 13

# Post-Event Activities

## Conducting the Post-Auction Audit

Even though the event is behind you, you have a few more steps to complete before your "tour of duty" is over. As important as it is to raise money, it is equally important to get that revenue in your bank as soon as possible so it can be spent supporting your cause. This cannot be completed until a post-event audit is conducted. The purpose of the audit is to accomplish six things:

1. Verify that all purchases have been accounted for by tracking each event-related successful bid, cash contribution/donation, and merchandise or raffle purchase to an attendee's bid number.
2. Double check that each successful bidder has a corresponding payment method on file, either credit card, check, or cash.
3. Compare all physical original bid forms and tracking sheets against database entries to be sure the official accounting in your database matches actual bids recorded at the event. This includes adding all last-minute and duplicated items that were added during the event.
4. Make sure all revenue (as listed on credit card statements or auction software statements) and any cash and checks received total correctly to the amount listed in post-event reports.
5. Make sure that the person listed as the purchaser was indeed the actual bidder who meant to buy that item.
6. Once all money is accounted for and the reports indicate each sale is tracked to the proper person, upload the credit card charges and deposit checks and cash into the bank.

You will also want to account for items that have not been sold, so you know exactly what has sold, to whom, and for how much. Knowing and accounting for the items that did not sell at the event serves two purposes:

1. It lets you know what categories of items did not sell well to your audience this time, so you can save time instead of trying to get similar items for the following event.
2. Nonsale items can be used as raffle and door prize items at volunteer appreciation parties after the event, or assigned to other events in the future.

Items that did not sell are generally not returned to their donors because, once donated, they belong to your organization. Title to the items changed hands when the donor made the contribution, so returning an unsold item is actually in poor taste and may insult the donor, who naturally will want to know why you were unable to sell "their" item. It is best to not go down that path. Of course, any items you may have taken on consignment must be returned, as you don't own those items unless they are sold and payment is made to the vendor or supplier.

It's also a good idea to remove the "catalog item" designation for any nonsold items in your database before you run your final yield reports. Your post-event yield report should include only items that actually sold; otherwise, you will be artificially holding down the yield percentage you earned for those items that did sell. This is because an unsold item still has value, but since it did not sell, there is no corresponding income from that item.

To conduct the post-event audit, start by making sure your database is up to date with all last-minute and duplicate items entered. If you are using good auction management software, you should be able to print a "Who Bought What by Catalog Number" report that will list all of the sold merchandise in order by catalog (e.g, Silent Auction items listed together, Live Auction, and so on). You can then compare this report to the original bid forms to be sure each item has been properly entered into the software. Often, you will find an incorrect entry during this step. Perhaps a bid number and bid amount were transposed, or a bid number such as 151 was entered as 115. As part of this process, you will want to make sure your cash contributions from your Fund-an-Item and your raffle and merchandise sales are also entered completely and accurately into the database. Making sure your paperwork corresponds to what appears in the computer is a critical step, and should not be bypassed.

After making sure all data is entered completely and accurately, it is important that all payments for the items sold can be completed. This requires that each successful bidder has either a credit card on file, a check for their purchases, or a credit for a cash payment. Each sale should be compared to the amount collected to be sure the bidder was neither overcharged nor undercharged. It is much easier to adjust a payment *before* charging the credit card than it is to make changes afterwards, when it becomes necessary to either get authorization to charge more or requires you to issue a credit. You will save many embarrassing phone calls if you take time to be sure that 100% of the amounts you charge to your guests' credit cards are accurate.

When you are certain that all charges are properly accounted for, all additional items are in the database and assigned to a bidder, and all bidders have a payment for their purchases and donations on file and for the proper amount, you are ready to upload the credit card charges and deposit the checks and cash into your bank. Once the money is in the bank and your post-event reports have all been run, your audit is completed.

## Hosting a Post-Event Recap Meeting

Assuming you and your committee have agreed that their current effort is not the end of the road, but represents just one step on the continuum of managing a successful business, you will want to conduct a post-event recap meeting. This meeting should be held as soon after the event as is practical. Some organizations actually hold some form of debriefing the day after the event—maybe over brunch the following morning—although this may not be practical for your organization. One fact is undeniable: The longer you wait to conduct this meeting, the less value it has.

Consider, for example, the Navy's elite flight demonstration team, the Blue Angels. They are known for their precision and grace flying high-performance FA-18 Hornet jets. Although they conduct more than 200 flying demonstrations each year, one routine they *never* bypass is their post-demonstration debrief. As soon as they exit their aircraft after their 30 minutes of exacting flight, they go immediately to the debrief room where they relive every moment of their flight. No detail is left off the table, and they conduct this debrief for one and a half hours, to allow enough time to put all issues in perspective. For them, it is a matter of safety—their lives literally hang in the balance. Despite conducting the very same routine hundreds of times, often on consecutive days, they still find issues to discuss and opportunities for improvement.

While your auction certainly isn't a life-or-death event, and you are not conducting more than 200 of these each year, it is still important to treat your post-event recap as serious business. Memory is clearest immediately after your auction is over. Each day that passes erodes your memory, rendering the information shared as less valuable. Imagine the loss in value for the Blue Angels if they waited a week after their flight to do their post-flight debrief! It would be nearly worthless. Therefore, recognize that a debrief conducted a month or two—even only a few weeks—after your event, will only hit the high points and gross errors. The real learning requires reviewing the details, and the details will surface only immediately after your event, while they are still fresh in everyone's minds.

With this in mind, we recommend that you conduct a post-event recap meeting the day after your event if at all possible, but certainly within a week. Meet before the memories fade and the interests of your committee turn elsewhere.

The post-event recap meeting should help you document answers and archive them for the next committee to use. Here are some tips for conducting the recap meeting. This is not an all-inclusive list by any means, and you will certainly want to add your own items to it:

- Capture the impressions of each of the committee chairs on paper and in a database.
- Identify the aspects of the event that occurred exactly as planned, and those that did not.
- Recap the performance of each of the vendors. Which did their jobs flawlessly and which did not perform as expected?
- Discuss the event logistics. Was there anything that could run more easily or smoothly had a little more planning been involved?
- Walk through the evening from the perspective of your guests. Did they get easy access, and did they have only few, if any, lines in which to stand, either on the way in or the way out? How were the registration and the cashiering processes? What could have been done better?
- How was the sound during the Silent and Live Auctions? Could the auctioneer be heard clearly?
- How was the lighting in the Silent Auction room? Were the bid forms easy to read, and were the displays properly illuminated?
- What could be done to display the items better the next time? How was the flow around the Silent Auction? Were guests able to get to the tables to bid, or did they encounter blockages or congestion that kept them from bidding?
- How was the catalog preparation, and was the catalog a useful tool for your bidders? Were the fonts and font size used readable, and the descriptions sufficient and adequate? Was the item content easy to read and accurate, including all necessary information and restrictions for your bidders to make informed decisions?
- Did the event stay on schedule? Did speakers stay within their allotted times? Did the event finish when it was supposed to, and did the Live Auction begin when it was supposed to?

- How did the guests respond to the event? Did they enjoying themselves? Was the "party" aspect a hit with your guests? What comments did guests share directly or were overheard?
- How did the preparation go leading up to the event date? Were auction items received in a timely manner, and did the RSVP process work well? Were bidder packets prepared in advance of the event? Were their any last-minute "crunches" or panic that caused stress?

Although jobs done well should be generously praised, the real purpose of this meeting is to catch, while fresh in everyone's memory, the impressions of your committee about how the actual event turned out, and the effectiveness of the planning that led up to it. This requires an open and honest exchange among all the committees, with no blaming, throwing of bombs, or oversensitivity. Fresh and accurate data is the first step toward continuous improvement, which is the goal of this recap. Once accurate data is captured, you can begin the improvement part of your process.

## Generating Thank-You Letters to Guests and Donors

You can never say "thank you" too early or too often. It is always a good idea to send a thank-you note to the donors immediately after they make their auction item donation. If you wait until after the event, the donor may not even remember that they made the donation, because they may have done so two, three, or even six months earlier. This would render a post-event "thank you" out of context with their act of generosity. It's best to send a donor thank-you note within a few days to a week after they make the donation, while it is still fresh in their memory. This accomplishes two important tasks:

1. It acknowledges the donation, so the donor gets an official confirmation of that donation in a timely manner.
2. It's an opportunity to begin building a stronger relationship for the future.

So few organizations send out thank-you notes in a timely manner (right after the donation is made is timely; right after the event is not), that by doing so, your organization will stand out in the donor's mind.

There is an old sales adage that to really get your message to sink in you must take a three-phase approach: "Tell them what you want to tell them; tell them; tell them what you told them." When approaching your thank-you letters, you should think in these same terms. Remember, you are not just managing an event this year, but you are managing a *business* that will be operational next year and into the future. Sending out an immediate acknowledgment and thank-you letter after a donation is made is just good business.

To build on that relationship with the donor, you should send out another thank-you letter after your event, letting the donor know how successful your event was and how their contribution was key to that success. This is the second time you get to say thank you. Then, when it's time to begin procurement for the next event, your solicitation letter should include an acknowledgment of their prior donation to remind them of their past generosity, and your stated wish that they continue the relationship. Note that by thanking the donor three times, each with a different purpose, you are building a relationship, and the donor will view your organization as different from others that merely come along once a year looking for something. Donors who receive continuous appreciation and reinforcement of their generosity are more likely to donate again, and sending three thank-you notes to a donor is a small price to pay for continuous support of your event and cause. By the way, good auction management software will track and even produce these thank-you letters automatically, so this three-touch approach should not be overly burdensome.

When sending thank-you letters to the guests that attended your event, you should use the same three-step approach. The first "thank you" is when the guest RSVPs for your event. You should acknowledge that RSVP with a note-card, e-mail, or some other written method that confirms you have their reservation and are looking forward to seeing them at the event. This is a good time to send out a hot sheet, if you're using one (see the Glossary for the definition), describing the bigger items and items that may have some complexity requiring prior consideration for active bidding. Or you may just want the note to just confirm the directions to and attire for the event, and the arrival time. This note would also be an excellent opportunity to refer the guest to your event Web site, where they can see a full catalog of the auction items if you are using MaestroWeb.com or cMarket.com for online catalog production and display. See the Resources section in this book for more information.

The second thank-you letter is sent to all attendees after the event (not only to those who purchased something), because you appreciate everyone who attended, not just those who spent money. Remember, you want to build relationships, and a guest who did not spend money this time might be a big spender at the next event, or may bring other guests who do. For those who did spend money, be sure to include a final statement and acknowledgment of their purchases with their thank-you letter. To conform to tax laws, you will need to do this for anyone making a cash or cash-equivalent contribution (e.g., for Fund-an-Item), so you might as well acknowledge all expenditures, not just those required by tax law. Again, if you are using auction management software, this task is automated and easily done, so don't bypass this step.

The third opportunity to say thank you is when you send out your Save-the-Date card for the following event. Having a customized version specifically for prior attendees is a nice touch and lets them know you remember that they attended the prior event. One line on that card, such as "As an attendee at our last event, we wanted to make sure you join us again for even more fun this year!" would be appropriate. You can save this step for the actual invitations, but the key is to acknowledge the guests' prior attendance. This shows your guests that they were not just faceless in the crowd—you are aware they attended, and you appreciate their support. This is all part of building a relationship and solidifying support for the future.

One final comment on thank-you letters, whether they are being sent to donors or to your guests: Some personalization is a must. Generic mass-produced letters are very impersonal and not worth the effort to send. Be sure each note has some personalization on it. For example, it would be easy for your volunteers to handwrite the addresses on the envelopes that are sent out to donors. Handwritten envelopes are more likely to be opened than those with mailing labels on them. On the letter, it would be nice if they were personally signed by the chair of the event. This sounds tedious, but remember, you are building a relationship and you can do the signing over several days while watching TV or taking a coffee break.

For larger donations, it is best that the donor be acknowledged with a special letter specific to their donation. In other words, a donation of a smaller Silent Auction item might result in a thank-you letter produced by the auction management software, but the person who donated a stay at their villa, a gourmet dinner for eight, a ride on their yacht, or their season tickets to the local pro sports team, should have a handwritten or at least personalized typed message, specific to what they donated. After all, they were significant contributors to your success, and the act of writing something special just for them helps show appreciation, builds the relationship, and increases the chances of getting that or a similar item from that donor the following year.

Remember, as you build your business, relationships become central to generating continuity and avoiding starting over each year. The simple act of thanking your supporters, whether they are donors, guests, volunteers, or committee members, is crucial to building your business.

## The Volunteer Party

Now that all the hard work of the auction is over, it's time to destress the committee, thank the volunteers, and begin planning for the following year. The volunteer party is your chance to offer up a great big hearty thank you to all those who generously gave their time to helping your business through a successful event. In the commercial world, this would be called an "office party'' or ''employee recognition party,'' and it's an important step in maintaining continuity from event to event. Retaining your key volunteers is just as important as retaining key employees, because having to start over by training new personnel each year is risky. It is much better to have volunteers who know the ropes, so to speak, because they have previously worked at the event or were involved during the event planning.

The party should be low-key with no auction business conducted beyond presenting some ''awards,'' which can be fun and humorous. Acknowledge the volunteers with some fun and inexpensive gifts to let them know you appreciate their hard work. Leftover items from the auction make perfect gifts to give volunteers. They can also be used as door prizes for a raffle at the party. Items that remained unsold generally did not sell for a reason; as such, they become a kind of ''white elephant'' type of item—perfect as a fun gift for door prizes at the party!

Here are some examples of some awards you could hand out at your party:

- The ''Who Turned Out the Lights Award'' for the last volunteer to leave the event
- The ''Who Turned On the Lights Award'' for the first volunteer to arrive for setup
- The ''Grace under Pressure Award'' for the volunteer who fielded the most problems with a cheery attitude
- The ''Jack of All Trades Award'' for the volunteer who jumped in to help in the most areas

You get the idea. Have some fun with it, create your own, personalize them, and keep them upbeat. Volunteers love to be acknowledged, and, like the guests at your party and the donors who contributed your auction items and cash, you can never say thank you too early or too often. The volunteer party is the beginning of the recruiting process for the following year. Wouldn't your job (or the job of your replacement) be easier if you knew most of your volunteers would be back for the following event?

# 14

# Planning for the Next Event

As we have stressed throughout this book, your success is measured not merely by what your single event accomplishes, but whether you are able to sustain that success through future events. Remember, we said right at the beginning that if you go into business, with the intent of going out of business the day after your first sale, you are really just throwing a party and hoping it makes money. True success comes from an attitude of accepting nothing but success, and then passing on to your successor what you have learned. The ability to prepare the table for those who follow in your footsteps will really be how you will be remembered, long after the memory of your party has faded and the money is in the bank. Clearly, you want to be remembered as the person who "set up our business process so we could have reliable funding from our event each year" rather than the person "who really knew how to throw a party!"

With this objective in mind, we enter the final step in our five-phase process, and that is the "pass the baton" phase. Actually, this phase began back in the early days of planning, when (hopefully) you preliminarily identified two or three possible successors to take over as cochairs of the event. They would have been recruited for the job early and would have had the opportunity to watch and learn along the way. One of the best ways to create fear, uncertainty, and doubt, as well as a lot of stress, is to suddenly throw responsibility on one or two folks without any warning and then hope they can handle it. This may have been what happened to you, but there is no reason you should continue that bad pattern! So begin recruiting early, and reassure your successors that the job will be made much easier for them because of the groundwork you have already done. Let them know their job this year is to observe, learn, and help where they can, and when they take over the following year, they will need only follow in your footsteps and manage the business. By creating continuity of this kind, you will remove much of the stress for your successor, find it much easier to recruit future volunteers, and create a legacy of which you can be proud.

With your assistance, your successors should recruit replacements for the Steering Committee as soon as possible. Remember, you no longer have just an "auction committee" that changes 100% each year; instead, you have a Steering Committee as a standing committee that does not go out of business. However, we have allowed for tours of duty to lapse, and certainly you will experience some natural attrition, too, as people move or other obligations take over. Getting the Steering Committee up and running at full strength is Job One. If at all possible, recruit leadership on the subcommittees from those individuals who worked on those committees previously in lesser roles. Rewarding and promoting from within is a basic business principle that also works on volunteer committees. When you must recruit new workers to replace the new leaders, assure the new volunteers that they have one year to work and observe before you will throw them into any leadership position. This will make recruiting volunteers easier as well.

At the same time you are recruiting the new committee, help the new leaders set the date for the next event, lock in the location, and book the auctioneer. The best venues and the best charity auctioneers will book up well in advance—up to a year in advance is not unusual on prime dates. If at all possible, if your new event leadership is known before your current event, it's a great idea to lock in the location before the current event occurs. This will allow you to announce both the chairs of the next event and the date and location of where it will be held to your guests. It really impresses guests when you can have an orderly transition of "power" by introducing your successor to your event's guests at the current event.

Once your date and location, and hopefully your auctioneer, are all in place, you should plan to meet one more time with the Steering Committee to introduce the new leaders and new members. It is not necessary to hold off on locking in the date and location of the following event until the first new Steering Committee meeting because too much time will have passed, and the opportunity to get the best dates and locations could have narrowed. Instead, assume the current (old) Steering Committee would make those determinations, and then pass that decision along to the new Steering Committee. Remember, since you are not changing all members each year, you already have continuity, so you are not taking the decision process away from the new committee. The newest members are not really in a position to make key decisions, such as date and location, anyway, as they are too new to the process. They will have the opportunity later in their term to affect the date and location for the event following their first term.

At this meeting of the new committee, quickly review the previous event's data, including:

- Net goal for event vs. actual net income (show your process works)
- The number of people who attended

- Your dollars per Buying Unit
- The number of items in the Live and Silent Auctions
- Additional revenue-enhancing elements you used
- Any logistical issues that occurred that need to be fixed
- Any personnel issues (volunteers or committee issues) that need to be addressed

As final activities during this meeting, you'll:

- Thank your committee for working so hard
- Sit down and let your successor take over from there (you are *done!*)

The new committee chair should now take your place and lead the Steering Committee through the steps for determining the new goal (based on dollars per Buying Unit, using your results as a baseline) and other forms of revenue that will all flow into the total event income. At this point, your job is over, but it is usually appreciated if your new status of Past Auction Chair allows you to serve in a consulting capacity to the new committees.

# PHASE V

# CONCLUSION

Congratulate yourself for a job well done. As you reach this point, you can feel confident that you have put in place processes that will truly transform your auction experience, not only this year, but year after year, as long as you continue to:

- Follow these proven processes (by now you should be a believer!)
- Continue to look for areas of improvement
- Be an advocate to put those improvements in place

While you have hopefully learned a great deal from this book, know that this is really only the tip of the iceberg. We have tried to cover many of the basics—those processes and issues to consider that make a critical difference between auctions that are successful and auctions that are not. But there is still plenty to learn, and once you have mastered these essentials, you can begin to explore areas where you can fine-tune your auction, change things up to keep things interesting, and continue to move the revenue line upwards and to the right.

There are many resources available to you and no shortage of people and companies with opinions of what is "right." In this book, we tried to share with you what we have seen as a formula for success, because the approaches we discussed are not theoretical, but are actual practices in place over thousands of events. Everything we discussed in this book has been proven, and the organizations that have embraced these concepts and processes have achieved great and sustained success. We encourage you to explore other ideas and test them for yourself.

Change is good and is, in fact, essential to sustain growth, so each year you should be open to new trends and suggestions that may help you achieve even greater results. We suggest, however, that you test each suggested idea against the basic core operating principles you have learned, so you are not taken too far away from what you know works. With that said, we wish you well, as we are confident you are now on the path toward great success and, most importantly, the satisfaction that you have created a legacy for your organization that will live on well after your leadership "tour" has concluded.

# RESOURCES
## Contacts

While there are certainly many excellent resources you can use, both on a local and national level, here are a few that can get you started. This list is not intended to be an endorsement or promotion for any of the vendors or sources that appear on it, but these are the sources with which we are most familiar and have direct experience.

**Auction Software**

AuctionMaestro Pro and GolfMaestro Pro

MaestroSoft, Inc.

1200 112th Ave. NE, Suite C250

Bellevue, WA 98004

www.maestrosoft.com

Phone: 800-438-6498

Fax: 425-688-0999

**Online Auction Software**

MaestroWeb

MaestroSoft, Inc.

1200 112th Ave. NE, Suite C250

Bellevue, WA 98004

www.maestrosoft.com

Phone: 800-438-6498

Fax: 425-688-0999

cMarket, Inc.
125 Cambridge Park Drive
Cambridge, MA 02140
www.cmarket.com
Phone: 866-621-0330
Fax: 617-374-9015

**Auctioneers/Auction Management/Consulting Help
(National/International Reach)**
Northwest Benefit Auctions, Inc.
1200 112th Ave. NE, Suite C250
Bellevue, WA 98004
www.auctionhelp.com
Phone: 425-688-1110
Fax: 425-688-0999
Toll-Free: 800-469-6305

**Consignment Items**
Auction Stuff Web site
http://auctionitems.maestroweb.com/

**Audio/Visual**
You may find excellent and reliable resources that can serve you locally.
Here are two resources for audio/visual services that have a national
reach:
AVP Nationwide Productions
131 Rental Court
Rock Hill, SC 29732
www.avpinc.net
Phone: 800-951-0555
Fax: 803-336-1024

Swank Audio Visuals
639E Gravois Bluffs
St. Louis, MO 63026
www.swankav.com
Phone: 877-792-6528

**Standards and Best Practices Related to Payment Processing**
PCI Security Standards Council
www.pcisecuritystandards.org

**Bid Cards, Bid Forms, Bid Card Holders, Silent/Live Auction Display Easels, and Other Supplies**
Northwest Benefit Auctions, Inc.
1200 112th Ave. NE, Suite C250
Bellevue, WA 98004
Phone: 425-688-1110
Fax: 425-688-0999
Toll-Free: 800-469-6305
www.auctionhelp.com

**Magazines**
*Chronicle of Philanthropy:* The Newspaper of the Nonprofit World
http://philanthropy.com/
*The NonProfit Times*
http://nptimes.com/

**Other Resources**
Raiser's Edge
Blackbaud, Inc.
2000 Daniel Island Drive
Charleston, SC, 29492-7541
Toll-Free: 800-443-9441
Fax: 843-216-6100
www.blackbaud.com

The National Auctioneers Association
www.auctioneers.org

The Northwest Benefit Auctions Web site
www.auctionhelp.com

This site contains many free tips, publications, sources for regional and local auctioneers, professional auction management staff, auction information, and more.

# A Budget Worksheet Template

**Note:** Highlighted field indicate variables on which other calculations are based.

This template represents working budget for a typical auction. A full budget template for your own use can be downloaded at www.auctionhelp. com/page13910.asp.

---

### Sample Auction Budget Template

| | Net Event Goal | $100,000 | | | |
|---|---|---|---|---|---|
| | | *Income* | | | |
| **Income, Pre-Auction** | | | **Budget** | **Actual** | **Variance** |
| ***Pre-Auction Revenue*** | | | | | |
| Underwriting–Corporate Cash Donations | | | $1,500 | $0 | ($1,500) |
| Underwriting–Non-cash Services or Materials (in kind) | | | $1,000 | $0 | ($1,000) |
| Underwriting–Individual Cash Donations | | | $1,000 | $0 | ($1,000) |
| Catalog Advertising | | | $5,000 | | ($5,000) |
| Sustaining Funds (Carryover from prior year) | | | $7,500 | | ($7,500) |
| Misc. Contributions | | | $1,000 | | ($1,000) |
| | | **Subtotal** | **$17,000** | | **($17,000)** |
| | Number of Guests | Cost/Person | | | |
| ***Admissions*** | | | | | |
| ***(Target 300–350)*** | 350 | | | | |
| General | 200 | $75 | $15,000 | | ($15,000) |
| Faculty or Special | 20 | $50 | $1,000 | | ($1,000) |
| Patron Level | 10 | $100 | $1,000 | | ($1,000) |
| Benefactor Level | 20 | $250 | $5,000 | | ($5,000) |
| Sponsorship Level | 5 | $500 | $2,500 | | ($2,500) |
| Table Sales (10 per) | 50 | $75 | $3,750 | | ($3,750) |
| Complimentary (honored guest) | 10 | $0 | $0 | | $0 |
| Other (media, staff) | 10 | $0 | $0 | | $0 |
| Total Guests | 325 | | | | |
| | | **Subtotal** | **$28,250** | | ($28,250) |
| **Total Income (Pre-Auction)** | | | **$45,250** | | ($45,250) |
| ***Income, Auction*** | | . . . | | | |
| Auction Revenue | | | | | |
| Limited Ticket Raffle–Donated Prize | | | $5,000 | | ($5,000) |
| Silent Auction | | | $20,000 | | ($20,000) |
| Live Auction | | | $40,000 | | ($40,000) |
| Fund-an-Item (20% of Live and Silent Income) | | | $13,800 | | ($13,800) |

| | | | | | |
|---|---|---|---|---|---|
| Grab Bags or Balloon Sales | | | | $1,500 | ($1,500) |
| Centerpiece Sales | | | | $1,500 | ($1,500) |
| Merchandise Sales | | | | $1,000 | ($1,000) |
| | | **Subtotal** | | **$82,800** | **($82,800)** |

*Planning Income Level Based on "Buying Units" (2 guests = 1 BU)*

| | | | | | |
|---|---|---|---|---|---|
| *$500/BU Average* | *Number of Buying Units* | 175 | | **$87,500** *(not in totals or* | |
| | | | | | *recap)* |

**Other Auction Revenue**

| | | | | |
|---|---|---|---|---|
| Guests' Employer Matching Funds | | | $10,000 | ($10,000) |
| (post-event) estimated | | | | |
| | **Subtotal** | | **$10,000** | **($10,000)** |
| **Total Income (Auction-Related)** | | | **$92,800** | **($92,800)** |
| ***Total Revenue, All Sources*** | | | **$138,050** | **($138,050)** |

***Expenses***

**Pre-Auction Expenses**

Printing

| | | | |
|---|---|---|---|
| Invitations | | $500 | ($500) |
| Letter Stock, Envelopes | | $100 | ($100) |
| Logo Design | | $150 | ($150) |
| Other | | $100 | ($100) |
| Procurement Forms | | $75 | ($75) |
| Save-the-Date Mailer | | $50 | ($50) |
| Signs | | $150 | ($150) |
| Deposits | | $1,500 | ($1,500) |
| Auction Database Software (1/3 cost, | | $500 | ($500) |
| amortized over 3 years) | | | |
| | **Subtotal** | **$3,125** | **($3,125)** |

**During and Post-Event Expenses**

| | | | | | |
|---|---|---|---|---|---|
| Catering (based on # of | 350 | Cost/Meal | $45 | $15,750 | ($15,750) |
| guests) | | | | | |
| Volunteer Buffet at Event | | | | $150 | ($150) |
| Clerical Staff | | | | $350 | ($350) |
| Decorations, including Centerpieces | | | | $1,000 | ($1,000) |
| Insurance (may not be required) | | | | $350 | ($350) |
| Liquor License (may not be required) | | | | $50 | ($50) |
| Bank Card Processing | 3.25% of CC used | | | $1,749 | ($1,749) |
| Fees @ | (all card types) | | | | |
| Office Supplies | | | | $100 | ($100) |
| Misc. | | | | $50 | ($50) |
| Postage (1,000 pieces) | | | | $350 | ($350) |
| Procurement Kickoff Party | | | | $250 | ($250) |
| Volunteer Party | | | | $500 | ($500) |
| | | **Subtotal** | | **$20,649** | **($20,649)** |
| | | | | | (*Continued*) |

---

### Sample Auction Budget Template

**Net Event Goal      $100,000**

**Income**

| Income, Pre-Auction | | Budget | Actual | Variance |
|---|---|---|---|---|
| ***Auction-Related Expenses*** | | | | |
| Printing | | | | |
| Catalog and Cover | | $2,000 | | ($2,000) |
| Addendum | | $50 | | ($50) |
| Silent Auction Bid Forms | | $75 | | ($75) |
| Live Auction Bid Forms | | $25 | | ($25) |
| Bid Cards (Numbers) | | $100 | | ($100) |
| Display (Live and Silent Auction) | | $250 | | ($250) |
| | **Subtotal** | **$2,500** | | ($2,500) |
| ***Other Event Expenses*** | | | | |
| Early Arrival Incentives (optional) | | $350 | | ($350) |
| Lighting System (optional) | | $350 | | ($350) |
| Security (optional) | | $250 | | ($250) |
| Sound System (not optional!) | | $1,000 | | ($1,000) |
| Video Rental (optional) | | $750 | | ($750) |
| Stage Rental (optional) | | $150 | | ($150) |
| Valet Parking (optional) | | $250 | | ($250) |
| Room Rental (may be included with catering) | | $500 | | ($500) |
| Other | | $500 | | ($500) |
| | **Subtotal** | **$4,100** | | ($4,100) |
| ***Professional Help*** | | | | |
| Professional Benefit Auctioneer (not optional!) | | $2,500 | | ($2,500) |
| Professional MC (optional) | | $350 | | ($350) |
| Professional Spotters (optional) | | $500 | | ($500) |
| Event Managers and Consulting (optional) | | $1,000 | | ($1,000) |
| | **Subtotal** | **$4,350** | | ($4,350) |
| ***Total Expenses (Event Related)*** | | **$34,724** | | ($34,724) |

### Income, Expense Recap

| | | | |
|---|---|---|---|
| Pre-Auction Revenue | | $17,000 | |
| Admissions | | $28,250 | |
| Auction Revenue | | $82,800 | |
| Other Auction Revenue | | $10,000 | |
| | Total Income | $138,050 | |
| Pre-Auction Expenses | | $3,125 | |
| During and Post-Event Expenses | | $20,649 | |
| Auction-Related Expenses | | $2,500 | |
| Other Event Expenses | | $4,100 | |
| Professional Help | | $4,350 | |
| | Total Expenses | $34,724 | |

| | |
|---|---|
| *Net Event Revenue* | *$103,326* |

Expenses as a Percentage of Gross Income                     25%
*(Includes all optional line items—may be lower without these optional items)*

This sample planning budget template is available as an Excel worksheet.
You may download it at www.auctionhelp.com.

---

## The ABCs of Auction Item Procurement

Following is an excerpt from the handout entitled ''The ABCs of Auction
Item Procurement.'' This excerpt is intended to get you started on ideas for
auction items you may want to get for your event. You can get the entire
document by registering at www.auctionhelp.com.

## Getting Items is as Easy as A, B, C . . .

### A is for . . .
1. Autographed sports stuff - footballs, baseballs, soccer balls, basketballs
2. Athletic equipment
3. Antiques
4. Appliances
5. Airline tickets
6. Autographed memorabilia
7. Airplane rides
8. Artwork (framed)

### B is for . . .
1. Beach houses for the week or weekend
2. Baseball and basketball clinics
3. Best seat in the house for graduation
4. Boats and boat rides
5. Beanie Baby assortment
6. Books
7. Bed and bath items
8. Bed and breakfast stays
9. Baby items

### C is for . . .
1. Camping equipment
2. Condos at the beach
3. Condos at a resort
4. Condos in the mountains
5. Cameras, digital or video
6. CDs
7. Character in a novel named after you or a family member
8. Cellular phones
9. Celebrity lunches
10. Collectable items (limited editions)
11. Computer systems with consultation
12. Car, new or used, or one year lease
13. Car for a weekend or a week
14. Cabin at the lake for a weekend
15. Certificates for anything
16. Carpentry services
17. Catered meals
18. Corvette, fully restored
19. Consulting services from professionals

### D is for . . .
1. Deed to a condo
2. Day trip
3. Duck hunting
4. DJ for a day
5. Dinners in your home
6. Dinners out
7. Dolls and doll houses
8. Dance lessons
9. Decorating services
10. Day on a sailboat
11. Detailing for your car
12. Drive a NASCAR Race Car

### E is for . . .
1. Emotional items and experiences
2. Emeralds
3. Easter baskets
4. Events of all kinds
5. Escapes and getaways
6. Electrician services
7. Elegant evenings
8. Earrings
9. Ego satisfying experiences
10. Experiences of all kinds

### F is for . . .
1. Fishing trips
2. Flag flown over the capitol
3. Fruit of the month club
4. Furniture
5. Floral arrangements
6. Fifty Lotto tickets
7. Fourth of July party
8. Fly fishing on a river
9. Friendly get-togethers
10. Fun experiences
11. Flowers for a year
12. Framed artwork and photos

### G is for . . .
1. Golf with a celebrity
2. Getaways
3. Garden tools
4. Gift certificates
5. Grass cutting for a year
6. Glass artwork
7. Golf tournaments
8. Golf vacations
9. Guided tours
10. Great stuff of all kinds

### H is for . . .
1. Horseback riding lessons
2. Home remodeling
3. Hang gliding lessons
4. Handmade items
5. Health club membership
6. High end artwork
7. Heavy equipment rental
8. Hilariously funny stuff
9. Hauling services
10. Heart shaped jewelry
11. Heart shaped anything
12. Harley Davidson motorcycle

### I is for . . .
1. Investment advice
2. Ice cream maker
3. Instruction of all kinds
4. Ice skating party
5. Irish Setter puppy
6. Ireland trip
7. Irish Coffee party

8. Indy 500 trip with race tickets
9. Incredible, one of kind anything

### J is for . . .
1. Jet Fighter Plane ride
2. Jewelry, "generic type"
3. Judge Judy Tickets
4. Just about anything exciting
5. J-Lo concert tickets

### K is for . . .
1. Kitchen appliances
2. Kids clothing
3. Keepsakes
4. Kinetic sculptures
5. Kids toys and experiences
6. Kids artwork and projects

### L is for . . .
1. Long weekend getaways
2. Ladies clothing
3. Loan of a sports car for the week
4. Local cabins and condos
5. Ladies' jewelry
6. Luscious gourmet meals
7. Labor for work on the house
8. Lessons for cooking, dancing
9. Lease on a new car

### M is for . . .
1. Motor home for a vacation
2. Mountain retreats
3. Most anything YOU would want
4. Mountain bike
5. Mother of all parties
6. Memorabilia

### N is for . . .
1. New items of all kinds
2. Northwest trip
3. Night on the town
4. Night with the Police K-9 unit
5. Nostalgia items
6. New York trip

### O is for . . .
1. Out of town relaxation
2. Opulent surroundings for a weekend
3. Organized scavenger hunt
4. Outlandish party
5. Original Art
6. One-of-a-kind experiences
7. Orange Bowl tickets

Copyright 2005 by Northwest Benefit Auctions, Inc.  Permission to copy may be obtained by contacting us at: 800.469.6305, by FAX at 425.688.0999,  or visiting our Website at www.auctionhelp.com

## P is for . . .
1. Parking space reserved for you
2. Pair of Harley Davidson motorcycles
3. Photo-shoot weekend
4. Party with a celebrity
5. Party at the Fire Station
6. Politician takes you to dinner
7. Pets, pure bred only
8. Pony rides for a kid's party
9. Prowler automobile
10. Pair of candlesticks, framed prints

## Q is for . . .
1. Queen for a day package
2. Quilts, handmade
3. Quality antiques
4. Quebec trip
5. Quiet cabin in the mountains
6. Quality memorabilia
7. Quests and adventures

## R is for . . .
1. Racing car driving experience
2. Rugs, Oriental
3. Real Antiques
4. Reliable used cars
5. Row boat trip on a quiet lake
6. Rental of a car for a year
7. Rose Bowl Tickets

## S is for . . .
1. Saturday Night Live tickets
2. Sensational meals
3. Special dinners
4. Send a kid to college baskets
5. Sushi Party, catered
6. Super Bowl tickets
7. Super Bowl party
8. Star Wars script, autographed
9. Spend the day with a detective, doctor, etc.
10. Stuffed animals

## T is for . . .
1. Travel, local and out of state
2. Tickets to the ballgame
3. Tickets to the Opera, Symphony
4. Telephone calls free for a year
5. Terrific, one-of-a-kind items
6. Toys and games

## U is for . . .
1. Unique experiences
2. Utility Vehicles, Sport (SUVs)
3. Unique items
4. Used cars, reliable only
5. Upscale parties
6. Upper Deck baseball cards

## V is for . . .
1. Video Movies, assorted
2. Video game systems
3. Very rare items and memorabilia
4. Vintage wine collections
5. Very friendly puppies
6. Vintage car, restored
7. Veterinarian services
8. Villa, private, in a luxury location

## W is for . . .
1. Whatever you can think of
2. Water ski outings
3. Wine collections
4. Wonderful meals
5. World wide trips
6. Wholesale buying sprees
7. World Series tickets
8. Wagon filled with toys

## X is for . . .
1. Xacto knife gift sets
2. Xactly the perfect gift
3. "X Files" autographed script
4. "X Files" set tour
5. Xenon outdoor lighting fixtures
6. Xtraordinary items
7. Xtreme experiences(rafting, sky diving, hang gliding, scuba diving)
8. Xylophone lessons

## Y is for . . .
1. Yellow Lab puppy
2. Yearly lawn care package
3. Yuppie stuff
4. "Yesterday" album cover, autographed by the Beatles

## Z is for . . .
1. Sub-Zero refrigerator
2. Zebra striped rug
3. Zanzibar trip
4. "Zoo Doo"
5. Zucchini bread

## Remember:

- **Avoid consignment items!**

- *Think unique!*

- *Ask for the bigger items first*
- *Take whatever you can get*

- *Don't be afraid to ask EVERYONE you meet*

- *Use the "peel the onion" technique*

- *Carry a procurement form with you everywhere*

- *Take extra forms with you on vacation (hotels, restaurants)*

- *Search your checkbook for ideas*

- *Write down what YOU would buy, and then go find it!*

- *Don't think small:  bigger items are often easier to get*

- *Try to get at least one item each week – make it fun!*

- *Turn the items in as soon as you get them to eliminate the last minute "crunch"*

- *Remember, every item you get adds value to the event.*

- *Get new items only, except for real antiques, used cars*

---

**Additional tips and assistance are available on our website at**
*www.auctionhelp.com*

---

Copyright 2005 by Northwest Benefit Auctions, Inc.  Permission to copy may be obtained by contacting us at: 800.469.6305, by FAX at 425.688.0999,  or visiting our Website at www.auctionhelp.com

## Procurement Letter Sample: School

The following letter is a sample of text that can be used to solicit donations for your upcoming auction. Edit it as needed, remembering that shorter letters are more effective than long ones—additional information can always be provided upon request. This letter is only to get the donors attention and pique their interest.

{date}

Dear Mr./Mrs./Mss {name} (or Supporter):

On {date}, {organization} will be hosting a fundraising event to benefit children in our community through the improvement of their education. This is the first year of a five-year plan to create repeatable income to further this cause. Your support for the improvement of education in our community is greatly appreciated. We ask that you get involved in this effort by making a donation toward this worthwhile goal. An item that can be auctioned would be wonderful, and there are a number of other ways you can get involved as well.

Attached is a donation/procurement form on which you can indicate the scope of your donation. Your generosity will be acknowledged in our program and on our Web site. In addition, if you wish, we can provide a link to your Web site from our online catalog, which will be prominently listing the donations as they are made. This additional visibility for your company will provide a worthwhile benefit to you as our way of saying thanks for your generosity. In addition to your auction item donation, we are grateful for cash contributions that will go toward under-writing the costs of our event. Several levels of sponsorships are also available, as are advertising opportunities. Please talk with an event representative for more details on how you can also benefit by being a supporter of our event.

All of the volunteers on our team would like to thank you in advance for stepping up to help our community by getting involved in our event at whatever level and in any capacity you wish. Of course, we would like to invite you to our event, and will gladly add your name to our invitation list so you may be notified when our invitations are sent. Should you require additional information or clarification, please contact me at any time. My e-mail and telephone number are listed below. On behalf of {organization}, I thank you for your positive consideration.

Sincerely,

{name}

Event Chair

{e-mail address}

{telephone number}

## Ultimate Auction Items

This list of items is the A List from Northwest Benefit Auctions, Inc.—
a selection of auction items that can take your event to a higher level.

- A popular sports car, like a new Thunderbird, Mustang, or Jaguar
- Dinner at a private home, with cooking lessons by Emeril Lagasse or Wolfgang Puck
- A ride on a private jet for four or eight to a golf resort with golf, dinner, and overnight accommodations
- A tour of the space shuttle launch facility with an astronaut, including watching a shuttle launch from the VIP viewing stands
- Tickets to attend the Super Bowl and some VIP parties with a celebrity
- A ride on a float in the Rose Bowl Parade
- A cruise around a NASCAR track with a top stock car driver at high speed, including a team jacket to wear
- A spot on the pit crew for a NASCAR race
- An on-stage performance during a rock concert with any popular rock star
- A cruise on an aircraft carrier for a few days, after which the winner is flown back to shore on the supply plane
- An evening gown created for you by a world-famous fashion designer
- Tickets to fly on a Boeing 777's inaugural flight as it is delivered to an overseas airline
- An aerobatic flight (loops, rolls, spins) with General Chuck Yeager
- Have a street or park named after you
- Have your name used as a character in a novel written by a famous author
- A performance as an extra in a movie with a top Hollywood actor
- Throwing the first pitch at a major league baseball game and spending the evening in the broadcast booth with the sports broadcasters
- Your own custom wine label, designed and affixed to several cases of specially selected fine wines for your cellar
- Attendance at the Hollywood premier of a major motion picture and at the cast party
- Spend the day with a top Hollywood director on the set, including your name listed in the credits of the movie as an "assistant director"
- Six laps around the Ford Motor Test Track with a test car driver in a not-yet-released experimental car
- Tickets to watch the Indianapolis 500 from one of the VIP suites, and pit passes to Gasoline Alley before the race
- A performance as an actor (extra) in a television commercial

- A round of golf with Arnold Palmer or Tiger Woods
- Tickets for your child to sit on the bench at a Lakers game and hand out towels to the players—plus, you get tickets to watch the game from courtside
- A trip to New York, with a stay at a first class hotel and tickets to a Broadway play, plus an invitation to ring the opening bell of the New York Stock Exchange
- Tickets to attend the Academy Awards, the Emmy Awards, or Grammy Awards and one of the after-parties, with limousine service included
- An "Instant Stock Portfolio" of Fortune 500 stock
- An invitation to the next White House Inaugural Ball
- An around-the-world cruise for two
- Your name mentioned in a nationally syndicated newspaper column (Larry King, Jeannie Williams, etc.)
- A one-year unlimited dining pass (good for a meal every day) at Ruth's Chris, Morton's, or any other popular restaurant
- The complete set of 100 best movies of all time on DVD
- A Harley-Davidson Fat Boy, Electra Glide, or Softail motorcycle with all of the riding leathers
- The ultimate guided fishing trip to Canada or Alaska: one week at a remote fishing lodge, flown in by float plane
- A ride on the Goodyear, Met Life, or similar blimp during the broadcast of the next major PGA/LPGA golf tournament in Palm Desert

## Sample Event Forms

### Silent Auction Bid Forms

This preprinted silent auction bid form includes 14 steps and a guaranteed purchase option. This full-page silent auction bid form includes 35 steps, plus the guaranteed purchase option.

Item Number:

**A 102**

Organization:
Legal Name: Northshore Rotary Foundation
Fed. TAX id #    95-123456

Fair Market Value:

**$250** Certificate Delivered ☐
* Certificate Required

Item Description:  **Police Canine Ride Along**

How fast can you run?  How about spending a shift with the Seattle Police Canine unit?  You go on all of the calls they go on.  Chase the bad guys.  Be part of the action as your two "officers" go after the crooks.  Listen to the siren.  Can't you just imagine what it will be like to ride along for a full 8 hour shift?  The best part is you get to sit in the FRONT seat!  Must be at least 18 years old.

Donor:    Seattle Police Department

Expiration Date: 12/18/2004

| Bid Number | Bid Amount | Bid Number | Bid Amount | Bid Number | Bid Amount |
|---|---|---|---|---|---|
| | $ 50 | | $ 165 | | $ 280 |
| | $ 73 | | $ 188 | | $ 303 |
| | $ 96 | | $ 211 | | $ 326 |
| | $ 119 | | $ 234 | | **Guaranteed Purchase** | |
| | $ 142 | | $ 257 | | $ 375 |

To enter a bid, just write your **bid number** next to any amount above. Skip down or across the form as you wish. Winner will be the number next to the highest bid amount at the conclusion of the silent auction. To see if you are the winner, check the pink copy on the table after the closing of the silent auction. Do not remove items until paid for.

To be the "instant winner" of this item, enter your bid number here. It will be yours!

Table Number

NWBA Form S1000L    © 2004 Northwest Benefit Auctions, Inc. Forms, Software and Consulting Assistance © (800) 469-6305 or www.auctionhelp.com

---

Item Number:

**A 103**

Organization:
Legal Name: Northshore Rotary Foundation
Fed. TAX id #    95-123456

Fair Market Value:

**$250** Certificate Delivered ☐

Item Description:  **Limited Edition Boeing Print**

Limited edition print from Boeing commemorating the golden anniversary of the first flight of the B-17.  Custom framing included.

Donor:    Big Airplane Company

Expiration Date:

| Bid Number | Bid Amount | Bid Number | Bid Amount | Bid Number | Bid Amount |
|---|---|---|---|---|---|
| | $ 50 | | $ 165 | | $ 280 |
| | $ 73 | | $ 188 | | $ 303 |
| | $ 96 | | $ 211 | | $ 326 |
| | $ 119 | | $ 234 | | **Guaranteed Purchase** | |
| | $ 142 | | $ 257 | | $ 375 |

To enter a bid, just write your **bid number** next to any amount above. Skip down or across the form as you wish. Winner will be the number next to the highest bid amount at the conclusion of the silent auction. To see if you are the winner, check the pink copy on the table after the closing of the silent auction. Do not remove items until paid for.

To be the "instant winner" of this item, enter your bid number here. It will be yours!

Table Number

NWBA Form S1000L    © 2004 Northwest Benefit Auctions, Inc. Forms, Software and Consulting Assistance © (800) 469-6305 or www.auctionhelp.com

## MaestroSoft Charitable Foundation

Sample Database Holiday Gala

*Red Silent Section #1*

| Item # |
| :---: |
| **A-101** |
| Value |
| **$200** |

**Ten hours of Bookkeeping Services**

Taxes coming up?  If you own and business and need to have your taxes done, let a bookkeeper do it.  They are up to date on all the IRS codes, restrictions, exemptions, and exeptions.  Guaranteed to relieve stress.
Restrictions: Does not guarantee that you will owe more taxes than last year.

**Donor(s)** Winfred R. Hatch Co.

| Bidder # / Signature | Bidder # / Signature | Bidder # / Signature |
| :--- | :--- | :--- |
| _____$60 | _____$186 | _____$312 |
| _____$70 | _____$196 | _____$322 |
| _____$79 | _____$206 | _____$332 |
| _____$89 | _____$215 | _____$342 |
| _____$99 | _____$225 | _____$351 |
| _____$109 | _____$235 | _____$361 |
| _____$118 | _____$244 | _____$371 |
| _____$128 | _____$254 | _____$380 |
| _____$138 | _____$264 | _____$390 |
| _____$147 | _____$274 | **Guaranteed Purchase** |
| _____$157 | _____$283 | **$400** |
| _____$167 | _____$293 | |
| _____$177 | _____$303 | |

Organization Legal Name:

Federal Employer Identification #:

* This Item Requires a Certificate

*MaestroSoft, Inc. © 2007*

*Sample Live Auction Bid Form*

NWBA Form **L1000L**      © 2003 Northwest Benefit Auctions, Inc. Forms, Software and Consulting Assistance @ (888) 469-6305 or www.auctionhelp.com

*Sample Fund-an-Item Recording Sheet*

## Cash Donation for Special Projects

| $5,000 | $2,500 | $1,000 | $500 | $250 | $100 | $100 | $50 | $50 |
|--------|--------|--------|------|------|------|------|-----|-----|
| Bidder # | Bidder # | Bidder # | Bidder # | Bidder # | Bidder # | Bidder # | Bidder # | Bidder # |
| $5,000 | $2,500 | $1,000 | $500 | $250 | $100 | $100 | $50 | $50 |
| $10,000 | $5,000 | $2,000 | $1,000 | $500 | $200 | $200 | $100 | $100 |
| $15,000 | $7,500 | $3,000 | $1,500 | $750 | $300 | $300 | $150 | $150 |
| $20,000 | $10,000 | $4,000 | $2,000 | $1,000 | $400 | $400 | $200 | $200 |
| $25,000 | $12,500 | $5,000 | $2,500 | $1,250 | $500 | $500 | $250 | $250 |
| $30,000 | $15,000 | $6,000 | $3,000 | $1,500 | $600 | $600 | $300 | $300 |
| $35,000 | $17,500 | $7,000 | $3,500 | $1,750 | $700 | $700 | $350 | $350 |
| $40,000 | $20,000 | $8,000 | $4,000 | $2,000 | $800 | $800 | $400 | $400 |
| $45,000 | $22,500 | $9,000 | $4,500 | $2,250 | $900 | $900 | $450 | $450 |
| $50,000 | $25,000 | $10,000 | $5,000 | $2,500 | $1,000 | $1,000 | $500 | $500 |
| $55,000 | $27,500 | $11,000 | $5,500 | $2,750 | $1,100 | $1,100 | $550 | $550 |
| $60,000 | $30,000 | $12,000 | $6,000 | $3,000 | $1,200 | $1,200 | $600 | $600 |
| $65,000 | $32,500 | $13,000 | $6,500 | $3,250 | $1,300 | $1,300 | $650 | $650 |
| $70,000 | $35,000 | $14,000 | $7,000 | $3,500 | $1,400 | $1,400 | $700 | $700 |
| $75,000 | $37,500 | $15,000 | $7,500 | $3,750 | $1,500 | $1,500 | $750 | $750 |
| $80,000 | $40,000 | $16,000 | $8,000 | $4,000 | $1,600 | $1,600 | $800 | $800 |
| $85,000 | $42,500 | $17,000 | $8,500 | $4,250 | $1,700 | $1,700 | $850 | $850 |
| $90,000 | $45,000 | $18,000 | $9,000 | $4,500 | $1,800 | $1,800 | $900 | $900 |
| $95,000 | $47,500 | $19,000 | $9,500 | $4,750 | $1,900 | $1,900 | $950 | $950 |
| $100,000 | $50,000 | $20,000 | $10,000 | $5,000 | $2,000 | $2,000 | $1,000 | $1,000 |
| Total | Total | Total | Total | Total | Total | Total | Total | Total |

*MaestroSoft - Fund-An-Item Bid Sheet*

# Glossary

**Auctioneer**   The person in charge of accepting the bids during the Live Auction. The auctioneer may also be involved in announcing closing times and key items during the Silent Auction. Some organizations may use a volunteer, but ideally this person is a professional specializing in charity auctions.

**Bidder**   An individual, couple, or company who has registered for the event and is able to place a bid on auction items. Volunteers may also be bidders.

**Bid Card**   The most common tool used by guests in benefit auctions today to indicate their acceptance of a called bid amount. The card has the bidder's number printed on one or both sides. If the bid number appears on only one side, the reverse side is frequently used for revenue-generating advertisements for sponsors or other supporters. Bid cards come in several different formats (full-size, half-size, pocket-size), depending on the number of guests, the size of the venue, or other important factors affecting visibility and readability.

**Bid-O-Gram**   A type of auction where guests submit a blind bid on a slip of paper. When the auction closes, the highest bid submitted is the successful bidder.

**Bidder Recognition**   The method used during the Live Auction bidding process when the auctioneer recognizes the successful bidder on each item by name. Sometimes, recognizing successful bidders includes "rewarding" them with some tangible gift, such as a special necklace, a bottle of wine or champagne, or some other visible thank you.

**Bidder Recognition System**   A computerized display that flashes the winning bid number and bidder name on a screen so the auctioneer or audience can acknowledge the winner of an item during the Live Auction.

**Bidding Frenzy**   One or more sections within the Live Auction where a collection of similar items (such as restaurant gift certificates, parties, gift baskets, etc.) are sold in a rapid-fire fashion for fair market value to the first bid card in the air.

**Buying Unit**   A typical unit of people sharing one bid number, used for the purposes of calculating expected bid yield. Typically, a buying unit is a husband and wife sharing one bid number, or an individual using one number.

**Catalog Number**   See *Item Number.*

**Constituent Management**   Typically, software that tracks all point of contact with donors and potential donors to produce a bigger picture of the relationship between that person and the benefiting organization.

**Emcee**  The Master (or Mistress) of Ceremonies (MC) for the event. This person will welcome the guests, introduce the dignitaries and program agenda, and typically work with the auctioneer during the Live Auction to describe the items up for bid.

**Express Checkout**  There are many names for this process, which is described in more detail under qCheck. Regardless of the name used at various events, the key definition is a prepayment authorization system that will allow the guests to stay until the event is over without needing to queue up at the cashiering tables at the end of the event.

**Fair Market Value**  The value of the item if the guest were to purchase it on the retail market. *Caution*: Many times the *fair market value* of the item is not the same as the *actual* value of the item, but is the amount that the IRS would allow as the basis of tax deductibility. Even "priceless" items must have an estimated fair market value upon which to base potential tax deductibility.

**Floor Auctioneer**  See *Spotter.*

**Fund-an-Item**  Pledges for direct cash contributions that are taken by the auctioneer during the Live Auction at different dollar amounts. Typically, these are fully tax-deductible donations for the guests. Also frequently known as "Fund-a-Need," "Fund-a-Mission," "Emotional Appeal," or "Raise the Paddle," this can be an exceptionally powerful method of increasing your revenue, as 10–20% of your auction income can come from this activity, and it can be augmented by guests' employers' matching funds.

**Greeter**  A volunteer who may know many of the guests, but whose primary job is to greet guests and direct them quickly to registration as they walk in the door to your event.

**Item Number**  The number assigned to an auction item or lot in the catalog for the Live Auction and Silent Auction. This number is separate from the *Tracking Number*, which is used to track donated items in the computer system.

**Live Auction**  The classic verbal auction, also called an "oral auction," where items are sold one at a time, in a predictable fashion, by an auctioneer to an active, present bidding audience.

**Lot**  An item or collection of items up for bid during the Live Auction. This commercial term is most often used for art, wine, or memorabilia auctions, but may also be used in some general-purpose charity auctions as well.

**MC**  See *emcee.*

**Mini-Live**  Also known as "Almost Live." A hybrid of Silent and Live Auction in which bidders initially use Silent Auction bids to prebid on items. The final bids are taken "live" by the auctioneer, generally at a point in the event just prior to the beginning of the Live Auction.

**Pot of Gold**  An auction item for the Live Auction that is collected from the guests at the event. Beginning with an empty fish bowl or similar container early in the event, volunteers ask guests to make contribution of cash, coins, gift cards, jewelry, watches, business cards with donated services, and anything else of value. This Pot of Gold is auctioned off as the last item in the Live Auction.

**Procurement**   The process of gathering the items to be sold at auction or used for raffle prizes. In-kind services, cash contributions, and underwriting may also occur during this process.

**qCheck™**   The preeminent method of guest prepayment, created by MaestroSoft, Inc., in which one or more credit cards of choice are securely scanned at registration prior to any purchases or donations. Because payment is made in advance through this method, guests' receipts and gift certificates can be delivered to the guests during the event, and the guests avoid waiting in a cashiering line at the end of the evening. Generally, if you use this method of prepayment, guests tend to be more generous during bidding because they are not penalized for their generosity by having to stand in a line to settle up at the end of the evening.

**Raise the Paddle**   See *Fund-an-Item.*

**Recorder**   One or more individuals responsible for recording all bid activity in the Live Auction. Ideally, there will be two or three to help "break ties" during possible problems with clearly hearing a bid amount or bidder number.

**Runner**   Typically a volunteer who serves as courier for transporting invoices and gift certificates to the various locations—such as taking receipts for winning bids to guests' table or bid forms to data entry—throughout the entire auction.

**Scrip**   Scrip—or auction scrip—is a discount on auction purchases, taking the form of coupons which are presented to certain attendees. Typically, scrip is a reward for a patron- or benefactor-level admission to offset the additional cost associated with the higher admission levels. Scrip is exchanged as a discount on auction purchases, therefore it generally loses its value at the end of the event, rarely is transferable, and never is refundable.

**Silent Auction**   An auction conducted in a silent (i.e., nonverbal) manner, in which items are displayed on tables along with bid forms. Guests indicate their bids by writing their bid numbers on the forms adjacent to their preferred bid. The highest bid shown at the time the Silent Auction closes is the winner of the item.

**Spotter**   A volunteer or professional that assists the auctioneer by "spotting" bids from within the audience. This is exceptionally important when the room in which you are conducting your audience has poor sight lines or blind spots for the auctioneer.

**Super Silent**   A Silent Auction with premier items that normally might qualify for Live Auction but may not be appropriate for the Live for a number of varying reasons—for example, there may be too many items in the Live already, or there may not be enough potential bidders for the item (although the item may be of premium value, there may not be enough general interest to make a successful

Live Auction item) and so on. Generally used as the last Silent Auction section, but sometimes closed in the early- to middle-parts of the Live Auction.

**Table Captain**   An individual or couple who agrees to come to the event and commits to help fill a table with bidding guests. The table captain is not expected to buy the whole table; instead, their job is to invite like-minded others who will typically pay their own way to attend and be supportive of the cause.

**Table Closer**   A volunteer or professional who closes the bidding in a Silent Auction section by circling winning bids, picking up bid forms from the tables, and bringing them to the data entry and filing area.

**Tiered Pricing**   Also known as multilevel pricing. Tiered pricing allows for guest recognition levels at a variety of entry costs above the basic admission. This affords guests who are willing to make an additional financial contribution for their admission to receive premium recognition for doing so, by being named as sponsors, benefactors, founders, and so on. *Auction Scrip* may be awarded to higher levels to offset some of the higher cost of admission.

**Tracking Number**   A sequential number assigned by auction software program to each item in the database. The tracking number helps keep track of the item and assists in packaging the item with others. This is not to be confused with the Silent or Live Auction *Item Number* assigned to the item for the catalog.

**Volunteer**   A person, typically a member of your organization but not always, who donates his time and energy to be involved in your event in a nonpaid supporting role.

**Yield**   The ratio of the *Fair Market Value* of an auction item to the actual bidding or sale price of that item. For example, an item that has a fair market value of $1,000 that sells for $800 has a yield of 80%.

# Index